LIVING FULLY IN THE

SHADOW OF DEATH

D1444069

LIVING FULLY IN THE SHADOW OF DEATH

ASSURANCE AND GUIDANCE TO FINISH WELL

SUSAN J. ZONNEBELT-SMEENGE, R.N., ED.D.

ROBERT C. DE VRIES, D.MIN., PH.D.

BakerBooks
Grand Rapids, Michigan

Published by Baker Books
a division of Baker Publishing Group
P.O. Box 6287, Grand Rapids, MI 49516-6287
www.bakerbooks.com

Printed in the United States of America

Library of Congress Cataloging-in-Publication Data
Zonnebelt-Smeenge, Susan J., 1948-
    Living fully in the shadow of death : assurance and guidance to finish well /
Susan J. Zonnebelt-Smeenge, Robert C. De Vries.
        p.   cm.
    Includes bibliographical references and index.
    ISBN 0-8010-6507-0 (pbk.)
    1. Death—Religious aspects—Christianity. I. DeVries, Robert C., 1942- II. Title.
BT825.Z66 2004
236′.1—dc22   2004001803

This book is dedicated
in loving memory to

D. Richard Smeenge
1946–1994

and

Charlene K. De Vries
1942–1993

who, in our first marriages, taught us
a great deal about dying
so we now embrace living more fully.

We also acknowledge the countless
others in Susan's clinical practice
and Bob's pastoral work
who, in their dying, taught us more about
the joys and sorrows of this earth's journey.

CONTENTS

TWO

The Knock at the Door

THREE

Midnight

The Day Has Ended

ACKNOWLEDGMENTS

A book never represents the work of an individual person, nor even (in this case) the collaboration of two people. Thoughts, ideas, perspectives—these are all influenced by a variety of other relationships. Susan's parents, William and Norma Zonnebelt, have been immensely helpful not only in serving as a sounding board for many of the ideas in this book but also in their faithful and dedicated support of our speaking and writing. Susan's daughter, Sarah, read the manuscript and made helpful suggestions from the perspective of both a teacher and a young adult. Matt Swanson consented to provide the artwork while his wife, Laurie Albers Swanson, read the manuscript as she valiantly battled bone cancer. Her parents, Robert Albers, M.D., and Rose Albers, lent their wisdom both from a medical perspective and as parents watching their daughter fight cancer.

Colleagues offered valuable support and insight. C. J. Weidaw, a friend, nurse, and psychologist in the Pittsburgh area, graciously read the manuscript, as did Patricia Cassell, a nurse, social worker, and friend in the Western Michigan area. These two professional women offered their perspectives on dying from both a clinical and a personal perspective.

Technical advice was gathered from a variety of other people. Attorneys Christopher Byrd of Atlanta and Jeffrey Helder of Holland, Michigan, gave direction on the legal aspects covered in the book. Martin Hollebeek, past president of the Michigan Funeral Directors Association, read the manuscript to ensure a fair and accurate representation of the funeral service industry. Gloria Brooks and her staff from the home office of Hospice of Michigan reviewed this book for accuracy and fairness in our representation of the hospice movement and the services they provide.

We also express a word of deep appreciation to Robert Hosack, senior acquisitions editor, for his faith in our work, and to Kristin Kornoelje, project editor, trade books, for giving a clear voice to our writing. These two people, as well as the entire staff of Baker Book House Company, have provided generous support and wise direction to this project.

We attempted to listen and accept the advice of all of these people as best we could. We truly believe their assistance has strengthened this work. On the other hand, we accept full responsibility for any errors or misrepresentation that may have inadvertently slipped into the following pages.

Much more could be written on this subject—we consider this just the beginning. We hope this book will be the beginning for you as well. We acknowledge you, the reader, for the contribution you are making through the purchase of this book in order to make conversation about death more natural and not something to be avoided.

Susan J. Zonnebelt-Smeenge
Robert C. De Vries

PREFACE

Light and dark.
Sweet or sour.
Big and small.
Each alone
But only understood together.
Life and death—
When one begins
Each begins.
The baby's first cry
Echoes tears of the grave.

R. De Vries and
S. Zonnebelt-Smeenge

There is only one liberty—to come to terms with death,
after which everything is possible.

Camus

The confronting of death gives the most positive reality to
life itself. It makes the individual existence real, absolute,
and concrete. Death is one fact of my life which is not
relative but absolute and my awareness of this gives my
existence and what I do each hour an absolute quality.

Rollo May

This book is about dying, which really isn't a popular subject. Most people think about death only when they or
a loved one face it directly. They usually don't read this
kind of book for pleasure or relaxation; instead, they will buy a good
mystery, a romance novel, or a work of classic literature.

So what motivates Bob and me to write such a book? Neither one of us is about to die as far as we know. Our lives are good. We have had a few brushes with potentially terminal diseases, but in every situation the lab results came back negative. "No cancer was found," the doctor would happily say. "The tests came back clear. You're good for another year." And so we live on, aware that some day we will face death but not knowing when or how our lives will end.

But we are convinced that being aware of the inevitability of death is a good thing. Robert Herhold said, "It is too bad that dying is the last thing we do, because it could teach us so much about living."[1] So this book is written for everybody, because at some point each one of us will face death. And as Herhold implies, we can live more fully if we face our own mortality.

This book will be of particular significance to those who know they are dying and those who walk with them as family, friends, or caregivers, as well as to anyone who simply has an interest in knowing how a person prepares for death. We all want to live a richer and more complete life. Both Bob and I are convinced that this is possible only when we look death squarely in the face, understand it, and reconcile ourselves to its inevitability.

As a clinical psychologist and a registered nurse, I have been processing data for many years from people who were diagnosed with a terminal illness and faced the likelihood of their own death. In my career as a nurse, I was at the bedside of many patients who were aware of their impending deaths. I worked with several other families who experienced the tragic and sudden death of a loved one. The wide variety of reactions they had to the prospect of dying sometimes troubled me, but this variety has been helpful in giving shape to this book. Some patients displayed a total confidence in their final destination; others were anxious and troubled. Still others didn't want to talk about the possibility of their death. Most people, however, expressed pain at the prospect of severing those special relationships they had with their loved ones.

In my late twenties and thirties, all four of my grandparents died. My thirty-three-year-old brother was killed in a plane crash. My first husband, Rick, was diagnosed with a malignant brain tumor at the age of thirty-two. Death certainly became real for me during that time. In our heads we all know we will die, but coming to grips with the emotions surrounding death can be devastating. While Rick was dying, I certainly gained valuable insights into life and death. The best doctors could not tell us with any certainty when Rick would die. At times they predicted he had five years to live; at other times the prognosis was two or three years at the most. In fact, he lived eighteen years after his original diagnosis. But the brain tumor eventually led to his last breath, and then he reached his final peace.

Now as a psychologist I work with individuals who are diagnosed with illnesses that may be potentially terminal, as well as with people who are in the process of dying. I counsel those family members who are supporting a dying person while struggling with their own anxieties and sadness over the possibility of their loved one's imminent death.

My hope is that this book will encourage each of us to come to terms with the inevitability of our own death, to prepare for it in a healthy way, and to live life more fully until we die. My intent is also that this book will help anyone who is facing death, either their own or that of a loved one. The supportive counsel in this book can provide clear information on what happens as one dies and help deal with the inevitable emotions that accompany the dying process. Wherever you are in life, I hope you will be encouraged by the knowledge that even while dying, you can richly embrace life and live in fullness.

Susan J. Zonnebelt-Smeenge, R.N., Ed.D.

Susan and I began writing together in 1996. Both of us had been widowed, myself in 1993 and Susan in 1994. (My first wife, Char, died after a nearly four-year battle with ovarian cancer.) In the writing and speaking Susan and I have done since then, we have become all the more convinced that American society would benefit from having a better education about dying and death. We find it ironic that everyone knows and is interested in the birth process. This process is surrounded by all kinds of voluntary and often mandatory education classes—future mothers learn how to breathe properly during delivery; future fathers learn how to coach and encourage their wives during delivery; and both learn about the proper feeding and bathing of newborns and the regulating of their sleep patterns.

But where is the education for dying? Do we know how to approach this equally important event on the opposite end of life that is as inevitable and irreversible as birth? Our hope and prayer is that you are taking the beginning steps in educating yourself about dying by reading this book, and subsequently that you will talk to your family and friends about dying in a more open and natural manner.

In all our writing and speaking, we strive to combine a sound mental health perspective with a solid spiritual base. We attempt to do this in a genuinely ecumenical Christian manner. Both of us were raised and trained in the Reformed Protestant tradition, which has long recognized the harmony that exists between one's mind and heart. Social sciences such as psychology, sociology, and anthropology need not contradict the spiritual life. Nor should one's spiritual life ignore or minimize the reality of the physical, social, and emotional aspects of life. One of the primary themes of our writing and speaking is that a person's faith should equip him or her to move *through* emotionally traumatic or painful events. On the other hand, we believe the world, and human beings, are subject not only to the physical laws of nature but to social and psychological principles that apply to everyone regardless of their particular religious practice. A spiritual life is not a life of escape—it is one that equips a person to face the realities of life in a way consistent with sound mental health practices.

This is the third book we have written together. In our first two books,[2] each chapter contained a section dealing with mental health practices followed by a separate section of spiritual reflection on selected themes of the chapter. We continue that format in this book because sound mental health principles combined with a deep spiritual base can provide the foundation for living and for dying.

The basic issues of living and dying are divided into three main sections. In the first section we focus on how to live life fully while physically healthy, prior to any potentially terminal diagnosis. This is our "normal" life in which we are consumed with our daily routines and relationships. We are healthy, and everything looks good—we are living in the **daylight**. We have the opportunity to plan for death before facing a disease. The second section addresses how to live life when confronted with the possibility of death—when a diagnosis or circumstance forces you to look death in the face. You might be able to avoid death, but you cannot run from the shadow it casts over your life. Daylight then turns to **dusk**. The third section addresses the issues raised when death is imminent—that moment when you realize there is no turning back. Death is near and inevitable. **Midnight** is pressing in.

At the end of each section, you will find a number of short Christian meditations. These meditations correlate with the issues of living and dying raised in that section. We recommend you read both the mental health sections and the meditation sections—preferably in combination with each other. We hope that in reading, your life will be enhanced, and the death you will die someday will be filled with grace and peace.

Robert C. De Vries, D.Min., Ph. D.

ONE

Daylight

Death Yet Unseen

Sunlight is bright.
Our steps are quick.
Hurry up!
Finish the chores,
So much to do.
Hugs and kisses.
Kids to tend.
The beach or the circus?
Quickly now!
Before life passes by—
Embrace it.
Daylight.

R. De Vries and
S. Zonnebelt-Smeenge

Here begins the open sea. Here begins the
glorious adventure, the only one abreast with
human curiosity, the only one that soars as
high as its highest longing. Let us accustom
ourselves to regard death as a form of life
which we do not yet understand; let us
learn to look upon it with the same eye that
looks upon birth; and soon our mind will be
accompanied to the steps of the tomb with the
same glad expectation as greets a birth.

Maurice Maeterlinck

THE MENTAL HEALTH
PERSPECTIVE ON LIFE

Death Is a Part of Life

Nightlife seems like an oxymoron. Sure, we might like to party a little. Live it up. But when we really analyze our lives, we know we live in the daylight. Alarms ring at 6:00 a.m., or perhaps 7:00. And dinner at 6:00 p.m., or perhaps 7:00, usually marks the end of our productive time. We punch in and out on the time clock. We produce through our individual routines day after day—almost endlessly through our twenties to our sixties. We have our challenges, of course. Some of them may be traumatic. Divorce. Chapter eleven. The kids don't call. But somehow we think we will always have tomorrow. We will try again. We will work harder. Maybe we'll call the kids ourselves—tomorrow.

But then something happens. In the United States (and, in a real way, in the rest of the world), September 11, 2001, eclipsed the daylight. Not only did the twin towers crumble, but for many, our "tomorrow" was called into question. Death muted the brilliance of the daylight.

You may not have known anyone who died in the tragedy of September 11, the Oklahoma City bombing, or any other national tragedy; maybe instead you read of the teenager who was killed in an auto accident in your town or the young woman who took her life out of sheer frustration with the pressures she faced.

But the next morning your alarm went off at its usual time. You put on your work clothes, gulped down breakfast, fast-tracked to wherever you needed to be. The routine swallowed the specter of death, and daylight returned again.

Yet just below the surface we still have this uneasy sense. We are now more aware than ever that death is as much a part of life as birth. But as a society we embrace birth much more than death. Look at all the preparation promoted by the medical profession and child care advocates on how to approach pregnancy, birthing, and newborn parenting. Is there any comparable educational process to help prepare us for death? No. Most of us like to think only of pleasant things. Death seems morbid, promotes despair, and is dark. We prefer to live in the daylight.

Society's Reluctance to Face the Reality of Death

As a society we tend to avoid talking about unpleasant things, and death is in that category. We want to focus on happy thoughts, the beginnings rather than the endings. We work hard to accumulate and achieve, striving to do our best among the many challenges and difficulties of daily life, and we don't want it to end. We don't want to lose everything we have attained, and we prefer not to think about this inevitability.

Not only do many of us play ostrich, sticking our head in the sand to avoid our own mortality, but we also are uncomfortable talking with others about the end of their lives. Friends do not typically invite other friends over for coffee and open the conversation with, "Well, have you thought about your death lately?" Rather, we try to maintain the pretense that somehow we will pull off the great escape and be the first human not to die.

So what is it going to take for *you* to consider that your life has both a beginning and an ending? First, let's accept the fact that talking about death, especially your own death, isn't very popular. You may think it will make others feel uncomfortable—or worse yet, yourself! But here is where a good psychological principle may help: Talking specifically about something that is uncomfortable or painful actually reduces rather than increases those feelings of discomfort. Talking concretely about troublesome areas helps most people dispel the anxiety, depression, or fear associated with those issues. So facing head-on the reality of dying may actually help you feel better about yourself and feel closer to those around you.

Dying and death are scary subjects for most people—largely because so much of it is shrouded in mystery. The unknown can bring shadows to the daylight, and the shadows won't go away by themselves. We need to learn to talk about death as freely as we talk about birth. Then and only then will the anxiety and discomfort surrounding death decrease.

Assessing Your Life to This Point

We often use milestones such as birthdays, anniversaries, or holidays such as New Year's Day as occasions to "take stock" of who we are and what we have done. This may be especially true for a person on his or her deathbed, looking back and wishing they had made different choices. In some respects this type of reflection is quite normal. The confrontation with death makes life assessment almost inevitable. (See sidebar 1)

At this time you may not be on your deathbed. Probably you are still living in the daylight. No potentially terminal illness may be threatening you. However, isn't it important for each of us to evaluate our life while we are still healthy, so that we can appreciate it? What successes have you had? Can you celebrate the good things of your life and allow the memories to soak into your pores like a sponge? Relishing what you

---

I WOULDN'T TRY TO BE SO PERFECT ❶

Anonymous

(The following was written years ago by an eighty-five-year-old man who learned he was dying.)

If I had my life to live over again,
I'd try to make more mistakes next time.
I wouldn't try to be so perfect. We all have
    perfection fetishes.
What difference does it make, if you let people
    know
you are imperfect? They can identify with you
    then.
Nobody can identify with perfection.

I would relax more. I'd be sillier than I've been
    on this trip.
In fact, I know very few things that I would
    take so seriously.
I'd be crazier. I'd be less hygienic. I'd take
    more chances.
I'd climb more mountains. I'd watch more
    sunsets.
I'd go more places I've never seen.
I'd eat more ice cream and fewer beans.
I'd have more actual troubles and fewer
    imaginary ones.

You see, I was one of those people
who lived sensibly and sanely

hour after hour and day after day.
Oh, I've had my moments,
and if I had it to do all over again,
I'd have more of those moments.
In fact, I'd try to have nothing but beautiful
    moments;
moment by moment by moment.
In case you didn't know it,
that's the stuff life is made of—only moments.
Don't miss the now.
I've been one of those people
who never went anywhere without a
    thermometer,
a hot water bottle, a gargle, a raincoat, and a
    parachute.
If I had it to do all over again,
I'd travel lighter next time.

If I had it to do all over again,
I'd start barefoot earlier in the spring
and stay that way until later in the fall.
I'd ride more merry-go-rounds,
I'd watch more sunrises,
and I'd play with more children.
If I had it to do over again. . . .

have learned, accomplished, and endured helps you feel as though your journey has been worth it. Life assessment also provides an opportunity to head in a new direction or incorporate some new elements into your life if you want to.

But life assessment doesn't always produce happy results. Sometimes such reflection uncovers a well of remorse and regret. To think that you might die without achieving some of your life's goals is tough. But each of us knows at some level what we still want to do, and this is the point of life assessment. Take time not only to assess what has been done but also to accept the fact that your own end will come. Your future is limited—daylight doesn't last forever. Now is the time to think through how you want to spend the remaining hours or years of the daylight in your life.

PRIORITIES AND VALUES ❷

Analyzing how you spend your time is a fairly good indicator of where your priorities and values lie. In addition to earning a living, how do you spend your time? On the *left* side of this list, write the approximate number of hours a week you spend in this activity. On the *right* side, rate the value of the activity for you on a scale of 1 to 5 with #1 being "most important." Several items can have the same rating. Please also add other items that occupy your time.

____ Spending time alone with my spouse ____

____ Spending time with my children ____

____ Spending time with my grandchildren ____

____ Working an extra job or overtime to provide greater financial security or to ____
         purchase things I want or need

____ Attending movies, plays, or concerts ____

____ Watching television or videos ____

____ Maintaining or repairing the home or apartment where I live ____

____ Shopping ____

____ Cooking ____

____ Engaging in domestic duties, such as housecleaning, laundry, etc. ____

____ Doing lawn care, gardening, or landscaping ____

____ Visiting with friends ____

____ Pursuing further education ____

____ Being involved in church activities or religious practices ____

____ Going for a walk or to the gym to work out ____

____ Volunteering ____

____ Other: ____

____ Other: ____

____ Other: ____

So how might a person approach a self-evaluation process? How can you assess your values and priorities, those things you most desire or want to protect? For some, these values or priorities might be the accumulation of material possessions or life's "fun" experiences. For others, the value might be the pursuit of a moral and ethical character marked by integrity, honesty, and dependability. Still others may pursue relationships that give meaning to their life. They establish friendships, develop closeness with their family, and perhaps make intimate relationships a priority. Any number of things can contribute to a person's values. Typically our values come from a combination of our genetic makeup and our environment or life experiences.

Perhaps as you read this you are realizing that you have never really intentionally thought about your values or priorities. Why not take time right now to make a list of what you have spent the most time and energy on? Use sidebar 2 to prioritize those things that are important to you. Doing this will assist you in determining your values. For example, some of us learn very early that we can receive our parents' approval by working hard, checking things off a list, and being productive. Others value social relationships and therefore make plans to include others in what they do. Whatever the driving forces have been, these likely represent your values. Goals then arise from what we value and represent what we work for. So ask yourself: "Do I like the direction I'm going and how I'm getting there? Are my values and goals consistent with each other?" The answers may provide the green light to continue toward your goals, or they may signal it's time to reformulate them.

Evaluating Your Past and Present Relationships

Assessing our personal relationships with other people is also healthy. Sometimes we just casually reflect on what we like and don't like in a particular relationship. But conducting a comprehensive assessment can be especially helpful. You can analyze the number of social relationships you have, the nature and frequency of those relationships, and how those people contribute to or enhance your life.

Each of us desires different levels of social contact. Part of understanding yourself is to assess your personal preference for being alone compared to being with others. We are referring here to your level of social desire. Some people like to be with others only occasionally, while other people may prefer to have more frequent contact with their family and friends. Certainly a person's comfort level with being his or her own best friend and spending quality time alone plays a significant part in

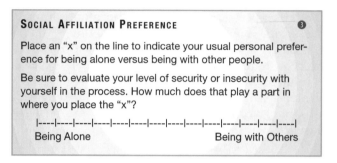

SOCIAL AFFILIATION PREFERENCE   ❸

Place an "x" on the line to indicate your usual personal preference for being alone versus being with other people.

Be sure to evaluate your level of security or insecurity with
yourself in the process. How much does that play a part in
where you place the "x"?

|----|----|----|----|----|----|----|----|----|----|----|----|----|
Being Alone   Being with Others

how much the person feels a need to be with others (social need) compared to simply wanting to be involved with others (social desire). Notice
we differentiate social *desire* from social *need*. How needy or insecure
a person is (social need) influences the number of social contacts he
or she wants. See sidebar 3 to rank your own personal preference for
being alone versus being with others.

To assess the nature of your relationships with significant people in
your life, use sidebar 4. List their names and estimate how often you
are with them on a weekly, monthly, or yearly basis. Then assess the
nature of the association you have with these people. Are they family
or friends? If they are family, how are they related to you? What roles
do they play in your life? What do they do with and for you, and you
for them? Are these relationships balanced, with equal give and take,
or are some of them one-sided (and if so, in which direction)? List the
positive ways each person enhances your life as well as the negative
aspects that may detract from your life. Obviously it is beneficial and
healthy when relationships add to our level of enjoyment or contentedness. Please note, however, that we do not derive our core happiness
from others—we find that in ourselves. You may want to expand your
list to additional pages in order to complete your thoughts and feelings
about specific relationships. Hopefully this exercise will help you to
realize what changes you would like to make in your relationships as
well as to embrace the positive aspects.

Another helpful exercise to evaluate your relationships is to draw a
series of concentric circles, as in sidebar 5. Put your own name in the
center circle. In the next ring out, put the names of one to three people
with whom you are the closest and feel best being around. If you decide no one in your life belongs in the ring closest to you, skip that ring
and determine where the person with whom you feel most connected
does belong. Continue to the outer circles with diminishing degrees of
closeness corresponding to the quality of the relationships you have
with these people. Then add arrows indicating where you would like

each relationship to be. Use an arrow pointing toward the center of the circle if you want the relationship to grow closer. Point the arrow away from the center if the relationship is no longer satisfying to you and you realize you need to put more distance in that relationship. This will give you some idea which relationships you wish to cultivate further. If you see many empty spaces and recognize that you do feel lonely much of the time, you might consider with whom you want to expand a present relationship, or you could explore building additional friendships with some new people.

ASSESSING THE NATURE OF YOUR RELATIONSHIPS WITH OTHER PEOPLE

List the person's name, the nature of your relationship, and how often you see or talk with each person. Then list the ways that person enhances (+) and/or detracts (-) from your life, giving explanations on the lines provided.

Name	Relationship/Roles	Frequency of Contact	+ or –	Explanation

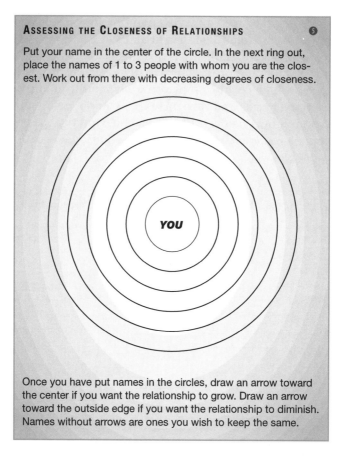

ASSESSING THE CLOSENESS OF RELATIONSHIPS

Put your name in the center of the circle. In the next ring out, place the names of 1 to 3 people with whom you are the closest. Work out from there with decreasing degrees of closeness.

YOU

Once you have put names in the circles, draw an arrow toward the center if you want the relationship to grow. Draw an arrow toward the outside edge if you want the relationship to diminish. Names without arrows are ones you wish to keep the same.

What Kind of Relationship Can You Have with Yourself?

How much a person likes himself or herself also makes a significant difference in facing the reality that one's life on earth will end. How we see ourselves is known as our *self-concept*. Do you describe yourself mostly in positive or negative terms? The other word often used to describe this is *self-esteem*. This term refers specifically to the value and worth we have for ourselves. Do you think other people matter more than you do or are more important than you are? Actually, to be able to say "I am a good and valuable person" is healthy. Recognizing and embracing your own value is an important step in developing healthy self-esteem. So if you like yourself and feel good about who you are, you will likely feel more confident, self-sufficient, and comfortable with yourself. Those strengths will assist you to some degree in facing a potentially terminal illness.

Maybe you think it sounds crazy or selfish to develop a relationship with yourself. This reaction may be a clue as to how you assess your own importance and worth. You may believe it is not even "right" to like yourself. Many people were raised by parents who stressed that being humble, modest, proper, or "religious" meant never thinking of yourself as being as important or valuable as other people.

But we the authors don't believe that having a healthy self-esteem is inconsistent with having a religious faith. Christians, for example, believe that people have been created in the very image of God! This belief allows people to think highly of themselves because of their relationship with God.

If you learned to focus on others and to emphasize their needs or wants and consider them first, you may now face a real personal dilemma. Who is this person inside your body? Do you actually matter? Maybe you've never given yourself permission to find out.

When it comes right down to it, each one of us walks this earthly journey most intimately with our self rather than with others. As we become adults, we assume total responsibility for ourselves. Yes, we may be in caring relationships with others. We want to be helpful and to collaborate in making wise choices or solving problems. And it feels good to have others express caring toward us. But ultimately "the buck stops here" for each one of us. In the end we each need to take responsibility for our own choices, our growth in living, and the contributions we have made.

Think about it. We definitely do two things in life solo—being born and dying. Obviously we have been birthed by our mothers, but we actually make the journey from the womb to breathing on our own in this world. We will hopefully have others near us as well when we die, but we will be on a solo journey in dying. No one completes the journey with us from start to finish. Now is the time to become your own best friend. Get to know yourself—after all, you are the one you will live with twenty-four hours a day, seven days a week, for the rest of your life. We have already indicated that liking yourself will lessen any loneliness you feel and probably decrease the need and desire to be with people all the time. You can then feel content and secure within yourself. Furthermore, to have a deep and intimate relationship with others, you need to know and love yourself first.

As a clinical psychologist, Susan often suggests that a person go away for a weekend alone. Don't visit someone else—go away by yourself. Even better, go to a new place you have never experienced before. That adventure may help you further discover who you are—what you like and don't like. You will develop a clearer sense of what you enjoy doing, where you like to stay, where and when you like to eat and sleep. Even how you decide those things is an important data-collecting experience and can help shed light on your values and sense of identity. Sometimes society insinuates that going somewhere alone denotes some inadequacy or deficiency rather than demonstrating a sense of comfort with yourself, assurance, and contentedness. You are, however, a complete and whole person, and you can do things alone. Achieving this type of self-reliance will help when you ultimately face your own death.

Planning for Your Death

Many of us have already learned the value of planning ahead. We often plan ways to celebrate the bigger milestones on our life journey. Take for example a twenty-first birthday or a special holiday celebration. What about the birth of a baby or a fortieth anniversary? Or career decisions or the purchase of a new home? We look ahead, anticipate, imagine, and plan for these future events. By doing this, we can better make the occasions live up to our expectations. Very few of us just let a special day or event arrive without some forethought.

Yet isn't it interesting that when it comes to planning for our death, we often think of it as morbid and shrink away from thinking about it or making any plans for it? We do look forward to some endings throughout our life, such as finishing high school or college or leaving the workforce for retirement. Our death will happen just as certainly as that milestone birthday, a holiday, the end of a phase of life, or the achievement of some goal. However, very early on—before we are even conscious of it—we seem to learn that hushed tones are appropriate surrounding death, and we adopt a predominantly negative attitude about dying.

But we the authors believe that people should view death as the completion of a well-lived life. Some cultures view dying as the final step toward life's completion, as a successful end to be celebrated. But even those who come from a religious or spiritual perspective often do not behave as if their own death is the victorious conclusion to a life well lived. We may believe it in the abstract, we may even say it at a loved one's funeral, but when it comes to practicing it by planning for our own physical end, death doesn't look very desirable.

We are fully familiar with life—this is all we know. And because we only die once, death is unfamiliar and unknown. There is very little to entice us to embrace it. But the point we want to make is that to deny or avoid the reality of our eventual death simply is not healthy. Planning for death at least gives a person some control over the final outcome of his or her life.

Planning for Your Legal and Financial Needs

In planning for your death, you need to consider four basic legal actions to ensure that your wishes will be fulfilled both in the process of dying and upon your death.

The first is to create a Durable Power of Attorney. This is a legal document naming a person(s) to make financial and managerial decisions if you are incapacitated or for some other reason are unable to personally manage your own affairs while still alive. This person can write checks and access the rest of your financial accounts.

A second instrument is the Durable Power of Attorney for Health Care. Through this document you identify the person(s) who will have the legal power to make health care decisions if you are no longer able to do it for yourself. This typically involves implementing your prescribed wishes about end-of-life issues, such as what type of (if any) extraordinary or life-sustaining means you want the doctors to use if you are in a life-threatening situation. That may include whether or not you want cardiac resuscitation should your heart stop, IVs , a feeding tube, or a respirator and other measures to prolong your life even though your prognosis is terminal. These personal wishes are often called an advanced directive, and federal law mandates that hospitals ask if you have this when you are admitted.

The other two legal instruments you need to consider are a Last Will and Testament and possibly a Living Trust. They clarify how you want your remaining estate (financial and material holdings) to be distributed upon your death. If you are married at the time of your death, typically the remainder of your estate becomes your spouse's property if you have documentation of joint ownership of your properties (i.e., holding title as "joint tenants" or "with rights of survivorship"). With documentation of joint ownership you can avoid some of the expenses associated with filing your will in probate court. If you do not have a will when you die, you are said to have died "intestate," which means that the laws of your state of legal residence (as administered by the courts) decide who receives what portion of your remaining estate. In some states this may mean that the surviving spouse will receive one-third of the estate with the remaining two-thirds divided among the children. In other states the surviving spouse may receive the first one hundred thousand dollars of the estate and 50 percent of everything over that amount with the other 50 percent divided among the children. Obviously you will want to check the laws in your state of legal residence. Therefore, having a will is very important, and you should seriously consider drawing one up so that you have control over the distribution of your assets.

If your total assets exceed one million dollars, a revocable trust is used not only to avoid probate but also to distribute your assets to your heirs (or other organizations) *over a period of time* after your death. In a revocable trust, as long as you are alive, you are the trustee and retain full control over your estate. When you die, however, the trust continues through a successor trustee whom you have already named when establishing the trust. That trustee manages your money in keeping with your wishes as stipulated in the trust. Therefore, through the trust you are able to avoid probate court as well as a number of other fees or taxes that may be associated with your death. For a summary of your legal and financial planning needs, see sidebar 6.

ARE YOU FAMILIAR WITH THE FOLLOWING LEGAL DOCUMENTS?   6

Durable Power of Attorney:

A legal document in which you authorize another person or persons to function for you financially and legally in the event you are not able to do so yourself.

Durable Power of Attorney for Health Care (which often contains an "advanced directive," "living will," or "health care proxy"):

A legal document in which you authorize another person or persons to make medical decisions for you in the event you are not able to do so yourself. It also explains how you want your body cared for medically should you not be able to make those decisions and what type of life-sustaining treatment (if any) you want as you near the end of your life. The document should also provide immunity to medical caregivers who follow your wishes and can be understood as your specific instructions to the Power of Attorney for Health Care for your treatment.

Last Will and Testament:

A legal document in which you provide instructions on how you wish your estate to be divided upon your death. This document is administered by the probate court in the area in which you live when there is no evidence of joint ownership to the heirs receiving the assets. Typically, the probate court assesses relatively minor fees to administer the will, but the executor's and attorney's fees can be somewhat expensive, and the process may take a considerable period of time. Even if you establish a trust hoping to avoid some of the expense of probate, you will need a will to cover other unforeseen contingencies. If you do not have a will, the state does, in effect, create one for you.

Living Trust:

A legal document by which you place all your financial assets in an entity that you will manage as a "trustee" until your death (or until you are incapacitated). You will have named successor trustees who will then assume control over your assets and administer them according to the provisions you elected when you created the trust. In many cases, this method avoids the heavy costs of administering an estate through probate court. Trusts are useful for minimizing taxes for people with an estate in excess of one million dollars. They are also useful for avoiding probate and managing your asset distribution *over a period* of time following your death even if your estate is less than one million dollars in value.

Planning Your Memorial or Funeral Service and Disposition of Your Body

Planning your memorial or funeral service and determining the method of disposition for your body is another way to acknowledge your life, to celebrate your value, and to recall your life's journey. The funeral visitation and service are the beginning of the grief process by which those who loved you can acknowledge your absence and the pain associated with your death. These are necessary and meaningful opportunities for the community of mourners to remember you and to offer each other emotional support.

When you design your funeral (or memorial) service, make certain that your life, work, values, relationships, activities, interests, beliefs, and passions are represented. This can be done through eulogies, an open microphone, a meditative message, Scripture passages, readings, songs, or pictures and other objects that are visible during the funeral service. Selecting what you would like ahead of time can provide a sense of comfort for those attending the service because these things will truly represent your values and tastes.

Hopefully you will also feel good knowing that at the end of your life, your loved ones will pay tribute to you. Of course, you don't have to wait until you are dying or dead to celebrate your life with them. But the funeral puts a final cap on your life. While this may all sound morbid or negative, we hope this book will help you decide what you want at the end of your life while you are still living in the daylight. When you get to the point of feeling more comfortable with your own death, you will be able to live life in a healthier and more satisfying way.

What Do You Think about the Dying Process, Death, and the Afterlife?

Your past undoubtedly has shaped some of your attitudes about death. Do you have memories of when you first encountered death? How old were you? What were the circumstances? Who or what died? How was the death explained to you? What other experiences have you had since that first experience?

Make a chronological list of the deaths you have experienced throughout your life (using sidebar 7) and then write about what you learned from each of them. As you do this, identify what you now think and feel about death. This process helps because it asks you to be concrete and specific. Do you think you had some experiences or were told things that did not give a very accurate or positive view of death? Maybe you were left to figure it out by yourself. If that is the case, you may have developed some inaccurate notions about dying. Maybe your picture of death was shaped by a dying person writhing in pain and the family wringing their hands in agony over seeing their loved one suffer. Or perhaps you remember a scene in which someone was so scared to die that they clung to a loved one, begging to be saved from death. In the absence of a healthy view of dying and death, we often imagine the final event to be far worse than it is.

Sometimes geographical distance separates family members, so you may not have experienced the actual death of a loved one firsthand. The lack of a personal experience in witnessing a death or in attending a funeral often increases a person's discomfort in thinking about his or her own dying and death. While you are still healthy, you have an excellent opportunity to reframe these distorted notions.

One good place to begin is to gather more accurate information about death. *Webster's* defines death as "a permanent ending of all life in a person, animal, or plant."[3] That doesn't have to be scary or painful. Don't shy away from being present when someone is dying. Attend funeral events of family and friends. You hopefully will learn to view death as the end of a race well run or the shutting off of a car at the end of a vacation trip. And it's important to remember that life is intermingled with pain, grief, hurt, and anger. Death not only ends good things but also ends pain, disharmony, and disappointments. The good and bad things of life all come to an end.

Death has an interesting counterpart—a new beginning. When one door closes, another door is opened. Another pathway appears on our

---

YOUR DEATH AWARENESS ASSESSMENT   ❼

We learn from our experiences. This is also true for deepening our understanding of death. Sometimes we learn from healthy examples. Sometimes we learn from unhealthy examples. What have you learned about death from the experiences you have had?

Who Died?	When? How Old Were You?	What Did You Learn about Death?	Does It Present an Accurate View?

journey. Many religious faiths embrace some concept of eternity—a new beginning that doesn't have the negative side to it. So as this life ends, we enter a new beginning—a very different and wonderful one.

When Susan was a young child, her grandmother would tell her a story that helped her understand death. When Susan wondered how sad a person must be to die and leave everyone behind, her grandmother said it was like a person leaving on a very long boat trip. Their family and friends stood on the departing shore seeing their loved one off on this special journey. Certainly they were all sad at the farewell, but as the home shoreline grew fainter and finally faded out of sight, the opposite shore where the ship was headed came into view. There the passenger could see scores of familiar faces eager for her arrival. An ending became a new beginning. Death is both a good-bye to the relationships we have on earth and a hello to an entirely new, never-ending life. An end and a beginning.

Many religious people embrace a sense of continuity between this life and the next. If this life is a prelude to a place of no more pain, no more sadness, no more bodily limitations, then it would seem we would want to get on with it and say good-bye to this world. With no cure for a critical illness or decreased quality of life because of old age, most of us would like to leave, except we like to hold on to the known, the familiar. This life is all we know, but this is where faith comes in. John Bunyan, in his classic book *Pilgrim's Progress*,[4] describes us as journeying through life, experiencing both exhilarating joys and devastating sorrows, but always with eyes looking toward the Celestial City, where there is no longer any type of pain or hardship.

As you read this, you may be healthy and far from dying. If that is the case, living life to the fullest is undoubtedly your aim. But if your body is deteriorating and increasing in pain with little hope of health again, the thought of death might even seem inviting. Perhaps you remember visiting an older person confined to bed because of a chronic, progressive illness who was eagerly awaiting his or her own death. It's very hard to relate to that perspective when life is good. However, when there is little hope left that one's quality of life might return and when being active and feeling good aren't really possible anymore, death may very well seem inviting. Most of us want to live long lives, but not just a quantity of years without quality.

Of course, dying and death may be elusive concepts to grasp when we are healthy. Part of that avoidance may arise from our anxiety about the future and what may happen as we approach our own death. What precipitates our uneasiness? It is helpful to assess exactly what you actually fear so you can do some problem solving and develop a plan of action. Do you *fear the unknown*? This concern is understandable, because death is an experience you have never had before. However, exploring your feelings about your own death helps illuminate some of the unknown. Perhaps the thought of having to *endure intense pain* is the real issue. But in the twenty-first century, medical science can provide medications for effective pain relief. Maybe the thought of how lonely the dying process might be, accompanied by the *fear of being alone* when you die, triggers discomfort. If this is the case, think about planning a visitation schedule with your family to ensure that people are with you as much as possible as you near the end of your life. *Loss of freedom and dependence* on others is almost always a fear as we age and approach death. It is important to remember that even as we age, we are still valuable.

Regardless of your specific fear, the first step is to face the fear squarely and name it for what it is. Once you have identified your fear, express your concerns to someone close to you. Hopefully you can work through the issues with this support person, understand your concerns better, and determine ways to decrease your anxiety. Actually, death is the only thing (other than birth) that we do only once. Therefore, we really can't learn from our own experience. In other words, there are no rehearsals. We may learn a little from others who have had a "near death" experience. Most of those reports seem comforting—seeing a bright light surrounded by a serene and peaceful atmosphere. Or we may learn some valuable lessons about dying from being with others at their passing. But the fact remains, we only die once ourselves.

What Is Dying Like Emotionally?

Even if you are not presently faced with a serious illness or actively dying, we think you should be aware of what that experience might be like emotionally. We all know the dying process can be scary, but what other emotions accompany this journey toward the end of life? Dr. Elisabeth Kubler-Ross[5] conducted groundbreaking research into this area in the 1960s and 1970s. She identified five stages of the dying process that are probably familiar to most people. These stages were first thought to be sequentially connected, with each stage following the preceding one. Now, however, many experts suggest that the stages are far more interrelated and integrated, more of an indicator of the type and range of the emotional responses a person may have while dying.

The danger of any stage theory is the expectation that everyone experiences all of the stages and goes through them in a particular predetermined order. This type of thinking is not only erroneous but can be hurtful if a dying person's behavior doesn't seem to follow the stages.

Someone might conclude that she or he is doing something wrong because they are not in the stage they are "supposed" to be at the time.

Such a situation occurred when Susan's first husband, Rick, was dying, because he wasn't feeling angry about his diagnosis (at least at that time) the way some people expected him to be. They told him to stop denying his anger and admit he had that feeling. So in cases such as this, information can be dangerous if it is not used for the purpose intended. Knowledge of the dying process is meant to give us an idea of the reactions or responses a dying person might experience in facing death, but it is not intended to make us judgmental toward the dying person.

Let's take a brief look at the stages that Kubler-Ross identified. They are: (1) denial or shock; (2) anger; (3) bargaining; (4) depression; and (5) acceptance (see sidebar 8).

Receiving the diagnosis of a potentially terminal illness is a shock to almost everyone who experiences it. Many people initially deny, at least emotionally, that they will eventually die. When a person hears that he or she has a potentially terminal illness and may die, perhaps soon, they feel both shock and denial, which constitutes Kubler-Ross's first stage. A common reaction is to say there must have been a mistake, a mix-up with someone else's test results. When denial no longer works because overwhelming evidence verifies the diagnosis, the person still feels numb over what is happening to them.

A problem develops when people continue to refuse to face their diagnosis and do something to help themselves. Some people will search far and wide to find medical or holistic health professionals who will disagree with the seriousness of the diagnosis. Others may bury themselves in their work or find some other way to distract themselves

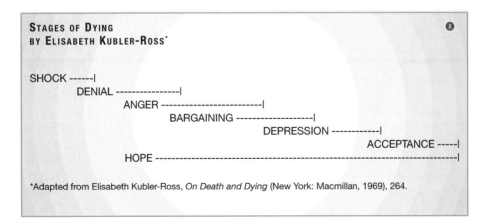

STAGES OF DYING
BY ELISABETH KUBLER-ROSS*   8

SHOCK ------|
          DENIAL ----------------|
                  ANGER -------------------------|
                          BARGAINING -------------------|
                                  DEPRESSION ------------|
                                                  ACCEPTANCE -----|
                  HOPE --|

*Adapted from Elisabeth Kubler-Ross, *On Death and Dying* (New York: Macmillan, 1969), 264.

from the reality of the diagnosis. Eventually anyone with a potentially terminal illness needs to recognize the diagnosis is real and find some healthy ways to respond.

The second stage is anger. The apparent injustice of a terminal illness is obvious to most of us. Questions such as "Why is this happening to me? Why now? What did I do to deserve this?" race to the forefront of our minds after hearing that our life may end. Sometimes the anger is directed inward for lack of self-care and sometimes at another family member who contributed to an unhealthy situation (such as smoking in the house or cooking unhealthy meals). Other times the anger lashes out at medical professionals, at God, or at anyone who happens to be there.

Many people are raised with the idea that you should not feel angry. Yet anger is a very normal and natural way to express feelings about a situation. Remember that anger isn't meant to be an end point. Anger is something to be expressed and worked through.

Kubler-Ross identified the third stage as bargaining. Bargaining refers to the desire to make deals with God or a higher power so that longer life will be granted. A person may resolve to live a better, more honest life if God will grant a few more years. Sometimes gifts made to charitable organizations are bartered for a longer life. Often the dying person hopes to attend or experience an important event before dying, such as a graduation, wedding, favorite holiday, vacation, or the birth of a grandchild. It does seem that motivation to attend an event or still see a certain person can positively impact the length of life at times. Bargaining takes motivation one step further by making some type of deal with God or a higher power. In exchange for a longer life, the dying person promises to do a particular thing.

The fourth stage is depression. Our life goals certainly don't include a potentially terminal illness. As the symptoms appear and worsen, most people experience some depression, which is understandable. The thought of death is unpleasant for most of us, even though we understand at some level that it happens to everyone and is not controlled by our time schedule. When we face difficult situations, depression can be a frequent visitor.

The last stage of Kubler-Ross's theory is acceptance—accepting the inevitability of the impending death. Depending on a person's perspective about what happens after this life, acceptance may be the belief that death is a transition. Pain will come both physically and emotionally, and in time the disease will take over the major organs required to sustain life, but eventually one moves to a better place. Most religions portray this better place as one free from all of the strife and pain of this life. Acceptance does not mean that a person needs to like the fact that he or she will die. And acceptance may be felt at some times but not as strongly at others; like the other stages, it can be transitory. Acceptance simply means that the person no longer resists the inevitable. Reaching the point of acceptance provides an easier transition from this life for both the dying person and his or her loved ones.

This brief introduction to Kubler-Ross's stages of the emotional responses to dying should help acquaint you with what may happen to anyone who has some warning that death is coming. Remember that most of what a person experiences is normal, unless the person is actively suicidal. These stages are not, as was said before, a prescribed sequence in which each stage becomes an end in itself. Rather, they represent emotions or experiences a dying person may have at various times during the dying journey. While you live in the daylight, use this information to better understand those you know who are actively dying.

How Do Children Think about Death?

Children are often exposed to sickness and death early in life. Shielding them from those realities is nearly impossible. And if we could, the children would not have an opportunity to form healthy coping mechanisms to handle difficult life traumas.

When families get together, they often have conversations about someone who is seriously ill or who recently died. How do we, as loving parents and family members, deal with children when these subjects come up? We the authors would encourage you to become comfortable talking about serious illness, dying, and death with your children within your family setting and use these conversations as a learning experience. Many people, however, often behave like Dick and Molly in the following scenario.

Molly's sister had been diagnosed with liver cancer several months ago. When friends asked Dick and Molly how she was doing, Dick and Molly quickly turned and said to their preadolescent daughters, "Why don't you run along and play outside?" They obviously didn't want to talk about the girls' aunt in front of them. The clearly implied message was "This is a serious conversation for adults only and something we don't want you to hear." But the children missed an opportunity to hear in a healthy way how others view serious illness and dying. Instead, they probably began to form the idea that death is something bad and to be dreaded.

It is important to recognize that children do not think about dying and death the same way adults do. Their view is dependent on their developmental level, including the capacity for abstract reasoning, as well as the limited amount of life experiences they have accrued. Yet children, as a part of the family unit, are often involved in some planned or unplanned ways when a loved one is dying. How do you talk with children about what is happening? How much involvement or exposure to the actual dying process should they have? Even when you or your family are not faced with a serious or terminal illness, how can (and should) you make conversation about death a normal activity with your children? Our children may be more tuned in to the reality of dying, death, and grief following the tragedy of September 11. Certainly they hear about death and dying at school, in church, or in their friends' families. So allowing children to observe grieving family members and including them in conversations about death in a manner in which they can understand helps them learn healthy coping strategies.

Exposing children to some of the harsh realities of life can be tough. After all, parents spend a great deal of time and effort trying to protect their children. They don't want them to watch violence on television or in the movies. They protect them from pornographic material. They keep track of whom they associate with and make sure they are not taking unnecessary risks. The topic of dying or death is a threat to the childhood innocence parents have worked hard to maintain. But remaining silent and refusing to talk about it is unhealthy. A parent's primary responsibility is to prepare children for life. And life includes death.

Decades ago children grew up closely connected with a grandparent or older family member who usually became increasingly debilitated and eventually died. The deceased was then "laid out" in the parlor, and people came to offer condolences and support. There was no avoiding the fact that death happened. Now our society attempts to make things nice, easy, and protected. We need to ask if this approach is ultimately helpful. We the authors think that facing reality and dealing with the tough stuff is a much more emotionally healthy way to manage a loved one's death.

Well-meaning attempts to shelter children from life's tragedies or harsh realities can be more confusing and frightening than a simple explanation of the truth. Children of all ages are quite perceptive and watch the behavior of adults closely. Even if they cannot understand our words, they respond to the emotional climate set by their primary caregivers. They often learn from what we do and how we behave (such as by our tone of voice, facial expressions, and body movements) more than from what we actually say. They need to know they are safe, they will be well cared for, and things are basically stable for them. Being truthful and answering their questions will help provide that stability.

If you or a loved one is terminally ill and you can't talk about the illness or death when the children are asking their questions because you are too emotional or it is not good timing, be sure to let them know specifically when you will get back to them. Also remember that as adults we can't fix or eliminate our children's pain. Feelings are healthy. Allowing children to be sad and cry or to feel angry is healthy. Let children know you understand that they feel sad or mad. Sit with them and listen to them. Children need time to work through their feelings.

How much information you give children depends on their age, their developmental level, and what they are asking (see sidebar 9). For example, a very young infant or a child of up to two years old has no concept of dying or death. This age group will react to their primary caregiver's emotions. If they sense distress or fear in their caregiver, they may respond in similar fashion by not sleeping well, clinging, or exhibiting "cranky" behavior. It may be helpful to begin teaching them "sad, mad, and glad" and talk about their feelings in simple terms. If the primary caregiver died, they would definitely miss that person and search for him or her. In that case you could tell them something like, "Mommy died. She can't come back." If you believe in an afterlife, you might add that "Mommy is in heaven. She was sad about having to go and didn't want to leave you." It is most important for them to feel loved by continuing in as normal a routine as possible.

Around the ages of three to five, children develop the ability to form a mental representation of an important attachment figure. In other words, they can picture a person without having to see him or her physically. They have developed some comprehension of the English language and can understand an explanation that a person is very sick and no longer able to do many things, but they may not perceive the severity of what is happening. They likely associate the meaning of

---

CHILDREN'S UNDERSTANDING OF DEATH: AGES 0–18 ❾

Infant–2 YRS.:	No concept of death.
2–5 YRS:	Death not permanent; is reversible.
5–8 YRS:	Death thought of in concrete terms.
8–12 YRS:	Finality of death understood; irreversible.
12–18 YRS:	Now able to use abstract reasoning.

Eventually all children need to understand that death is:

- permanent
- a biological process
- inevitable
- universal

dying and death with sleeping a lot, and they are typically very curious and may say things like, "How come Grandma doesn't get up and play with me anymore?"

Children of this age may ask spiritual questions about what happens to the dead body and where that person really is when he or she dies. A child of this age does understand, based on others' reactions, that a traumatic or difficult event has occurred but may seem personally unaffected by it. One of the reasons for this is that they do not see death as permanent. They view death as reversible—similar to the person who has gone on a trip or is sleeping. A child between the ages of three and five might say something like, "Grandpa has gone away for a while, but not for long. He will come back." Children up to the age of five believe that when a loved one dies, he or she can still eat, hear, and see. A good way to help a child of this age understand death is to explain that being dead is when the heart stops beating and the person stops breathing. Using the example of a dead animal, bird, or bug is also a helpful way to show that there is no longer movement or signs of life.

Children between the ages of three and six tend to incorporate magical thinking into their perceptions. They believe that if they wish or think something hard enough, they have the power to make it happen. If they had been angry with the deceased person, they may feel worried or guilty that their negative feelings caused the death.

Children between the ages of five and eight connect death concretely to its causes. They might think, for example, that Dad died because he was very, very sick. Or a sister died because she was very, very hurt when she rode her bike into the path of a car. Or Grandma died because she was very, very old. According to children of this age, being sick, hurt, or old are three common reasons why people die. These children are curious about what specifically caused the person's death and have a tendency to think that the causes came mostly from an outside source. They also tend to personify death and associate it with ghosts, monsters, goblins, darkness, or nighttime. However, they reason that if a person is clever enough, he or she can probably escape dying.

When adults express their emotions of grief in a strong or powerful way, children between the ages of two and eight may feel frightened and helpless. They may deal with these feelings by either withdrawing or behaving aggressively. They may have nightmares, demonstrate moodiness, or want to carry around a belonging from the sick or deceased person. They have a strong curiosity about death, including what happens to the body and why it is buried. Children of this age don't understand that someday they too will die, either by becoming very sick or by a sudden cause, so their search for information rises primarily from a factual curiosity rather than a fear base.

Somewhere between the ages of eight and twelve years, children begin to understand the finality of death. They recognize that death is irreversible. They also understand death as a biological process and therefore a scientific inevitability for all people. Children then begin to develop an increased awareness of their own mortality, but they also believe that death won't happen to them for a very long time.

Children of this age will probably be more concerned about what changes or consequences will occur for them personally as a result of the loved one's death and the absence it creates in their lives. These changes will be in direct relation to what the dying person has done for him or her in the past and obviously can no longer do. They will probably ask questions like "Who will take care of me?" and "How will I possibly manage without this person?" They may become upset or angry with the deceased because he or she died and deserted them. They may also develop a fear of going to school or complain of physical symptoms or an illness following a loved one's death. Sometimes they put the dead loved one on a pedestal, which makes working through loss issues more difficult.

The gruesome aspects of death are of special interest to preadolescents, including the nitty-gritty, "blood and guts" of what happens to the body. Sometimes children of this age also get the idea (often from adults) that they should be caretakers to the people feeling sad and upset. Because preadolescents now have a deeper understanding of the body and soul, they tend to focus more prominently on God when thinking about death and the afterlife. A multitude of questions may surround all of these components of death and need to be handled with accuracy and sensitivity by caring adults.

Adolescence offers an entirely new challenge in dealing with a dying person or with an actual death. On the one hand, most child development experts agree that this is when a person's abstract reasoning ability begins, and the dying process and death certainly involve abstract concepts that even adults struggle with. Adolescents perceive death as the destruction of life, of one's body, and of the corresponding hopes and dreams for the future. They can begin to understand the idea of the transition from life to death. In many ways their reaction may be similar to that of adults, but they probably have had little or no experience prior to this trauma to learn how to deal with really bad or sad things in their lives. They likely have developed few coping strategies and will therefore watch how adults manage their emotions.

Adolescents do comprehend the universal nature of death—that it happens to all living things. However, they don't necessarily generalize death to include themselves because of their sense of invulnerability and immortality. In addition, the teenage years are turbulent and stressful as identity issues arise, peer relations become more important, and major decisions about educational and career goals need to be made. Adolescence is a fairly self-focused and difficult time, and so the serious illness or death of a loved one may compound their stress and overwhelm teenagers to the point of wanting to distract themselves, avoid their feelings, or withdraw from adults and not talk about what is happening. They may need encouragement to speak with the dying person and express some of their feelings related to their grief rather than internalizing them, which may result in some other physical or emotional problem at a later point.

We should also say a word about young adults, ages twenty through twenty-nine. Facing the death of a loved one is never easy, but young adults have a special challenge in this regard. As their adult life begins, they spend much of their energy contemplating career choices, learning how to develop intimacy with others (including dating and marriage), and separating from their parents not only physically and financially but also psychologically. They are "coming into their own" in the adult world. When an important adult figure in their life dies, the very stability against which they push in order to establish their identity is gone (which is true for adolescents as well). Young adults have enough emotional baggage to sort through without the myriad of feelings that accompany the death of someone they love. Hopefully, because they are emerging adults, they may be open to talking with you about their feelings, especially if you approach them in a loving and supportive manner.

Another way to understand how children, adolescents, and young adults manage grief is to recognize that they do so incrementally and developmentally. At times it may appear as if young children don't care about the dying or deceased person very much because they return quickly to playing. An older child or adolescent may cry initially and then appear to be done with grieving. A young adult may appear to be engaged (or distracted) by the pressing issues of their daily life. These interruptions with grieving have more to do with the power of the other things that are vying for their attention at the time than with a lack of caring for the deceased person or the conclusion of grieving.

Children, adolescents, and young adults will most likely return to the work of grieving periodically over several years as they experience various developmental changes. This intermittent grieving comes because they miss this significant person at important times of their lives. These include life transitions or milestones such as graduations, weddings, establishing careers, various personal accomplishments, and the birth of children. As they grow into adulthood and begin to understand the deeper significance of holidays or other special events, the absence of their loved one may trigger some sadness on these occasions.[6] The goal is that every bereaved person will arrive at a point in adulthood where they have finished dealing with all the identifiable aspects of their loss and will no longer feel pain as a result of their loved one's death.

In trying to understand grief in children and adolescents, we need to recognize that age and developmental levels impact grieving behaviors immensely. In addition to those factors, all of us have our own ways of dealing with death and grief based on our personalities, our specific life circumstances, and our coping strategies. The theory of multiple intelligences as articulated by Howard Gardner and associates is another way to understand and help children deal with their grief.[7] Gardner theorized that we all possess a variety of forms of intelligence in differing combinations. When Gardner originally developed his theory of "multiple intelligences," he identified seven basic forms. Everyone possesses each one, though each person may excel in certain areas and be weaker in others. The application to assisting children, adolescents, and young adults in their grief is simply to realize they have a number of avenues for expressing grief available to them. Each person may select a different route to grief expression, but each route may be legitimate at that time for that person. We have provided a list of the original seven basic forms of intelligence identified by Gardner along with a brief description of each and examples of how you can use each form to help a child or young person move through his or her grief.

Linguistic	Using words, either written or spoken.	Have children tell a story, read a story, or (for older children) write a letter, a poem, or a journal entry.
Logical	Using the sequence of thought, including mathematics or scientific knowledge.	Help them engage in research to better understand the illness, death, or other questions they may have.
Spatial	Using shapes, forms, or art material.	Invite children to draw a picture, make a scrapbook, or create some other art project either of the person or the funeral.
Musical	Using either vocal or musical forms.	Listen to music or participate in singing or playing an instrument; be involved with music at the funeral.
Bodily	Using the physical body, such as with dance, sports, or crafts.	Children can use physical games to release energy, create skits to express their feelings, or make a handicraft to express their emotions.

| Interpersonal | Having "insights" almost intuitively into the thoughts and feelings of others. | Be sensitive that children may reflect the feelings they sense in the adults around them; answer their questions honestly, as appropriate to their age level. |
| Intrapersonal | Developing self-awareness or the ability to understand and accept one's own feelings, ideas, and values. | Invite children to be introspective by asking open-ended questions, especially ones that invite them to "wonder" about what is happening. |

Along with understanding the various developmental levels of children, we must acknowledge the wide variety of ways they express their grief based on how they best comprehend and deal with life.

So how can you help children, adolescents, and young adults face the reality that dying and death are an integral part of living and life? The general principle is to engage them in conversation about these issues at a level appropriate to their age and allow them to participate in activities with a person who is dying as the opportunity may present itself. If they have had a pet die, or even seen a dead bug, you can use this as a helpful precursor to explaining various aspects of dying and death to them. They will probably have many questions that need to be answered honestly at their level of understanding. Being honest is crucial because honesty is a fundamental ingredient in establishing a trusting and secure environment. Honesty will also decrease a child's anxiety and tension. Sometimes adults underestimate a child's ability to understand, so a helpful approach is to first ascertain what the child or adolescent thinks or feels about the dying person or death before answering their questions. Some helpful books you can use to educate children of various ages about the specifics of dying and death are found in the appendix to this book.

You probably know the good feeling that comes from helping another person. We are often geared in our culture to be "doers." Children may think they are insignificant when it comes to helping a dying person. If someone they love is dying, try to identify some things children and adolescents can do that will be supportive and meaningful to them and to the dying person. We all like to feel useful, and being involved in someone's dying process or death will help young people deal with their feelings. They might color a picture, pick flowers, bring a water bottle, make a card, lend a stuffed animal, read to the person, or play an instrument for them. The person dying may also want to give the child something as a concrete reminder of their special relationship. Children, adolescents, and young adults also need to realize the art of "being oneself" with others. Let children know that being with a person is often more appreciated and helpful than anything else. People who are dying often comment that the most meaningful thing a person can do for them is to sit and listen. After the death, help children or adolescents become involved in some part of funeral planning in a way appropriate to their age. A young person might find it helpful to put an object special to him or her in their loved one's casket to express closeness and caring.

As you live life in the daylight, it is also an appropriate time to reflect on what we believe to be one of the most significant purposes of parenting and grandparenting—to be healthy role models for your offspring in handling the challenges and traumas of life. Talk with children and adolescents about your feelings, and express your emotions. It's fine to cry when you feel sad. That is how children and teenagers learn to express their own emotions. But guard against expressing emotion in such an intense way that it becomes frightening for them. Being open about your emotions helps them learn healthy ways to express their own. Particularly when someone is dying, be aware that children are observing adults' methods of managing their feelings and behaviors.

Death also triggers spiritual questions for children and adolescents in ways similar to adults. "Forever" is a difficult term to comprehend. Many questions rise to the surface, such as, "What is it like to die?" "What happens to the person?" "What is the soul and where does it go?" and "What about heaven and hell?" Remember that children *don't* become more frightened by factual information. What they imagine is usually far worse than what actually happened if they are told about it in words they can understand.

Above all, make certain that children and adolescents feel loved and are emotionally secure. No matter what the circumstances surrounding a potential death, let them know they probably will feel awful for a while because grieving takes time, but they can eventually work through their loss and feel better. Reassure them that people will always be in their life who love them and will be there for them.

If I Were to Die, What Would Happen Then?

We have addressed several issues associated with going through a loved one's dying process. Even if you never face a terminal illness yourself, you will at some point die, perhaps unexpectedly. Having thought about the reality of your own death and having made some plans in advance while you are healthy will help those you leave behind and will remove any hesitancy to live fully right now. Some people don't take risks (even such as flying on airplanes) because they may die. Living this way greatly restricts a person's life and gives that particular fear a lot of power. We truly believe you can have a deeper sense of peace and a greater confidence to embrace life fully if you have looked squarely at the fact you will someday die—maybe sooner than you think—and dealt with whatever fears you may still have about dying and death.

Some of us may have a lingering concern about what happens *after* we die. Some people believe that life totally ends at one's death. We simply cease to exist. Other people hold to a theory of reincarnation, believing we return in some other form of life. Still others embrace a belief in an afterlife. This can create either an air of excitement or a sense of fear, depending on the person's own view of God. But because we have never died before, what we think happens after we die is an act of faith for all of us. No one else who has died before us has come back to let us know what it is like. Death is our own personal journey. Like any other trip, making plans ahead of time makes the journey go better.

We admit that this subject is not the most popular. As a society we have a natural tendency to avoid what is perceived as negative or uncomfortable. We don't like to take bad-tasting medicine as a child. We avoid uncomfortable social situations as adults. Why think about death when surrounded so nicely by life? The best (and maybe the only) answer is simply this: because you cannot avoid it. You will die. We all do. Death is as much a part of life as birth. Sooner or later, the sun will begin to set. The shadows of dusk will come. No one ultimately avoids their own death. So while you live in the daylight, take a closer look at the horizon. Be prepared for the inevitable. Hopefully your preparation will be far in advance of the time when you will actually die. But to have thought these things through and reprioritized your living to prepare yourself for death is healthy. We believe it is the key to living a full and rewarding life as long as you are here on this earth. Sooner or later the sun will begin to set. The shadows of dusk will come. No one ultimately avoids his or her own death.

CHRISTIAN MEDITATIONS ON LIFE

For you created my inmost being;
  you knit me together in my mother's womb.
I praise you because I am fearfully and wonderfully made;
  your works are wonderful,
  I know that full well.
My frame was not hidden from you
  when I was made in the secret place.
When I was woven together in the depths of the earth,
  your eyes saw my unformed body.
All the days ordained for me
  were written in your book
  before one of them came to be.

Psalm 139:13–16

I have come that they may have life, and have it to the full.

John 10:10

Forty Days and Forty Nights

Then Jesus was led by the Spirit into the desert to be tempted by the devil. After fasting forty days and forty nights, he was hungry.

Matthew 4:1–2

How do I understand the seasons of my life?

orty days. That may not seem very long to you. It's just a little over a month. On the other hand, forty days is 960 hours, or 57,600 minutes, or even worse, 3.5 million seconds! When you put it that way, 40 days is a long time! In 40 days you can cook over 19,000 "three-minute" eggs one at a time.

The fascinating thing about forty days is that the Bible often uses this to represent a period of testing or trial. In this passage of Matthew 4, Jesus is led into the wilderness to be tested prior to beginning his public ministry. Earlier in the Bible, Noah was in a boat for around forty days. In another biblical account, forty days turned into years when the Israelites were forced to wander in the wilderness for forty years on their way to the Promised Land.

There are forty meditations in this book. We selected this number especially because of its association with trials. In these meditations we hope to demonstrate how God walks beside us through our difficulties, how he provides for our needs, and how he uses these circumstances for our growth. You don't need to be facing a particularly difficult time in life to recognize that we all go through periods of trial or stress. Some of those challenges are traumatic, although you might not yet have experienced such an event. This book deals largely with the time when our health is challenged by a potentially terminal illness. We also deal with death itself. But before we get to that point, we need to understand the rhythm of life and the fact that in the end each of us will die.

The forty days theme in Scripture doesn't refer only to the bad things that may happen to us. Even good things can cause us some anxiety or worry. There is the due date for the baby's birth or the wedding plans for your oldest daughter. Jesus in the wilderness, Israel in the wilderness, or Noah in the boat—all of these were stressful, but all of them also had a grace-filled, God-powered ending.

We invite you to ponder the two verses found at the beginning of this meditation. Read them slowly, because some important spiritual lessons are embedded in this story. Notice, for example, that Jesus was led by the Spirit into this wilderness. That "Spirit" is the Holy Spirit—God himself. One of the biggest mysteries of faith is trying to understand God's role in our lives versus our own responsibility. Throughout these meditations, we will return several times to this mystery. If God is all powerful, all loving, and all merciful, why do bad things happen? If I am responsible for making wise choices, is it my fault that I might be sick and possibly facing death? These tough questions cry out for answers. Hopefully your journey of "forty days" will help you think through them more carefully.

You should also notice that while Jesus was led by the Spirit into the wilderness, he was tempted by the devil. The devil was the one attempting to lure Christ away from his appointed task. Flip Wilson, a comedian from the 1970s and 1980s, was well known for his catchphrase "The devil made me do it." The devil was certainly trying to do that in this scriptural account. Jesus came face-to-face with the enemy. You and I also come face-to-face with this enemy, and sometimes the enemy's face looks like disease—cancer, heart defects, or any other life-threatening illness. When you are faced with a life-threatening situation, you must realize that you are engaged not only in a medical or physical battle but also in a spiritual and emotional one. You will lock horns with the evil one. Hopefully, your journey of forty days will help you be both realistic and positive about this battle when it occurs in your life.

Jesus' battle didn't begin right away. As a matter of fact, the face-to-face confrontation came only at the end. For forty days and nights Jesus was in the wilderness fasting. This was a spiritual discipline used in both the Old and New Testaments to help the believer focus all his or her senses on the grace and power of God. Jesus, in his human nature, needed to prepare for his work. He had to hone and sharpen his spiritual senses before the battle was engaged. Perhaps the lesson for us is that we ought not delay our spiritual readiness. While we are still healthy, or at least feeling strong, we need to practice our spiritual disciplines. Living in the daylight is the time to plot our course. Nothing bad has happened to us yet. Why not get prepared for some difficult seas ahead? If you've ever gone on a cruise, you know that before casting off from shore to enjoy their long-anticipated vacation, the passengers undergo a lifeboat drill so they are prepared in case of an emergency. They don't wait until the tragedy happens. Our challenge is that we get ready. Our forty-day journey will take us to the throne of God, to the cross of Christ, and to the point at which we will have to learn what it truly means to "wait upon the Lord."

And at the end of Jesus' forty days, "he was hungry." Of course he was. Forty days and forty nights without food. Who wouldn't be hungry? How odd that the very spiritual discipline that was to equip him for the battle seems to us, as human beings, to be the very thing that would make him more vulnerable. The devil moves right in with the first temptation. Hungry? Turn these stones into bread. Sick? Might be dying? Panic! Question God's goodness! Throw it all away since your faith doesn't seem to be working anyway.

At first that may be the real temptation. But a faith that works only during the good times isn't really faith at all. Our faith needs to stand up to the test. The final test comes when we begin to realize that we too will die. We offer these forty days of meditations with the prayer that they will strengthen your faith, bolster your resolve, and equip you to move, when you are forced to by illness, from the day on through the dusk and into the darkness of death—firm in your faith that the eternal light of Christ waits on the other side.

PRAYER: *God of life and light, I praise you for the life you have given me. I am aware of and grateful for so many good things that have happened in my life. But I am increasingly aware that death is a part of life, and I want to understand death better. As I begin this journey to search out the deeper meaning of my life and my eventual death, surround me with your life-giving Spirit. I want to embrace the life you have given me. I want to understand the death I will someday face. And I want the faith to know your presence both in life and in death. Amen.*

Taking Charge of Life

*Then the Devil came and said to him, "If you are the Son
of God, change these stones into loaves of bread." But
Jesus told him, "No! The Scriptures say, 'People need more
than bread for their life; they must feed on every word of
God.'"*

Matthew 4:3–4 NLT[8]

Am I really in charge of my life?

esus is sitting in the wilderness. For forty days he has gone
without food. He is tired, probably weak, and certainly
hungry. Temptations and trials seem to be all the more
powerful when we are vulnerable. So the devil comes to Jesus with
his first temptation. His invitation sounds so reasonable: Take matters
into your own hands. You've waited long enough. You're hungry—make
some bread. No yeast or flour? Not a problem for the Son of God! Use
the stones. Command them to become delicious loaves of bread. Can't
you smell them baking now? Go ahead. You're God. You're in charge
here. Just do it!

What would you have done? That might be a hard question to answer
because, in fact, you probably aren't sitting in the middle of a wilderness
having fasted for forty days. Maybe you have never fasted, and right
now you are sitting in a pretty nice house (at least one adequate to your
needs). Your cupboards are full of good things to eat; your refrigerator
is well stocked with fresh milk, eggs, and produce. When you're hungry,

all you need to do is pop open a can of Pringles, bite an apple, or phone for pizza delivery. No problem here.

When our lives are moving along in a normal fashion, this temptation of Jesus is pretty hard to understand. After all, we often live as if we were in charge of our lives. We get what we want, when we want. If we can't have it right away, we do whatever we can to get it as soon as possible. The evidence of this is seen in the fact that the average credit card balance in America often runs around $3,000. Along with Nike shoes, we "just do it."

We sometimes carry this attitude into the area of our health. We have been taught that we are entitled to live a completely healthy and happy life, regardless of what life may actually hold for us. Over-the-counter products are promoted to solve all our medical problems. Natural products, healthy foods, and low-fat items all suggest that full and complete health is just a bite away. We are responsible for our own health. And we are, at least in part, what we eat.

This first temptation of Jesus shows the lie in this attitude. There is no doubt that Jesus could have turned those stones into bread. There is little doubt that he would have liked to, for he was not only totally divine but also completely human as well, and therefore hungry—after all, that is what made it a temptation in the first place. But Jesus' response tells the full story: "People need more than bread for their life; they must feed on every word from God" (Matt. 4:4 NLT). This doesn't mean that bread isn't important. Jesus later teaches his disciples to pray daily for their bread. But where does the bread come from? Where do all the things we need for our daily life originate? They find their genesis in the grace of God. We are totally dependent on him for everything. Much of what Jesus preached soon after returning from the wilderness, in what we now call "The Sermon on the Mount," is about how we must rely on him daily for everything. Isn't it ironic that so soon after leaving the wilderness, he tells those listening to him, "Do not worry about your life, what you will eat or drink; or about your body, what you will wear. Is not life more important than clothes?" (Matt. 6:25). And he concluded the section by saying, "Seek first his kingdom and his righteousness, and all these things will be given to you as well" (Matt. 6:33).

About three months after Bob was first widowed, he read Richard J. Foster's book *Freedom of Simplicity*.[9] Foster challenges his readers to distinguish between wants and needs—and to recognize that, especially for those living in North America, we have very few real needs. We may *want* to have a lot of things, but we *need* very few, at least when we are talking about things like bread (or stones!). God has provided for us in rich abundance. This provision may not be as immediate as we would like. No quick fix here. Nor will this provision necessarily come in the form we may like. We may pray for health, but he may give us persever-ance instead. Jesus is now saying that this provision of bread is a physical sign of a spiritual truth—that God will also provide for all of our other needs as well. Just as surely as bread shows up on our table regularly, so certainly God will provide for all our other needs. But seek first his kingdom. Feed on his Word. This is the ideal spiritual lifestyle.

PRAYER: *Bread of Life, feed me till I want no more. Give me this day my daily bread. I realize I usually have more than enough to eat and to drink. But I need your daily care in every aspect of my life. Keep me from the temptation of trying to fill my needs through ways you do not provide. Strengthen my faith so that I have confidence that you will give me everything I need while I seek your kingdom to your glory and honor. Amen.*

To Life!

The LORD God formed a man's body from the dust of the ground and breathed into it the breath of life. And the man became a living person.

Genesis 2:7 NLT

There was no companion suitable for him. So the LORD God caused Adam to fall into a deep sleep. He took one of Adam's ribs and closed up the place from which he had taken it. Then the LORD God made a woman from the rib and brought her to Adam.

Genesis 2:20–22 NLT

What is "life"?

"LeChaim!" To life! This ancient Jewish toast lifts the glass in celebration of life. We rarely use the term *life* alone, in stark isolation from other words, except when we hear the cry of a newborn baby. Life, with placenta still attached, is at first confined to the embryonic sack. Then comes the first breath, raw and pure, the first gasp of air coursing into tender lungs. *Life.* Pure. No adjectives yet. We're not ready to talk about the "good" life, or the "happy" life, or even the "troubled" life. The adjectives come later. Now is the time for the first breath, the first cry, the first suck on the mother's breast. This is life, real life!

But what is life? Does it mean simply to be alive, to be animate rather than inanimate—to breathe and move, in contrast to being, say, a rock? Christians and Jews agree that life has its beginning and foundation in the Creator God. No big bang. No accident of science. No amoeba evolving into a higher, more complex life-form. Life begins by the declaring word of the Creator God. Without God there is no life. With God there is life, and that in rich abundance.

The first chapters of the book of Genesis tell a truly amazing story, never to be repeated again. God speaks reality into existence. In the words of Charles Wilson,

> The power of his word burst forth to carry out that which the word commanded. And the world was filled with every kind of running, crawling, flying, swimming, jumping critter. They were all colors: brown, pink, red, yellow—some were multi-colored, and some even changed color. They were covered with fur, feather or scale. Growing and replenishing themselves; changing and interacting with each other. There was the whale and the rhinoceros; the hippopotamus, the kangaroo mouse, grasshopper and lady bug; swallow and dinosaur; mosquito and the great, proud Arabian stallion. There were puppy dogs and white-faced calves; turtles and bobcats; eagles and armadillos. And to the glory of God, and in praise of his Holy name, they scampered, galloped, darted and soared. And God looked and he said, "Ahh! . . . That is good indeed!"[10]

And then God played in the dirt, fashioning the form of a man. Just dust and dirt. Inanimate. But something amazing happened. God leaned over from his majestic throne and, in an act of divine resuscitation, breathed into this lump of dust the breath of life. Adam and then Eve became living souls. And so, by the account of the Bible, life began.

Fast-forward through the centuries. Turn down your street. Enter your house. And guess what—there is life! The original breath of God into Adam and Eve has never ceased. Passed on from birth to birth, his breath has continued uninterrupted and now rests in your lungs, resides in your life. You are his creation just as much as Adam and Eve were. His breath brings life to you as it did to this first couple. "In him," reports Paul, "we live and move and have our being" (Acts 17:28).

Think of the infant's life once again. We said that here we find life in its most unspoiled form—before all the adjectives are added. Also notice, however, that an infant cannot sustain life long all by itself. The child depends completely on parents for food, cleanliness, security, and emotional nurture. That is what God is also saying to us here. Before we get too excited about adding adjectives like "good," "successful," or "rewarding" to our lives, we need to remember that the life we live depends entirely on God in a way similar to that of an infant's dependence on his or her parents.

Your life may become encrusted with adjectives over time. We talk more about what kind of life we have. Are we happy or healthy, hearty or hurting? Put the adjectives aside for a moment. Consider life—your life—in its purest, most naked form. You are God's creature, his creation. You are a product of his breath. We invite you to embrace that life. Live it to the fullest for as long as you have time on this earth. Live in the power of the Holy Spirit. Embrace God and live for him. Celebrate the life he has given you. *LeChaim!*

PRAYER: *O God, the Giver of Life, I praise your name. Without your sustaining breath, I would be nothing. Breathe on me, O Spirit of God. Let me feel your animating power within me. May I celebrate life, living fully in the power of your Holy Spirit. Amen.*

I Can Do Everything!

I can do everything through him who gives me strength.

Philippians 4:13

What am I really capable of doing, and how?

God is in charge, there is no doubt about that. The classic spiritual reminds us that "He's Got the Whole World in His Hands." But where does that leave us? We have an innate resistance to thinking that we are mere machines—pawns in the hands of a sovereign God. Can we not exercise our own wills? Can we not discover, create, plan, dream, and build? Of course we can! We have traveled to the moon, created the Internet, wiped out polio, and provided instant cell phone communication for millions of people around the world.

Unlike the other creatures God has created, we have been given the capacity for creativity. Using our imaginations, we can see things that are not yet invented and bring them into existence. True, we can't do it the way God did—out of nothing at all. But we can create scores of things out of the materials God has given us in this world.

We are not able to do it perfectly, of course. We have not yet learned how to control or change many of the things that still plague us. Wars continue to flare up around the globe. HIV and AIDS affect millions of people. Couples divorce, illicit drugs ruin families, the environment is polluted, and hungry people sleep in cardboard boxes under our interstate highway bridges. But we cling to the dream of EPCOT, the Environmental Prototype Community of Tomorrow, in Florida's Walt Disney World. The basic principle of this theme park is simple: Given enough time and sufficient resources, we can solve any problem we face. We can grow food without soil, we can create energy from almost any source, and we can find a remedy for nearly any ailment that might strike us.

When Paul wrote "I can do everything," this wasn't exactly what he had in mind. Quite the contrary. Paul was talking about being centered in Christ, for he quickly added the phrase "through him [Christ] who gives me strength" (Phil. 4:13). You might want to read the verses preceding this phrase, for Paul is also asserting that he has learned a secret! "I have learned to be content whatever the circumstances. I know what it is to be in need, and I know what it is to have plenty. I have learned the secret of being content in any and every situation, whether well fed or hungry, whether living in plenty or in want" (Phil. 4:12).

Paul reverses the order of things in this passage. The world says that strength leads to contentment. Paul says that contentment in Christ leads to strength. Which comes first in your life? Some of us assume that all we need is a little more money, leisure, time, love (or you fill in the blank!), and then we will be content. Paul says that the opposite is true. It doesn't matter if I am rich or poor, well fed or hungry, married or single, healthy or ill—I will be content, and this Christ-centered contentment will provide me all the strength I need, because then "I can do everything through him who gives me strength."

Let's not misunderstand what Paul is saying. He is *not* saying that you should be connected to Christ *in order to* get what you want. Christ is not the means by which you become rich, powerful, successful, beautiful, or healthy. Rather, you love Christ for his own sake. You love Christ because of what he has done for you on the cross. You love Christ because he first loved you. With that attitude, you can do everything. When the job promotion comes along, you can say, "I can do this through Christ who gives me the strength." When the pink slip comes and you pack your desk and prepare to apply for unemployment, you can still say, "I can do this through Christ who gives me the strength." When you are healthy and set out to climb to the top of Long's Peak in Colorado, you can say, "I can do this through Christ who gives me the strength." But when the MRI shows a mass growing in your abdomen, you also can say then, "I can do this through Christ who gives me the strength."

Paul wrote these words while he was under house arrest. He was getting older, nearing the end of his life. He was writing to a rather wealthy church in Philippi—people who tended to be proud of the fact they were part of the Roman Empire. Many were retired military people. They probably thought they had all the reason in the world to be proud of who they were and what they were doing. In many ways their situation seems somewhat parallel to North America. The gospel comes, in large part, to people who are proud of who they are and what they have done. But this prisoner of Christ tells us that our allegiance must shift from ourselves to Christ. Isn't that what Christ also said? "Seek first his kingdom and his righteousness, and all these things will be given to you as well" (Matt. 6:33).

PRAYER: *O God, you are my refuge and my strength. Help me believe in your strength more completely each day, confident that I will also become more content in this life. You know my joys, my sorrows, and my challenges. I am counting on you to give me strength in each of these situations and for what may lie in my future, for you are my all-powerful God. Amen.*

Day 5

Living in His Presence

But seek first his kingdom and his righteousness, and all these things will be given to you as well.

Matthew 6:33

How do I determine my priorities and spiritual values?

Jesus pits two things against everything else in life. The contest is the combination of "his kingdom" and "his righteousness" versus everything else. In his Sermon on the Mount, Jesus tells his listeners that the Christian life represents certain basic values. This business of his kingdom and his righteousness is a spiritual priority that comes before anything and everything else. And if you read the preceding verses, you will find that "everything else" refers to some pretty basic stuff—like food, clothing, and something to drink.

Setting priorities for one's life can be a pretty difficult matter. Who wouldn't say that taking care of our basic needs is important? Putting food on the table, keeping the family clothed, making certain we have a good roof over our heads—these all seem to be very legitimate goals. We work hard to provide for ourselves and our families.

But Jesus is saying that even under normal circumstances, these priorities may be out of order. His advice was not to worry about that sort of stuff, "for the pagans run after all these things" (Matt. 6:32). What makes you different as a Christian? What distinguishes you from the rest of the crowd? The answer: his kingdom and his righteousness.

So what does this passage mean for our day-to-day living? What does it mean for our dying as well? How can we be a people of faith when the concerns and pressures of daily life never seem to subside? Does this mean that worrying is a sin? Or does it imply that I don't have a strong enough faith if I do worry? Curbing worry may be something to work on, but that isn't exactly what Jesus is talking about here. Consider it from this perspective.

If you truly seek to live under the lordship of Jesus Christ (to seek his kingdom) and truly attempt to live a life that is holy and obedient (seek his righteousness), you will find that the rest of your life will fall into place. Jesus is asking you to focus on him and his kingdom rather than worrying about not worrying. If we are truly plugged into Christ, then everything else will be taken care of.

Go back to Matthew 6 and read from verse 25. Notice the comparison Jesus uses to illustrate his point! He talks about sparrows and lilies. Birds and flowers! And he asks, "Is not life more important than food, and the body more important than clothes?" (v. 25). He concludes the section with the strange advice, "Therefore do not worry about tomorrow, for tomorrow will worry about itself. Each day has enough trouble of its own" (v. 34).

The antidote for worry is faith—faith that once you have the basics set right, the rest of your life will be okay. The Bible clearly teaches us that if you love the Lord your God with all your heart, soul, mind, and strength and love your neighbor as yourself, you are basically seeking his kingdom and his righteousness. But something else comes before that, because if that were all there was to the Christian life, none of us would ever have peace of mind. We cannot love God in that perfect way. We certainly can't love other people like that. We may try, but we know we will fail. Others may be hurt, offended, or disappointed by what we have done. We certainly can't be perfect the way God wants us to be.

So what comes before all that? God's grace. We can seek his kingdom and his righteousness because "in him we have redemption through his blood, the forgiveness of sins, in accordance with the riches of God's grace that he lavished on us with all wisdom and understanding" (Eph. 1:7–8). God's grace was bestowed on us in sending Christ to die for us and cover our sins.

We, the authors of this book, both know that we are far from perfect. But since both of us have experienced the death of a spouse, we also know that God's grace was the unmovable foundation that brought us through that terrible trauma. When our spouses were ill and later died, suddenly food and clothing were not very important at all. Accumulating all the "stuff" of the world suddenly paled in significance. Many people who have gone through that experience relate the same thing—very few worldly things are of importance any longer. Oh, certainly, we still have to work for our food and clothing. We still need to take care of ourselves and our needs. We need to do our part to make positive things happen, like keeping physically fit and applying for that job. But since God took care of us through the pain of our spouses' illnesses, the decrease of physical function in our partners, and the grief following their deaths, we are confident that he will certainly take care of us through any other difficult experiences in life.

Jesus is telling us that, in a certain sense, living the Christian life is very simple. Just rest in God's grace. Be like the birds of the air or the flowers of the field. Fly free. Bloom on the hillside of your life. Have faith that no matter what happens in your life, you are a child of the King. And as you seek the King's "kingdom" and his lifestyle, you will discover that all the rest of your needs will be taken care of. He will work through you and with you to use your gifts and abilities, as well as your circumstances, to provide for your every need. "Trust me," says Christ, "I *really* will take care of you."

PRAYER: *Dear Lord, I must admit that trusting you alone is a pretty big challenge. Deep in my heart I believe fully that you will care for me regardless of my situation. But I also know that my attention can be easily diverted from that trust. Sometimes I feel very much like the man Jesus met who confessed, "I believe; help me overcome my unbelief!" (Mark 9:24). Strengthen my ability to trust you, because only you know what lies in my future, and only you can ultimately help me through my earthly life into the eternal home you have promised. Amen.*

Mirror, Mirror, on the Wall

So God created people in his own image; God patterned them after himself; male and female he created them.

Genesis 1:27 NLT

What does it mean to be created in God's image?

*W*hat do you see when you look in the mirror? Often we see someone who is too large, or too small; has too little hair, or at least the wrong color; has a nose that is too big or ears that are too small. We tend to be very critical of ourselves as the media strives to promote the image of how we "should" look. The cosmetics and weight reduction industries have, of course, cashed in on this desire to improve our looks.

Why do you think we tend to be so concerned about how we look? Most of us aren't models who need to keep in shape for magazine photos or the fashion runway. We're ordinary people living ordinary lives. Sure, we want to look and feel good about ourselves. But we realize that we'll never make the front page of a magazine or need to worry about our "star appeal." We probably wouldn't want that anyway.

Yet many times we tend to put ourselves down. We think we are not smart enough, strong enough, powerful enough, or influential enough to make a difference in our own life or in the lives of other people. We might pick out a hero (maybe a successful businessperson, sports star, singer, or actor) who has "made it." They become our role model; they have the life we would like to live. So we swoon at their concerts, race to get an autograph, and pin up their 8 x 10 glossy on our bedroom wall.

Well, maybe we aren't quite that obvious about it. We use other people as a model in subtler ways. The most destructive way is to see someone else's life and think that our life should look like theirs. It really doesn't matter what we like about their life—what really matters is that we think they have it better than we do.

The creation story challenges head-on this approach to life. You probably know the story quite well. You might believe that God literally shaped human beings from the dust of the ground and actually played in the dirt the way we might build a sand castle. Or you may believe the story is a beautiful metaphor or symbol. People tend to fight theological battles, split churches, and alienate family members over the debate. But the real point of the passage isn't whether or not God literally knelt in the dust. The important word is *image*. Mirror. Reflection. God created us to reflect certain qualities of himself to the rest of this world. There is nothing on this earth equal to our intelligence, that can develop our sense of morality, that will yearn to have a spiritual relationship with God, or that can become creative in its own right. When you really understand that we were created in God's image, when you develop this "self-concept," then you have every reason to also value yourself very highly. This is true Christian "self-esteem."

Christian self-esteem doesn't mean that we are arrogant, self-made people. Some popular how-to books may leave the impression that we create our own self-esteem by becoming better than others or that we simply feel good about ourselves because we have an inflated view of how wonderful we are. Christian self-esteem arises quite simply from a recognition that in God's eyes no one on the face of this earth is more valuable than his human family. And the implication is that you must be very valuable to God because you are personally and individually a product of his creative will. Be careful, however, since recognizing this has a number of implications for how you live your life. If you do recognize that you are God's valuable creature, you first of all understand true humility. Christian self-esteem is not proud. Christian humility recognizes that I am always the *creature* of the eternally powerful Creator. The scriptural image is that he is the potter and we are the clay (Isa. 64:8).

Christian self-esteem also means that you accept your rightful place at the head of everything God has created. He has placed us in charge of this world. This means you are to be responsible, both for the rest of the world and for yourself. You need to take care of the ozone layer, avert global warming, feed the hungry, and work for justice in the world. You must also watch what you eat, get enough sleep, secure proper medical care, avoid undue stress, develop appropriate moral behaviors, and seek after God.

The one other thing Christian self-esteem means is implied in the phrase "male and female he created them." How we view, accept, and love ourselves is intricately tied up with our sexuality. Everything you do, think, say, or feel is affected by your gender. This may be God's way of reminding us that we are not alone in this world. We need both God and others in our lives to complete that picture. Other people also want a relationship with us. That is an important part of our life. You are here on this earth to complement (fit into) other people's lives. We're not talking about marriage alone, because not all of us get married. This passage simply means we are social beings. We are here for others even as they are here for us.

When you look in the mirror tomorrow morning, what will you see? You may tend to focus on the emerging gray hairs or the blemish appearing under the right eye. But look again. Study the face closely, because if you look with the eyes of faith, you will see reflected in your mirror another reflection—you will see a reflection of God himself, for we are the image of God. That means we are ever in the process of molding our lives into what he is and wants us to become.

PRAYER: *Dear Lord, polish the mirror of my soul so I can brilliantly reflect your glory and beauty to others through how you have made me. May I be able to love and value myself because you love and value me as the crown of everything you have created. Build within me the confidence that comes from knowing I am your treasure through all that Christ has done for me. Amen.*

Day 7

Loving God, Loving Me, Loving You

*He answered: "'Love the Lord your God with all your heart
and with all your soul and with all your strength and with
all your mind'; and, 'Love your neighbor as yourself.'"*

Luke 10:27

What is a Christian perspective on loving God, myself, and others?

ove, they say, makes the world go 'round. Probably the deepest
human emotion, love expresses itself in a myriad of forms. We
love sunsets, pizza, our dog, a good concert, our mother, our
spouse, and God. The trouble with the English language, however, is
that we really have only one word for love. And what spouse wants to
be loved with the same love you have for pizza? The Greek language in
which the New Testament was written uses several different words for
love to distinguish between love for a pizza and love for God. Love for
a brother differs from love for a spouse. And love for your pet differs
from love for classical jazz or the bebop of the 1950s.

We also know that love requires a pair—a lover and that which is
loved. The focus of one's love can be an object, a conviction, a habit, or
another person. But, as the classic love song says, it takes two to tango.
Not only does love involve two poles attracted to each other like the poles
of a magnet, but we know that love is a special form of attachment or
bonding. This is especially true of love between two people, so let's put
aside talk about pizza and pets for a while. We are talking now about
love between people who experience this powerful bond and affection
for one another.

But even here love takes a variety of shapes. On the one hand, you have the natural and almost irresistible love a woman has for her newborn infant inhaling its first breath. They haven't "fallen in love." There is no romance here, no reciprocity, no give and take. But this love is powerful and, under normal and healthy circumstances, lasts a lifetime.

Siblings experience a different kind of love. The hearty relationship of brothers or the deep sharing of emotions between sisters is hard to duplicate in other relationships.

And then there is the love of romance—the nearly irrational, powerful attraction between lovers gazing into each other's eyes in total rapture. They "fall" in love almost as if it were an accident. "We couldn't help ourselves," lovers often say as they melt into each other's arms. Hopefully, however, this attraction is also based on logic and reason as well as emotion.

You may wonder why we need to talk about love in a book about dying and death. Love is for those who are living. Love is the core of what makes life worthwhile for most of us. But love is also what *causes* grief. If we didn't attach, didn't value the other person, had no relationship with others at all, death would be nothing. We grieve because we *love* our spouse, brother, sister, parent, grandparent, or friend. Breaking the bond of love hurts more than breaking anything else, such as a leg or an arm. Theoretically we might think, then, that we can just avoid the whole experience of grief by not getting close to others. C. S. Lewis is right—the only way to avoid the pain of grief is to avoid loving.[11] But he dismisses this approach as ridiculous.

In order to live life fully and then to die happily, we should kindle three distinct types of love in our life. They were summarized by the Master of Love, Jesus Christ. These three loves are love for God, love for yourself, and love for others. Like loving pizza, your papa, and peace, these three types of love are each different. Yet they are also intricately woven together, as the summary of the Law affirmed by Christ in Luke 10:27 suggests. Look at it again before reading on.

Love for God. In this case, love recognizes the value and beauty of God, accepts the awesome gift of gracious redemption in Christ, and loves him out of gratitude for that gift. Imagine yourself in God's place for a minute. (We know this is difficult because we are so imperfect, but try.) You are all powerful. You are holy and pure. You are the Creator of every single thing that exists. And then something goes wrong because you allowed a human choice. Your creation, through sin, rebels against you. Everything gets messed up. But you made it all. You can't just walk away. You love what you made so much, you'll do anything to set it straight again. Anything! God loved us so much that he decided to send his very own Son to rescue us from the mess we created for ourselves through Adam and Eve. So Christ died and rose again, and through faith in him you and I can become a "new creation" in him (2 Cor. 5:17). That is how much he loves us.

Love for yourself. Whoops—that's not the next thing in the text, is it? Read the text again, carefully. The command to love others is based on loving them "as yourself." So loving yourself precedes loving others; we need to love ourselves before we can genuinely love others. We are not talking here about a self-indulgent, humanistic sort of self-love. This isn't narcissism taken to the ultimate degree. What the Bible is really saying is simply this: If you can begin to understand just a little bit of God's love for us, then because of his love you can also love yourself. In this case love is recognizing the value you now have because of God's investment in you. I should love myself at least enough not to tarnish, abuse, put down, or otherwise hurt what God considers to be a valuable treasure. For Christ's sake I will watch what I eat. For Christ's sake I'll quit smoking, get enough rest, exercise regularly, decrease my alcohol intake, take my vitamins, and think of myself from a positive perspective. If I do it for no other reason, I ought to do this because I am the one Christ loved enough to die for.

But this love of ourselves through Christ really goes much deeper. When love is properly understood, the Christian really develops a sense of self-confidence, self-esteem, courage, and purpose because of what he or she has become in Christ.

Love for others. The love of self (based on God's love for us) then spills over to everyone else. No longer do you only search for that one special person whom you will love, although you still may do that too because of your personal desire for a romantic attachment. But we have been imbued with God's love, which has filled us up with his grace to the point at which it splashes over everyone who comes near us. It fuels our desire to relate to and be connected with other human beings. Just look around you.

This three-pronged love (God-self-others) is what makes life rich, rewarding, and fulfilling. But doesn't this also make the end of life even harder to endure? Certainly in some ways it does. If you love little in life, you lose little in death. If you love much, you lose much. But there is something deeper and more mysterious here than the economics of love. Our life on earth will end someday; others may die before us. But don't lose sight of God. He is eternal. He has conquered death and the grave. He assures us now that life and love exist beyond the grave. We don't know what shape they will take. We won't have our present life connections (such as spouse or family), so those types of love will be different. But the source of all love is there—God himself. We know that everything in heaven will surpass anything on this earth in splendor, beauty, and intensity. The loves we experience on this earth give us only the slightest hint of what heavenly love will be like. That is why, we think, Jesus asked us to love God first and above all—because in doing this, we will be able to better love ourselves and others as a way to foreshadow what heavenly love will really be.

PRAYER: *You are the source of all love, Holy God. As Father, Son, and Holy Spirit, you live in an eternal love bond that never ends. Now I also recognize that through your Son, Jesus, I have been taken into that love bond, now better able to love others even as you have loved me. Help me endure the sadness and pain that will come when these loving relationships on earth end through death. Reassure me that your eternal love will be waiting for me and those I love on the other side of the grave. I pray this in the name of my resurrected Jesus. Amen.*

Day 8

Are Loved Ones and Friends Ours Forever?

But Ruth replied, "Don't urge me to leave you or to turn back from you. Where you go I will go, and where you stay I will stay. Your people will be my people and your God my God. Where you die I will die, and there I will be buried. May the LORD deal with me, be it ever so severely, if anything but death separates you and me."

Ruth 1:16–17

What are the qualities and characteristics of Christian friendships?

We really find it difficult to understand those people, largely in the Middle Ages, who totally withdrew from society in order to quietly contemplate God in total isolation. The ascetics, as they were called, would go off into the desert or live on top of a pole in order to free themselves from all worldly concern. But God didn't create us to be isolated from each other. On the contrary, God created us to live in a variety of social relationships—some more intimate and others more casual. But all of our relationships serve to remind us of the important roles other people play in our lives.

This doesn't mean we wouldn't sometimes just as soon go off by ourselves for quiet contemplation. Who doesn't like to spend a quiet summer afternoon reading a good book under a stately tree? But we go off seeking solitude with the confidence that our family and friends will be there when we return.

One of the basic values in the Christian's life is to develop close relationships with others. While we titled this meditation "loved ones and friends," we are really talking about all kinds of relationships. As a matter of fact, the passage of this meditation has often been used at wedding ceremonies as a bride and groom swear loyalty to each other. The sentiment may be healthy, but this passage isn't talking about husbands and wives. This passage is talking about *kinship*—an old English word describing a relationship of emotional bonding between two people that can withstand all kinds of forces that try to break them apart.

Potentially terminal illnesses have a way of putting relationships under stress. Couples at the marriage altar often vow to be faithful to one another "in sickness and in health, till death do us part," but they usually do this without really focusing on the sickness or death part of the vow during the ceremony. So when the crisis occurs, the relationship can become strained under the stress of serious illness. Even in our usual type of friendships, jealousy, competition, changing values, or differing behaviors can have a way of eroding friendships.

Perhaps you already realize the fragility of life and, therefore, its relationships. Maybe you have previously experienced the death of a loved one. The grief that follows a death is generally defined as the breaking of the deep emotional attachment we had with someone else. Whether that be a parent, spouse, sibling, child, or friend, once they die we are "alone" without them. The loneliness comes precisely because we begin to realize they will never come back. The memories will live on in our minds and hearts, but the relationship as we knew it is over.

So we should be concerned about keeping relationships with family and friends alive and vital. We can't just go off and "do our own thing" without concerning ourselves in the least about what other people may think or feel about us. God created us to be in relationship with others. And he did this as a reflection of himself. The Bible teaches that God himself is a mysterious "Trinity"—three persons in one God. We can't fully explain how, but the Father, the Son, and the Holy Spirit are all one God. They exist together in perfect harmony. This Triune God created a male and a female—a sexual couple designed to reflect the perfect, complementary harmony of God himself. Even if we don't actually get married, our very sexuality is a sign that we are on this earth to complement (fit together with) others. The physical sexual union of a man and a woman is the highest level of the emotional and social union we can have with someone else. But there are also many other levels and types of intimacy we have with family and friends.

Someday you may hear a doctor announce that something has gone terribly wrong with your health (or maybe you have already heard that message). One of the relatively common reactions people have to that dreaded news is withdrawal. The person who is ill may decide to pull back, remove him or herself from the normal activities of life (if they

still have the energy to continue on), and refuse to be vulnerable and
open with others. How often have we seen people with a serious diagnosis keep that news from their family and friends for as long as they
possibly can? Or even if they don't keep the basic diagnosis quiet, they
won't talk about the progress of the disease.

Ruth, in her commitment to Naomi, is demonstrating true friendship:
"Nothing but death will separate us. I'm in for the long haul. You can
count on me." That is true friendship. Think for a moment how important
that kind of commitment might be for someone who is dying. Traveling
the road toward death can be very lonely and isolating. And things can
be complicated even further for someone dying from HIV/AIDS or some
other socially shunned illness. Don't you think these dying individuals
need caring relationships more than ever?

Or turn the situation around. If you were (or are) dying, how could
you still be in healthy relationships with others? How can you remain
loyal, honest, and open with your family? Many of the patriarchs in
the Old Testament did it by talking about their impending death and
by blessing others. Perhaps the blessing of others is the last great act
of love and friendship a person can perform before they die. A blessing
is passing on your faith, entrusting your values to others, affirming the
beautiful qualities they have, embracing their friendship. Heirlooms
may be fine—a grandfather clock, a ring, or a favorite picture. But if
you are truly a friend (even with your family members), don't forget the
blessing. You may choose to talk about it or perhaps write it in the form
of an ethical will. If you don't know what to say as a blessing, just use
the words of Aaron: "The LORD bless you and keep you; the LORD make
his face shine upon you and be gracious to you; the LORD turn his face
toward you and give you peace" (Num. 6:24–26). Look your loved ones
in the eyes, say or read those words, and see the glimmer of God's glory
shine in their faces. That is true friendship.

As people grow older, they often realize all the more the value of
relationships and may regret not having spent more time and energy
on developing them earlier in life. Remember the song "Cat's in the
Cradle"?[12] The main theme of this popular song is the realization that
precious time was lost when it wasn't spent with loved ones, and it was
too late for the father to have the time he wanted to have with his son.
As you live in the daylight, remind yourself of the value of prioritizing
relationships with others. This is an investment in the future and something God has provided so that each of us need not live alone. Cultivate
relationships with your family. Develop other friendships. Enrich your
life with others with whom you can connect. Where two or three are
gathered in his name, God is there with them. Seek out others who
care for you, and you will see in them the face of God. God wants us

to commune first and foremost with him but also to be in relationship with others.

PRAYER: *I have sung the song "What a Friend We Have in Jesus." Dear Lord, you are that friend—the one who is loyal, constantly by my side, and completely reliable. Thank you for that. Thank you as well for everyone in my family and for all my other friends who also want to be loyal and reliable. May I demonstrate those qualities for them as well. Being a friend is much more difficult, dear Lord, when I am facing trouble. Please reassure me that your friendship will never end. That will help me continue to be a friend to others regardless of our situations. Amen.*

Kids Say the Darndest Things

*By faith Jacob, when he was dying, blessed each of
Joseph's sons, and worshiped as he leaned on the top of
his staff.*

Hebrews 11:21

How can I develop childlike curiosity and faith?

Facing the prospect of your own death is tough enough. Helping smaller children understand what is happening is another challenge. How can they even begin to understand the deep mysteries of life and death? How can they begin to know what it feels like to face the end of this life—especially when you aren't so sure you even know how you will face it yourself? And little kids tend to ask a lot of questions. Maybe you remember Art Linkletter's television show featuring interviews with small children. He's the one who popularized the phrase "Kids say the darndest things." They ask the darndest things too!

Can you just imagine six-year-old Heather wondering what will happen to your body when you are buried? Remember, to her the earth is just a big pile of dirt and worms and other bugs. "Will the worms get in the box?" "How will you keep warm?" "Will you miss me?" "When I get there, will you still recognize me?" "How old will you be when you're in heaven?"

So the questions come, one after another. Actually, regardless of our age, we all ask these kinds of questions. Maybe we don't want to admit it.

Maybe we don't say them out loud. But perhaps you are wondering about them yourself. We have questions too, but usually not the answers.

The beauty of being a child is that the questions are asked with naive innocence and curiosity. As we get older (starting even in our teenage years) the questions may be the same, but they are asked with a bite to them. These inquiries are layered with emotions, expectations, or fears. They are no longer just curious questions.

Maybe we can learn something about heaven from children. They tend to have a simple, uncomplicated view. In fact, children usually see heaven in pretty much the same way they experience this earth—except that everything will be perfect. For children, heaven is not a mystery. Heaven is the place where God lives, and if he lives there, then heaven has to be a very, very special place.

What generally troubles children (and most of us) is the fact that heaven and earth are cut off from each other. Sure, modern psychics and some new religions want us to believe we can communicate with the dead. But we, like children, really sense that when someone dies they totally lose touch with this earth. They may live happily in Jesus' house (see John 14:2–3), but they no longer sit at the dinner table at my house. That's where the pain comes from. We really have to say good-bye.

A very interesting child's story that helps us understand the natural but unbridgeable divide between heaven and earth is *Water Bugs and Dragonflies*.[13] This intriguing little book tells of the quandary the water bugs have when they realize that every once in a while one of them swims to the surface, suddenly leaves, and never returns. They never hear from the water bug again. No letters, no phone calls, no return visits. Finally they promise each other that if this ever happens to one of them again, that water bug will immediately come back to tell the rest where they went and what it was like. However, when it does happen to one of them, the water bug on this new adventure realizes that she has turned into a dragonfly and to return to the water now that she has wings is absolutely impossible.

Death is a transition to another form of life that is totally separate from this form of existence. A deceased person can't come back to earth again to tell us about the journey and what heaven is like. So the new form of life to come remains somewhat of a mystery. It is beyond our imagination in its beauty, fulfillment, and rewards.

The point is that we really don't know the answers to most of the questions children ask. How old will I be? Will you still be my grandpa? Will my dog be there? We really can't answer those questions, at least not directly. What the Bible does say is that heaven is a place of inexpressible joy and peace. Heaven is a place where everything that has afflicted us in this life is gone and where everything that was rewarding, enriching, lovely, beautiful, and sacred will be infinitely more so. That's why it's hard to talk about heaven or to answer questions about it. It's easier to write poems about heaven—or to sing about it.

> When we've been there ten thousand years
> Bright shining as the sun,
> We've no less days to sing God's praise
> Than when we'd first begun.[14]

PRAYER: *Dear Father, I am one of your children. Just as it is hard for children on earth to understand things like death and heaven, I'm having a real challenge too. You are so much greater than I am. Heaven sounds like a perfectly wonderful place, but I also love this world and all the people you have put in my life. Thank you that I can enjoy this world, but also help me prepare for your eternal home, which I believe is so much better than this one. Amen.*

The Manna Syndrome: Waiting and Trusting

Because of the LORD's great love we are not consumed, for his compassions never fail. They are new every morning; great is your faithfulness. I say to myself, "The LORD is my portion; therefore I will wait for him." The LORD is good to those whose hope is in him, to the one who seeks him; it is good to wait quietly for the salvation of the LORD.

Lamentations 3:22–26

What is the nature of God's daily grace?

The word *new* usually piques our interest rather quickly. Who doesn't like to think about getting a new car or a new suit? For the most part we like to go to new places, have new experiences, and make new friends. Unless we are in the grip of depression or grief or smothered by a dull routine, the rising of the sun in the eastern sky holds the promise of a new day. Christians confess daily, "This is the day the LORD has made; let us rejoice and be glad in it" (Ps. 118:24). The words of Lamentations assert that God's mercies are new every morning and great is his faithfulness.

Is that how you live your life—your daily routine? In the course of normal living, have you been able to rise with the sun filled with an awareness that each day is a new, grace-filled opportunity to live under the mercies of God? Ideally that would be true of how we live. Sometimes it is. But many other times we wake not to the rising of the sun and a reminder of God's grace but to the siren of the alarm, the edginess of the kids who don't want to get up yet, and the bustle of showers, dressing, breakfast, gathering everything we need to take, and scurrying out the door for another hectic day. God's mercies and great faithfulness, if in our consciousness at all, are pushed to the back burner.

Maybe this busy pattern is acceptable some of the time. After all, God does call us to be responsible in the small matters of life. Being a Christian doesn't mean engaging in quiet meditation all day long. We are just as responsible for pouring the bran flakes into the cereal bowl for the morning breakfast as we are for meditating on God's goodness in some quiet place. The challenge for the Christian, however, is to find evidence of God's grace in the busy daily routine of life as well as looking for it in the quiet places.

But then there are those times in our lives when the routine itself is no longer there. The reality that death is a part of life comes through a loved one's dying or through our own struggle for life after a threatening diagnosis. The events of September 11 remind us that we could die by sudden or catastrophic means. Even if we have good odds of staying healthy most of our life or surviving the diagnosis for another year or even decade, the thought of our potential death reveals the shallowness of our daily routine. Our life here is really very fragile and fleeting. Life itself takes on new value. Knowing that we may not be here to hug the children every morning on the way out the door makes the hugs that much more important. And if we could ever just get back to that routine—an autopilot life in which we wouldn't have to struggle with these deeper issues—then we might have peace again.

Yet this passage reminds us that even in the course of daily living, not to mention during those times of distress or anxiety, we need to find ways to tune into the grace of God. "It is good to wait quietly for the salvation of the LORD" (Lam. 3:26). This verse contains a word we don't like to hear: *wait*. We are frustrated by the word especially when we are dealing with a situation that we know isn't what we want for our lives. We both remember how we had to play the waiting game. When our spouses were ill and their health was deteriorating, we'd have to wait for the test results, doctors' appointments, the medication to work, or the insurance company's approval for the next procedure. We often had to wait to sense God's answer to our prayers, whether we were praying for strength to endure the day, relief from pain for our loved one, or a sense of closeness to God—even those prayers were not answered immediately or necessarily the way we hoped they would be.

"It is good to wait quietly for the salvation of the LORD" (Lam. 3:26). Why is this waiting a good thing? You can probably find a number of reasons why this might have value. However, the primary answer is one of the themes of this book's forty meditations: *Waiting reminds us that God is in control.* He is sovereign over all. He is the King and Lord; we must wait for him. And why should we wait "quietly"? This word really doesn't refer so much to lack of noise as to waiting in peace and patience. This is a matter of faithful confidence, like that of the Israelites wandering in the wilderness for forty years who were told to wait on the Lord (see Exodus 16). God still provided for them during the waiting time in the wilderness. The provision did not come in advance, nor in excess. God gave his people exactly what they needed in the right amount for that day only. Then they had to trust that he would be gracious enough to do it again the next day. A number of years ago, Kellogg's Corn Flakes ran an advertisement inviting you to "taste them again for the first time." Like the manna in the wilderness that was to be collected new each morning, God invites us to taste his mercies new every morning. Why not try it today? Taste God's mercies again, but have a fresh taste in your mouth like it was the first time.

If we really know that God is in control, then we can wait a little more patiently, a little more quietly. Maybe you are healthy right now and are waiting to start your family, to get that job, or to finally buy a home. You are waiting, in a sense, for all that to happen. More importantly, however, remember what we are waiting for from a biblical perspective: "the salvation of our LORD." He will redeem. He will save. No, not always immediately (in fact, he usually doesn't work that way). But he walks with us through the valley of the shadow of death (Ps. 23:4) and turns evil to our profit (Rom. 8:28), even though (as with the Old Testament people of God) seeing his salvation may take forty years of wandering. Of course, he probably won't make you wait forty years if you are seeking something that is in line with his will, for "the LORD is good to those whose hope is in him" (Lam. 3:25). But this doesn't mean that our prayers are always answered on a regular basis the way we want.

Even if you now are fortunate enough to live in the daylight with no threat to your life, learn to wait on the Lord. Learn to trust him for everything. Trust that he will be there for you in the good times and in the bad. He will guide you through shadows when they come. Then no matter what happens in your life, you will be ready to face the challenge of midnight. Tragedy and death can come suddenly, without warning. Like cruise ship passengers learning about lifeboats, be prepared for a disaster. You know who your lifeline is—the same one who calms the seas.

I am more and more aware of the fact that those whom you healed may have been waiting a long time for you to touch them. And the reality is that you don't cure anyone physically forever. Someday I will have to die. Help me wait on you—both when times are good and when my life might be threatened by disease. I place my life in your care today, just as I must do each day. Grant me the patience to wait on you. Amen.

Heads or Tails? Are Decisions God's or Ours?

*Therefore, my dear friends, as you have always obeyed—
not only in my presence, but now much more in my
absence—continue to work out your salvation with fear
and trembling, for it is God who works in you to will and
to act according to his good purpose.*

Philippians 2:12–13

How do I make responsible decisions?

How do you usually go about making decisions? Let's say you're trying to decide which movie to see or what restaurant you want to eat in. And let's assume you need to make that decision with someone else. How do you go about doing it? Flip a coin? Draw straws? Maybe do rock, scissors, paper? Or maybe you talk it through, evaluating your options, discussing them thoroughly, rating your preference on a scale of 1 to 5, and developing a consensus. Whatever mode you might select, your aim is to make the decision so you can move on to the activity.

Those types of decisions may be pretty superficial and rather easy to make. Other decisions are more complex and difficult. Should I accept the offer for a new job? Should we move to another city? How can I help my son face his gambling problem? Should I remain a member of this congregation or parish even if I don't agree with all the changes that are being introduced? Am I financially ready to retire now or must I work longer? Would it be best for me to opt for chemotherapy?

One key factor in these difficult decisions (though it certainly isn't absent in the "lesser" decisions of life) is what you and I might discern to be God's role and will in these matters. It's tough to get a fix on the degree to which we are responsible for our own decisions versus recognizing and accepting God's sovereign rule over every aspect of our lives. This theological point has divided many churches. One extreme position is that God has so controlled everything in our lives (minute by minute!) that even if we think we have decided something, the whole thing has been predetermined by God. We really did not have any choice in the matter (though it may have seemed that way to us). In support of this position, people often quote Jesus' teaching that "even the very hairs of your head are numbered," and that, like sparrows, "not one of them will fall to the ground apart from the will of your Father" (Matt. 10:30, 29).

On the other end of the scale are those who figure that we are free to do what we want without any interference from God. They argue that God equipped us all with a "free will" to make our own choices. While God controls the ultimate outcome of this world, we are free to do what we want as we move along. In this view God is like the engineer on a train. He will get us all to our destination, but in the meantime we are totally free to decide where we sit, what we do, how we spend our time, and how we behave while on the journey.

In writing to the church in Philippi, Paul makes a very interesting statement. He advises us to work out our own salvation with fear and trembling (which sounds like something we have to do ourselves) because God is working in us both to will and to do his good pleasure (which sounds like God will be doing it). This is actually one of the mysteries of faith. As human beings, we assume that a person is responsible for any action he or she takes. When a window in our house is broken, *one* person is responsible. Sure, someone else may have contributed to it, but we need to identify the one who really did it.

But in the matter of God working within us, the issue isn't so neatly divided when we think about making actual decisions in our daily life. God isn't like a parent teaching a child to ride a bicycle by holding on to the rear fender, steadying the ride. The parent isn't really riding the bike; the child is. Mom or Dad may be helping, but they really aren't controlling the bike. God has a bigger role than that in how we live our lives.

Perhaps a better analogy, though still limited, is the kind of inspiration an artist or musician might experience. They often testify that an inspiration overcomes them so that their work of art comes into existence. Think about what the Bible teaches us. On the one hand we are told that Christians are "in Christ." On the other hand we are told that the Spirit of Christ is "in us." Who is in whom? Another mystery! But the way it seems to work out in our lives is that we and God (the Father, the Son, and the Holy Spirit) are not adversaries vying for the right to make decisions. Rather, the believer and God are so much one (each "in" the other) that we often have a hard time discerning which one made the decision.

Because we are not perfect, our decision-making process isn't always so effortless and efficient. On the contrary, we tend to exercise our will against that of God. We want things God doesn't want us to have, or we want things at a time when God knows they are inappropriate for us. That's where we feel the rub.

So the apostle Paul reminds us that in a perfect, sanctified relationship, a harmony characterizes the relationship between the believer and God. Adam and Eve experienced that in the Garden of Eden before they fell into sin. They communed with God, and only when they rebelled did they sense the need to hide in the bushes out of shame and fear of God.

The Bible also talks about a time when there will again be this perfect harmony. The Hebrew word is *shalom*—roughly translated as "peace" but much richer in meaning. *Shalom* means a perfect harmony, a state of perfect peace in which (as in the original creation) all the pieces of creation work together in harmony.

Paul urges us to work toward that perfect, harmonious peace in our own lives, especially in making decisions. It really isn't a matter of our will against God's will. This is really a matter of so tuning ourselves to the notes of God that our lives are a perfect harmonic symphony with our Lord.

Daily living is an exercise in practicing that harmony. Work out your salvation—not only your conversion but living a consistent Christian life. Write a symphony with God's Spirit. Perhaps that is why Paul was also able to conclude his short letter to the Philippians with the words "Do not be anxious about anything, but in everything, by prayer and petition, with thanksgiving, present your requests to God. And the 'peace' [the New Testament parallel to the Hebrew *shalom*] of God, which transcends all understanding, will guard your hearts and your minds in Christ Jesus" (Phil. 4:6–7).

PRAYER: *You ultimately bring peace to this world, Holy Father, through your Son, Jesus Christ. You have also brought peace to my heart because of Christ's sacrifice and death at Calvary. But I must confess that there are times when I may not be at peace. I want to do things my way and on my time schedule. I have a tendency to take credit for things that go my way, but I might blame others (even you!) when they go another way. Blend my spirit with your Spirit that I may feel your divine harmony in my life. Amen.*

How Long Do I Have?

All our days pass away under your wrath; we finish our years with a moan. The length of our days is seventy years—or eighty, if we have the strength; yet their span is but trouble and sorrow, for they quickly pass, and we fly away. Who knows the power of your anger? For your wrath is as great as the fear that is due you. Teach us to number our days aright, that we may gain a heart of wisdom.

Psalm 90:9–12

What makes for a full and happy life?

You need to recall the story of Moses in order to understand Psalm 90. Moses wrote the psalm near the end of his life, after he had wandered for forty years in the wilderness and after he had seen all the affliction the Israelites suffered in Egypt and on their journey to the Promised Land. Now Moses is looking at Canaan, knowing that he would not live to set foot on the land he had dreamed about for so many years. As you read the psalm, perhaps you can feel in the pit of your stomach the tension he felt in his. On the one hand, he praises God for being his "dwelling place," the constant source of comfort and security (v. 1). But he also feels the heavy hand of God pressing down on him. "You turn men back to dust," he says (v. 3); "We are consumed by your anger" (v. 7); "Relent, O LORD! How long will it be? Have compassion on your servants" (v. 13).

Most of us struggle with life—especially with trying to find that balance between embracing the love and security of God while still recognizing that bad things happen to us intermittently throughout our life. Simply listening to the evening news report reminds us of the terror in the world. Children are kidnapped, wars rage in various hot spots around the globe, the economy shifts more quickly than sands in the desert. Families do not always love each other the way we would like. Marriages fail. Health deteriorates. So we can relate to what Moses says: "You sweep people away like dreams that disappear or like grass that springs up in the morning. In the morning it blooms and flourishes, but by evening it is dry and withered" (Ps. 90:5–6 NLT).

So how do we go about living a long, fulfilled, and happy life—especially when so many things can go wrong? If you use Psalm 90 to instruct you, then you must first understand that this psalm is future oriented. Even though our days might be short, Moses says, "Teach us to number our days aright, that we may gain a heart of wisdom" (v. 12). Have you figured out your "number"? How do you estimate the number of your days? Actually this psalm is not making promises about chronological years, as if a really good life would be one of seventy or eighty years. What Moses is suggesting is that seventy or eighty years is an awfully *short* period of time, especially compared to the eternity of God. Moses is coming to that realization. Can you hear Moses asking God the question, "Was my life worth something? Were these few short years I spent on earth of value to you, O Lord?" His closing prayer is that God will satisfy us in the morning with his unfailing love and that he will establish the work of our hands (vv. 14, 17).

Earlier in the psalm Moses identified the key element in this business of numbering our days: God doesn't count the way we do. "A thousand years in your sight are like a day that has just gone by" (v. 4). Or go back to the story of God calling Moses by the burning bush. When Moses wanted to know how he was to identify God to the people of Israel, God gave him the strange response: "This is what you are to say to the Israelites: 'I AM has sent me to you'" (Exod. 3:14). Elsewhere God is identified as the almighty one "who was, and is, and is to come" (Rev. 4:8). All of these added together give us the picture that God is eternal—a difficult, yes impossible, phenomenon for us to comprehend. God's time is different from our time. But he *always* was and *always* will be!

The message is pretty clear. We can count days and weeks and months and years. But we had better remember that these categories of time are part of creation—part of this earthly world. Our time is calculated by revolutions of the earth on its axis and seasons by the orbit of the earth around the sun. God is outside of that. He not only holds the world in his hands, he holds our time in his hands. When our days are numbered on this earth and we face our imminent death, then we really begin our life—an eternal life with Christ our Savior.

After Bob's first wife died, he was asked to speak to the children at the elementary school where she had been teaching. He told a story about a ride at the Wonderful World of Energy at EPCOT Center in Disney World. After having stood for over an hour in a long line, guests were finally ushered to luxurious seats. Then they watched a movie shown on a 360-degree screen, surrounded by magnificent sound. They learned about the marvels of what can be done with all forms of energy. As the movie came to an end, the spectators were in awe from the experience. The lights slowly came up, and just as people were about ready to stand up to leave the auditorium, a voice boomed over the loudspeaker, "Everyone please remain in your seats—the real show begins in one minute." And then, all of a sudden, the curtains in the front of the auditorium opened and the chairs on which the people were sitting turned into cars that took them past the screen and on a ride through the wonderful world of energy. This earthly world, Bob explained, is like the movie. This life is a prelude. Our experiences here are rich and wonderful. We love people. We enjoy the beauty of the earth. But the day will come when we all pass through the wall to the other side, where our real, eternal life is waiting for us.

Your life may be good right now. Perhaps you are enjoying yourself to the fullest. Or perhaps the warning of the end has already been sounded. But even death, for the Christian, is not the end. Physical death is only the end of the beginning. When a Christian dies, the real (eternal) life continues. Numbering our days on this earth, then, is more like the countdown to when the real show begins. That will be a fantastic show. So we need not be afraid if we are in Christ. God promised.

PRAYER: *Give me eyes to see beyond the walls of this life to know the glory in which you live, dear Father. I want to live a long and happy life. You have given me so many people to love and who love me. There are a multitude of challenges to keep my life interesting. But help me remember that living this life isn't the final goal. All of this life leads me to an even greater, more glorious life with you for all eternity. Help me be prepared for the transition from this world to the next—whenever that may come. For none of us know the day or hour of our death. Nor do we know when you will return. Getting ready means having my priorities straight in you. Stay with me and do your work through me, I pray. Amen.*

TWO

Dusk

The Knock at the Door

Ever so slowly dusk comes,
Extinguishing the light.
No way to delay it.
The warning of darkness around the corner.
Little time left to mow the lawn.
Quick! Hurry!
Too many jobs waiting.
Time to focus.
The day is soon ending.
Sun is setting,
Shadows steal in
To cover the light.
Dusk.

S. Zonnebelt-Smeenge
and R. De Vries

Since we live with death, we ought to think of it while
living. To settle accounts, to draw a balance, is important
and useful. The pastors should make it clear that it can
be anyone's turn next; that everyone's turn comes at some
point; that to prepare oneself is good.

Peter Noll

THE MENTAL HEALTH
PERSPECTIVE ON FACING
THE POSSIBILITY OF DYING

PART ONE:
WHAT DO YOU DO WHEN
THE NEWS ISN'T GOOD?

*B*oth of us have had the earthshaking experience of hearing a dreaded diagnosis given to our spouses. Susan's thirty-two-year-old husband, Rick, experienced a grand mal seizure while driving with her and their eighteen-month-old daughter, Sarah, to visit relatives just before the Christmas holiday. Somber-faced doctors, detecting a brain mass on the CAT scan, warned them that he might die during surgery. "Get your affairs in order," they urged. Rick survived the surgery, only to hear the doctors' grave news: "You might have only another two, possibly five, years to live—maybe more, maybe less. Some of the tumor could not be removed because of the fingerlike cancerous projections. Radiation is the treatment of choice. You never know what new medical advances will come in the next few years. But ultimately, people rarely survive a malignant brain tumor of this nature for very long. Yes, this is serious, but don't give up hope." So Susan, Rick, and Sarah began nearly two decades of trying to balance hope and despair while battling Rick's brain tumor.

"This doesn't look good! There seems to be a huge mass down here in your abdomen." The emergency room doctor didn't win an award for how he broke the news to Char, then forty-eight years old, and Bob that Thursday night before Easter. They thought she might have had appendicitis or at worst a bowel obstruction. But while moving the ultrasound sensor around her stomach, the physician found cancer—ovarian cancer, stage IV. For nearly four years Char would get very close to winning the battle only to have the disease rear its ugly head again.

Perhaps your health experiences haven't been as traumatic as these two events, especially if you are young or middle aged. Sometimes the doctor may simply find that you or your loved one suffers from migraines or infected sinuses. At another time you might have an intestinal flu. As you get older, you may need surgery for torn cartilage, an inflamed appendix, or a kidney stone. You don't like to deal with an imperfect body, but you learn that eventually you will likely need some medical intervention to correct your physical ailments. Though these situations may be very stressful and unpleasant, full health is usually restored. You return once again to the daylight.

Other health problems are more chronic, such as arthritis, colitis, or a back problem. These may produce frustrating or unpleasant symptoms when they flare up, but you can quickly develop coping strategies to manage them. You can still enjoy much of your future life.

However, in this section of the book we are talking about a set of circumstances in which the diagnosis falls into a more troublesome and often traumatic area. This type of diagnosis may include cancer of some organ, pulmonary disease (such as emphysema or chronic obstructive disease), heart disease (such as congestive heart failure or coronary disease), kidney failure, AIDs, multiple sclerosis, leukemia, Lou Gehrig's disease, or Alzheimer's disease. These diagnoses are serious and potentially terminal but probably not immediately life threatening, although they could eventually lead to your death. They are likely treatable to some extent, at least to reduce the symptoms. Many people live for years with these illnesses. But your body is failing to some degree. The future looks more guarded than before the diagnosis. The daylight fades from your life as the dusk of potential death begins to cast its shadow. The reality of death has now come closer.

Other diagnoses can be even more serious, almost like a death sentence. They are grave, sobering realities—a fast-growing cancer of the brain, lungs, or pancreas, a massive coronary, or a debilitating stroke. Life as you know it probably won't last much longer. You will soon move through the dusk into the dark night of your life—into the darkness of midnight.

In the first half of this section, we will discuss how you can manage your reactions to hearing a potentially terminal diagnosis. In the second half of this section, we will look at what you will want to do now that the diagnosis has been made.

What's Going on Here? Understanding the Diagnosis

Doctors may or may not be optimistic about your prognosis. You may not know how forthright the doctor is being in telling you about your condition. Many doctors are frustrated when they confront an illness that doesn't respond to treatment. They might even consider their inability to cure as a personal failure. Of course, we are not blaming the medical industry. Doctors are here to solve physical problems whenever they possibly can. But we also need to recognize the limits of medicine. Only so much can be done for any disease. Facing that reality can be very tough.

Hearing a diagnosis that may be potentially terminal is an extremely traumatic event. You may not be able to think very clearly at that moment—even for days, or possibly weeks, after you receive the initial report. You may have a hard time thinking through all your options. Just remember, your physician is there to clarify information so that you can make wise choices. But you are still the one who finally has to make the decisions. We urge you to take charge of your medical situation in consultation with your physician. If you want to have some idea of how this disease will progress, you may have to be fairly assertive with your doctor to find out what he or she thinks about your prognosis and how much longer you might have to live. Medical professionals can help you gather information based on their research and medical experience. But they are also human beings, and none of us knows what ultimately will happen—especially if you are beginning to ask the question about how much longer you may have to live.

Isn't There Hope? Looking at the Positive and Negative Aspects

Will this illness be terminal? A dreaded thought! You just heard a diagnosis that could signal the end of your life (or that of a loved one). Now you face a dilemma. Do you focus on the hope that you can still conquer this disease? Or do you give in to the crushing news of the diagnosis, give up hope, and let despair overwhelm you? Your reactions can be as varied as the flowers of the field. You will likely hear stories of others who have survived. Our society is good at distracting or avoiding issues associated with a potentially terminal illness. The American Cancer Society says that the biggest obstacle to early detection of cancer is people's denial of the symptoms. We don't want to entertain the possibility of bad news.

The problem with most diagnoses is that the disease can develop in so many different directions. For example, cancer of the breast, liver, prostate, or gastrointestinal tract may be terminal or may not be. The potentially terminal nature of the disease needs to be taken seriously without losing hope for a partial or full recovery.

Preparing for the worst-case scenario is wise both mentally and spiritually. As a licensed psychologist, Susan frequently works with patients facing a potentially terminal disease to help them process their anxiety or depression associated with the diagnosis. Her clients often discover that they (along with the medical profession) have focused primarily on the "hope" or positive side of the equation and have ignored the potentially negative or "despair" side. The spectrum ranges from "I will get better again" to "I will die because of this illness." If both ends of the continuum (hope and despair) are not equally addressed, psychological problems can develop. The public seems to have adopted the premise that a positive attitude leads to a good prognosis. While research lends some credibility to the "positive attitude" theory, we believe this positive attitude must be tempered with a realistic approach. Balance is achieved only after exploring both the hopeful and the despairing sides. You may well live many more productive years, or you may have only a short time to live. Preparing for both possibilities can be extremely beneficial. Arriving at a balance seems to be the best option to give you some peace of mind regardless of which direction the disease may take. Once you have prepared for your death, life can be lived more freely and completely. Each one of us needs to realize that we are not immune to death. We will all surely die, sometime. Because death is inevitable, why not get mentally and spiritually prepared for it?

Learning More about Your Diagnosis

The medical field was very different twenty-five years ago. In those days Susan had to teach her nursing students to keep medical information away from the patient. They were not even to know their own vital signs (blood pressure, temperature, pulse rate, etc.) or any other medical information unless it came directly from their doctor. The thinking was that a layperson wouldn't be able to understand the medical jargon anyway. Today all this information is readily available to the patient. In fact, individuals are encouraged and expected to know all about their own health status. You can buy your own blood pressure equipment, take your own glucose readings, and perform a myriad of other medical tests in the privacy of your home. The medical profession now recognizes that the more people know about how the body functions, the more likely they will choose to take good care of their own bodies.

Yet many people think they don't have the expertise to be involved in what is happening to them. Patients often withdraw from the treatment process after describing their symptoms. They relinquish the decision making to the doctors. But if you are facing a disease, don't give up in making critical decisions about your life. Stick with it. Be a vital, active part in determining the treatment of your disease. Go to the bookstores or search the Internet. Learn all you can about your body, the disease, and the treatment options available to you.

This also means that you need to partner with your physician. As your physician is making the diagnosis or outlining a preferred course of treatment, listen carefully. Ask questions. Don't hesitate to say that you don't understand something and ask for a clear explanation in terms you can understand. Have your doctor draw a picture to help you visualize what is being said. Write down medical terms so you can look them up later on. When you leave the doctor's office, have as much information about what is happening in your body stored in your mind and on paper as possible. Even take a tape recorder along to record your conversation so you can play it back later. You will likely think of other questions after your doctor's appointment has ended. Write these questions down. Call your physician and ask your questions. Being your own medical advocate is healthy. You have every right. After all, it is your body and your life.

This is undoubtedly a very stressful time in your life. This is now up close and personal—it's about *you* this time! You may have learned about the diagnosis when you least expected it. You may have been alone in the doctor's office getting a routine annual physical exam when your doctor discovered some type of potential growth or abnormality. The shock of such unexpected news likely made it difficult to think of all the questions now flooding your mind. Even if the diagnosis wasn't a complete surprise because you were experiencing some symptoms, had been through a series of tests, and then made an appointment to see your physician, you probably still were not ready to hear the diagnosis. We would urge you to select a support person to accompany you to your next appointment to also learn with you about your medical problem—someone who is objective, can listen carefully, and will be able to retain the information accurately to discuss it with you afterward and to serve as part of your support network.

To learn more about your diagnosis, we suggest you investigate the following five questions (see sidebar 10). Ask them of your physician. Perhaps write them out before your appointment and then take notes or tape-record your conversation with the doctor.

QUESTIONS TO ASK ABOUT YOUR DIAGNOSIS ⑩
1. What happened in my body?
2. Do I really need to treat this condition?
3. How can I balance quantity with quality of life?
4. What treatment options are available for me?
5. What are the potential side effects of these options?

Question #1: What Happened in My Body?

You may want a quick refresher course in physiology because you need to know how your body normally functions and what has now gone wrong with it. This isn't done to assign blame or create guilt ("I shouldn't have put on so much weight," or "This is my brother-in-law's fault because he smoked so much in our house!"). You simply need to know what went wrong so you can understand it and explain it to others. Knowing about your condition generally decreases anxiety or worry. It can keep you from playing the "what if" game, which can be time consuming, stressful, and exhausting and forces a person to go round and round the issues or options.

Question #2: Do I Really Need to Treat This Condition?

The answer may be obvious to some. They would say: "That's simple—ignoring this would mean I may have a lot of pain or lose function more rapidly. I don't want to live like that." But maybe you are without pain or discomfort right now, so doing nothing about the illness sounds better to you. That certainly is your choice, although no treatment may not be the wisest decision. You will need to ask your physician what the outcome would likely be if you chose to do nothing right now. Then weigh your options. Later we will address how you determine when treatment has run its course and probably should be terminated. That is a different issue for further along in the disease process. The issue here is to identify what went wrong with your body and what you want to do about it now.

Question #3: How Can I Balance Quantity with Quality of Life?

Eighteen years before Rick's death, he underwent his first surgery to explore the mass in his brain. The surgeons wanted some idea of how much of the tumor (if they actually found one) they should remove if that might jeopardize the quality of body functioning. Rick had to make the tough decision of quantity versus quality of life. The more they removed, the longer he might live. But conversely, the more they removed, the less function he might have (depending on the site). In deciding whether or not to seek treatment for your disease, you face the issue of how much longer you would live without any intervention compared to receiving some type of treatment. Would you have several more months (or years!) in which you could still engage, even in a limited way, in your favorite activities? Would you still be able to vacation, travel, or spend time making memories with your loved ones? Or would the disease progress so rapidly without treatment that the quality of your life would quickly suffer? These questions are certainly difficult to answer, but discussing them with your medical professionals as well as gathering information from other medical resources may help shed light on these questions. At least asking the questions opens up discussion and may help you and your family come to some workable conclusion.

Question #4: What Treatment Options Are Available for Me?

Treatment options can vary widely. Sometimes surgery may be recommended. If the disease is cancer, surgery may or may not be followed by radiation or chemotherapy. At other times a specific medication regime may be suggested. Some people may want to investigate alternative treatments, such as holistic medicine or a spiritual-meditative approach. Experimental treatment for your disease may be available at a research-oriented medical facility. Your physician may know about these latest researched treatment methods and could make a referral if you want that. You can also check the Internet for treatment options, although you need to be very careful about the accuracy of that information. To ensure quality of medical information, check only those web sites that originate from credible sources. See sidebar 11 for a few sites to begin your search.

You should at least be aware of your options, even if you think you will ultimately decide on a more traditional or conservative approach. In many cases, opinions about the nature of the problem and treatment options vary greatly. If this is true of your particular situation, consider getting a second opinion from a qualified but independent physician. "Independent" means a physician outside your own doctor's medical group, possibly even in a larger city nearby. You can find a referral for a second opinion on your own, or your physician may refer you to a nearby teaching hospital, a medical school, or a major medical institution known for treating patients with your specific diagnosis. Getting a second opinion is not being disloyal to your doctor. Most physicians support this practice, especially in situations in which the diagnosis

---

MEDICAL INFORMATION AVAILABLE ON THE WEB   ⑪

A wealth of medical information is available through the Internet. Be cautious about what you read, and check out the creators of the website carefully. A few reliable sites that you can use to begin your search are listed below. Also use your favorite search engine to see what else you can uncover.

Medline Plus is a joint site provided by the National Institute of Health and the U.S. National Library of Medicine. You can link with them at www.medlineplus.gov.

Health Finder is a site that links you to more than 1,800 health-related organizations at www.healthfinder.gov.

Stanford University Medical Center maintains a useful site called Health Library, accessed at Healthlibrary.stanford.edu. You can also call them at (800) 295-5177. They will create for you free of charge a one-time personal packet on the specific disease you are researching geared to your age, gender, and the status of your disease.

Mayo Clinic has long been recognized as a leader in the field of medical care. Check out their website at www.mayoclinic.org and click on "medical services" and/or "health information" to research your personal medical questions.

---

and treatment plan are not obvious. If your doctor is offended by the request, consider if you want to continue treatment with him or her. How can more information or gaining another perspective have negative consequences? Securing a second opinion can give you the confidence that you are doing all you can to successfully deal with this illness.

In addition to requesting a second opinion, be sure to check with the physician you are planning to work with to ensure that he or she feels confident about treating the illness with which you are diagnosed. Find out if he or she has regularly performed these procedures or administered these treatments. This is your life you are dealing with, and you want the best expertise. Ask the doctor what he or she considers to be both the most aggressive and the most conservative approaches to treatment and what would be the wisest strategy, in fact, the one he or she might select in the same situation.

Don't be dismayed if, after making a decision, you hear someone question your choice. They might encourage you to choose the route one of their friends or family members took in a similar situation. The world is full of stories of successful outcomes. You might be tempted to look for that pot of gold at the end of the rainbow. That is a normal desire because we want to beat the diagnosis and live. However, you need to be realistic about your options, make your own decisions, and discover how to handle others who might try to convince you to go in another direction. Learn to respond kindly but directly with words like "Thank you for your concern and willingness to offer suggestions. However, I have looked at all the options and decided that this route is best for me right now." On the other hand, after listening to others' suggestions, you may want to check out some of them to see if they do indeed apply to your situation. Someone else may have a beneficial idea you had not considered. Make a phone call or do an Internet search to check it out. As the person with a serious illness, you need to be comfortable with your treatment plan. Hopefully this plan will also be supported by the other significant people in your life.

Question #5: What Are the Potential Side Effects of These Options?

Obviously you will want to choose the treatment that has the best potential prognosis for you. After all, if you are going to select a treatment that has significant side effects, you want a good chance of eradicating the disease. A friend of Bob's died of lung cancer. When he was first diagnosed, the surgeons removed his entire right lung. When cancer reappeared three years later in the left lung, he decided to receive no further treatments—no chemotherapy, no radiation. The only treatments he would allow were palliative (painkilling) in nature. The reason for his decision: If he had six months to live, he wanted to live them "his way." He liked to work outdoors, enjoyed golf, and wanted to play with his grandchildren. For sixteen weeks his strength was sufficient to do these things. Each person's situation is unique. You need to make your own decision, because the essential decision is how to balance hope with reality. Bob's friend chose a course he thought was realistic and would give him the highest quality of life for the time he had left. You must ultimately be comfortable and feel at peace with your choices, including choices about what kind of side effects you are willing to face.

Who Will Go through This with Me?

So now you know the diagnosis. As you left the physician's office, you may have been numb and unable to comprehend what the doctor said about your situation. You need to sort through the shocking information. Letting down your defenses to become vulnerable by sharing this bad news is extremely difficult. But putting up an emotional shield can only protect you temporarily. Eventually you can't avoid the reality of the situation.

Now you need to think about who else should hear this news. Hopefully you have some people with whom you are intimately connected. In the "Daylight" section we encouraged you to evaluate the relationships you have in your life. The exercises in sidebars 3, 4, and 5 were designed to help you assess the number and quality of the relationships you have. These exercises may now help you decide with whom to share the news of this diagnosis. You will probably want to tell those individuals who are really close to you first. This may also be an opportunity to rebuild other relationships that have weakened over time.

If someone went with you to the doctor's office, you can initially talk about this upsetting news with him or her and clarify what you didn't understand. Then can you explain it to someone else? You might want to rehearse what you will say. Practice it out loud. Test how you might answer the questions others might ask. Remember, you don't have to go into details about your condition or diagnosis if you aren't ready to share them. Statements such as "I'm not ready to discuss that yet" set healthy boundaries.

You may want to keep the news of a diagnosis quiet for a short period of time. Maybe you need to verify the diagnosis, or you may just want to let the fog clear for a day or two to sort through things before letting others know the news. How you decide to control the timing of telling others is certainly your prerogative. Digesting the initial diagnosis takes time and work. However, many others care about you and will want to be as supportive as possible. People in our lives who love us dearly want to be there for us at such a critical time. Sharing painful news with them is a way of feeling closer to each other.

If you have dependent children living with you, you also need to decide when and what to tell them. You may not want to say anything for a day or two until you feel more settled with the news yourself. What and how you tell them needs to be within their range of comprehension. You may not understand the full ramifications of the diagnosis yourself. The one cardinal rule we have in talking with children is *be honest*. Children can quickly discern when an adult is misleading them. Also try to say only what is necessary at the time. You may want to review what we wrote in the Daylight section regarding talking with children and adolescents about dying and death. Giving too much information at once can be overwhelming for anyone, especially for young people.

Some people choose not to talk about their diagnosis because they don't want to cause pain for others or themselves by focusing on the problem. This is probably one of the most unhealthy things that can happen. Some individuals have been taught to think that they shouldn't talk about anything that is painful because it will only make the other person feel worse. Didn't many of us learn as children that "if you can't say anything nice, don't say anything at all"? We interpret this to mean, "Keep quiet; it's better that way," and in the process we are not only hurting ourselves but also diminishing the quality of our relationship with the other person. Remember, secrets are ultimately unhealthy and put distance between you and others. And you then have to endure your pain in silence. The other negative ramification of keeping feelings inside is that you may eventually experience other physical or emotional problems by storing such stressful news. Talking with those who care about you can help you feel better. We all need to feel the support and caring of other people in times of crisis.

Many of us live as though we have all the time in the world to tell people how important they are to us. We aren't always intentional about saying or showing it before a terminal illness strikes. Generally speaking, when someone becomes seriously ill, family members and friends are quickly reminded of how valuable and important that person is to them. The same is true in reverse—the one who is ill now recognizes all the more the value of his or her family or friends. The lesson is to recognize at all times how fragile life is and how precious the people in our lives are to us. Talking about our feelings can bring people closer and enhance our relationships. We often feel more connected because we understand better the depth of the other person's heart and soul. Hopefully recognizing this will help overcome the obstacles that might prevent you from sharing your thoughts, feelings, and desires with others.

When you tell your family and friends about your diagnosis, they will likely shower you with offers to help in "any way possible." You will need to decide what kind of help you will want and from whom you want to receive it. People who care about you often want to be supportive. However, they sometimes don't recognize that their offer to assist you might be so general that it is hard to know what to accept. Try to hear all offers of help as genuine, and let the person know specifically what kind of assistance you would like from them. Or you could simply give them a list of things that you and your family already know you will need help with and let them choose what they can do from that.

Relationships with others can be one of life's greatest joys, but at times and under certain circumstances, they can be among the most hurtful areas of life. Many times that happens because of misunderstandings or not talking about feelings and what truly matters to us. We long to be loved for who we are. Receiving love and acceptance is all the more important when a person faces the possibility that his or her life is coming to an end. So what do you do when the news isn't good? Talk! Talk honestly and openly with those you love. Especially learn to talk about your feelings, because in the long run that will strengthen your relationship with your family and friends and help create a team approach to assist you in handling this potentially terminal disease.

How Do I Manage My Life's Goals, Values, and Priorities?

We call them "life-altering events"—those events that have such a major impact on your life that your goals, values, or behaviors could be dramatically changed. Life-altering events are usually neither totally positive nor totally negative. The birth of a child, for example, is often an eagerly anticipated life-altering event. Yet the addition of a child might impact negatively the amount of time a couple has alone together. A child increases their responsibility, introduces a higher level of structure into their lives, and certainly increases their financial obligations. This is only one example of the many events in our lives that combine both positive and negative factors.

Receiving a potentially terminal medical diagnosis is also a life-altering event. This type of diagnosis is almost universally seen as completely negative. One very common reaction is, "What's going to happen to my life now?" Many more questions follow. "What will happen to my children?" "Will we still be able to retire to Fort Myers Beach?" "If I should die, are my finances really secure enough to provide for my loved ones?" "What can I do about all my unfulfilled dreams and goals?"

Life Questions—Am I Pursuing Goals That Are Based on What I Value Most?

In the section "Daylight" we encouraged you to identify your values and long-term goals. Revisit them now to see how you might wish to reprioritize them in light of your potentially terminal diagnosis. When the stark reality of the diagnosis comes, we begin to realize we are fallible and finite. An alarm goes off within us: "Oh no! It can't be so! I haven't had a chance to do this or that!" Most of the time we have so much more we want to do. Our lives seem incomplete and imper-

---

LIFE QUESTIONS   ⑫

1   Why was I born?

2. What has my life consisted of up to now? What has been positive? What has been negative?

3. What are the purposes of my life?

4. What good have I contributed to this world?

5. What is the meaning of life? Of death?

6. What is my role in this diagnosis?

7. How do I want to spend the next month? Six months? Year?

fect—we need to add more finishing touches. Perhaps you have put off the serious questions such as "What is my purpose in this life? Why was I born? What good have I contributed to others or this world?" Maybe you thought you would have time in your old age to reflect on these questions. Maybe in retirement you were going to work on some of your unrealized goals.

But this diagnosis may have caught you off guard. You are too young. You haven't focused on some of the important things in your life yet. Now the time has come to answer some of life's deeper questions. They inevitably force themselves on you. How will you answer them?

So now you ask yourself: "What do I want my life to look like if I have only one month to live? Or six months? Or a year?" Start by journaling about your life up until now, what you have learned and what is important to you. Then ask yourself, using the "life questions" in sidebar 12, what you would like to do with the time you have left. Maybe you want to return to a few of your favorite places, have a family reunion, or travel to see a friend across the country whom you always wanted to visit. More than likely you will want to review your financial situation and perhaps make some changes to provide an easier transition for your loved ones. Remember, you are doing this only because there is the *possibility* that your life may end. The *possibility* is itself the life-altering event. Under normal circumstances, we rarely wake up in the morning with the sense that we might die soon. But now you have the doctor's word that this might happen to you. Your life has changed. The questions get bigger and more significant.

Spiritual Questions—Where Am I Spiritually and How Will This Impact My Potential Death?

A potentially terminal diagnosis not only raises questions about life but also, for many people, elicits questions about the "afterlife." What, if anything, comes after I die? This is a deeply spiritual issue. By "spiritual" we mean all those questions that deal with issues beyond this world (see sidebar 13). Is there a God? What kind of control does God exercise over my life? Is God good, loving, and powerful? If so, why does God allow these things to happen? (Some people may even believe God causes bad things to happen, although we do not come from that perspective.) Does God care for me personally? If I die, what happens to *me*—not just my body but *me* as a person? And what about my soul? Will my "new body" be anything like the present one to which I have become so attached, even though I may dislike it right now because it isn't functioning in a reliable manner?

SPIRITUAL QUESTIONS   ⑬

1. Is there a God?

2. Is God a real person?

3. Is God good, loving, and powerful?

4. If so, why does God allow these things to happen?

5. Does God care about me personally?

6. What is God's role in my diagnosis?

7. What do I believe will happen to me when I die?

Many religions believe in a life beyond the grave. Christians often have questions about what happens to their physical body as it goes to the grave. People from other traditions, such as the Jewish faith, focus far less on the afterlife and more on working faithfully in this life. But the question of the afterlife still pushes its way into their consciousness.

There is also the issue of eternity—a concept that is very difficult to grasp. In this world we experience a definite beginning and a definite end. We live with it daily—the sun comes up, the alarm clock goes off. At the end of the day, the sun goes down and we go to sleep. Time passes. But to live in a place where there is no time, or at least where time never ends, seems incomprehensible. Yet many people cling to this as a hope, believing that this impending physical death (not a spiritual one) is the only one they will ever face. After this death, they believe, they will live forever. That sounds good in so many ways, but the pain of severing the relationships we value so much can temporarily taint the joy of eternity. Maybe as you read this, you don't believe there is anything at all after death. This then really is all there is. If you do believe in an eternal life, nonetheless the joy of what is to come is still coupled with the deep pain of death. The joy and pain stand side by side as the daylight fades into dusk and then finally to midnight.

As a Family Member: To Tell or Not Tell the Diagnosis to Your Seriously Ill Loved One

Perhaps you are a family member of the person who has a potentially terminal diagnosis. The doctor may have talked with you and predicted a relatively short life span, but your loved one, who is terminally ill, hasn't heard that news yet. Perhaps he or she was too sick at the time, and no one has told him or her. You are debating whether or not you should break the news. You wonder if telling your loved one might cause him or her to "give up" if they hear the prognosis. Many people think that way—as if keeping the truth from someone might actually make the situation better. However, both research and our own experience indicate that the dying person almost always senses the truth of their situation before you tell them. They suspect what is happening, and if you do not talk openly and candidly about the situation, you may cause a growing distance between you and them. Then they might not be willing to broach the subject themselves. What a predicament to be in! This is a classic example of silent, parallel sufferers who are putting distance between each other because of their fear of talking.

We believe every person deserves to be told the truth about his or her potentially impending death. Do you as a family member think you have the right to keep such significant information from your loved one who may be dying sooner than they may realize? Telling the person the truth does not cause the person to die. On the other hand, not clearly informing a person of his or her prognosis may lead to an inappropriate decision about medical treatment or future goals. Or it may prevent your loved one from making some final preparation he or she would make if they knew the gravity of their situation. So now we need to turn our attention to the second main part of this section. When a person knows and understands that the diagnosis is potentially terminal, then the question arises: "What do I need to attend to now?"

THE MENTAL HEALTH PERSPECTIVE ON FACING THE POSSIBILITY OF DYING

PART TWO: SUMMARIZING YOUR LIFE— WHAT DO I NEED TO ATTEND TO?

We have been saying all along that a diagnosis that could result in death may seem unbelievable and overwhelming. Many people tend to avoid thinking about what might actually happen to them and refuse to deal with it. As a result no one really addresses what that person's potential death will mean. Maybe you know people who never talked about or planned for their death even though they knew their condition was likely terminal. They may have distracted themselves by keeping busy or pretending nothing happened. But these behaviors are neither healthy nor helpful. If your illness is potentially terminal, you need to prepare for the end, even if you still have hope to win the battle. Look closely at what you need to do as the daylight is overshadowed by your potentially terminal diagnosis. You have moved to the dusk of day because you realize that this diagnosis could lead to your death. So take the time to summarize your life and identify what you need to do as the shadows creep in.

You may have followed our suggestion in the "Daylight" section to put the important things in your life in order even while you were healthy. Now that the circumstances of your life have changed, you may want to review and revise the instructions and plans you wrote. Review your financial profile, your assignment of people to Durable Power of Attorney and Durable Power of Attorney for Health Care, and review your funeral plans. Because of your diagnosis you may now have a clearer idea of the approximate time you may have left to live, and you can more accurately plan your future. These tasks of planning for your death may appear far less theoretical than when you did them before, because your plans might now truly be your *final* wishes. This may be your last chance to decide what you want for yourself and your loved ones.

You can organize your planning around three main areas: (1) financial and legal matters, (2) dying and funeral events, and (3) issues of family involvement.

Money, Property, and Legal Issues

In section one we briefly described a number of financial and legal instruments that we believe everyone, healthy or not, should keep updated and in their possession. If you are not yet familiar with these instruments, turn back to their descriptions in the Daylight section. We want to encourage you to consider final adjustments to these documents in preparation for your possible death.

The agent appointed as your Durable Power of Attorney and your Durable Power of Attorney for Health Care may be the same or different persons. Make certain you have complete confidence in these people, because you may get to the point at which you will not be able to make complex decisions about your financial and health needs. In naming the Durable Power of Attorney, you are giving someone else permission to make financial decisions for you when you are no longer mentally or physically competent. This is more than simply having someone write checks for you. This person can decide when and where you will go for nursing care (if you can't take care of yourself), when to spend your savings, or when to sell your investments to help cover your expenses. If you are married, your spouse will likely be the person you name to be your Durable Power of Attorney. She or he will then be able to manage, and eventually inherit, your joint assets. If you are unmarried, the Durable Power of Attorney decides when and how to deal with all your assets including your property. In some states retaining ownership of your home during your lifetime may be the wisest choice. Consult an Elder Law attorney in your area. Make certain you choose a person for the Durable Power of Attorney who either has the same financial and life values you have or a person who will remain true to your wishes regardless of their perspective. Choosing two people to implement your wishes can provide a check and balance for each other. That may give you greater assurance that your wishes will be honored. However, selecting two people can also complicate the matter. An impasse may develop over a disagreement, creating a deadlock. As a result, you may want to appoint a third person who would be called upon to break a deadlock. Be sure to discuss your choice with the people you select to ensure they are willing to assume this responsibility, that they are willing to work together, and that they understand your wishes.

You can use a similar selection process to choose your Durable Power of Attorney for Health Care. This person must feel comfortable carrying out your wishes about life support. These advanced directives revolve around the type of life support you want, if any. Do you want to be resuscitated in the event your heart stops? Should they use intravenous treatment to fight infection or to hydrate you? How about a respirator to help you breathe or a feeding tube if you are no longer able to take nourishment any other way? Where would you prefer to be when death seems inevitable? If you are going to eventually use hospice, you will then have to sign a hospice advanced directive indicating you no longer desire any curative treatment to prolong your life. It is a "comfort only" directive.

You've probably heard stories about the struggle a family sometimes has in deciding to pull the feeding tube, remove an IV, or turn off the respirator when an advanced directive was not written ahead of time. Removal of any or all of these life supports certainly signals the nearness of death. The person with the Power of Attorney for Health Care must be fully instructed regarding your wishes if you cannot recuperate and your quality of life is now compromised before acting on your behalf. Hopefully the rest of the family will not object to the decision, but the person with the Power of Attorney for Health Care has the final responsibility precisely because there can be so many different opinions on what to do. If you are in a potentially terminal situation, you should recognize how critical the choice of this person is for carrying out your final wishes. So choose wisely, and discuss your wishes with the person(s) you have chosen.

A Last Will and Testament and possibly a Living Trust are used to distribute your material possessions and investments after you die. This is your final word on who gets what—whether you give your estate to family members, friends, and/or charitable organizations. If you haven't reviewed your will for some time, we encourage you to do so now. Also make certain that the beneficiaries named on your life insurance policy and other investments are consistent with your wishes. If you do not have a will or a will and trust combination, your survivors may be liable for higher taxes on your estate and any court costs. We encourage you to consult an attorney who is familiar with the laws of your state or province. If you are married, don't assume that everything will automatically go to your surviving spouse. You need to make special provisions by stating those desires specifically in your will and trust. Careful planning now will avoid major problems at your death and will be a meaningful parting gift for those to whom you wish to bequeath your estate.

You can attach special distribution instructions to your Last Will and Testament; in them you list specific personal possessions to be given directly to certain members of your family or friends. The will typically records amounts or percentages for the distribution of your major assets and financial holdings, such as your home, condo, cottage, boat, car, savings, or investments. The special distribution attachment permits you to list a number of smaller, perhaps senti-mental, items such as your jewelry, family heirlooms, china pieces, or anything else you treasure that you think another person may want as a keepsake. Sometimes people have put sticky notes on the bottom of items to be found following their death. This method is hardly official and may lead to some confusion about why a certain person was designated as the recipient of an item while someone else seemingly was not considered. If you choose, you could personally give the items to your loved ones before you die as a way to enhance their memory of that keepsake. By doing it that way, you are assured your wishes are carried out. You certainly don't need to do this with everything you own. But why not ask the special people in your life if there is a particular memento that would be especially meaningful to them and then select that or something else of significance to give directly to them? People are often more ready to accept your deci-sions about the distribution of sentimental items before you die, and this can minimize hurt feelings (and even arguments) among your relatives after you have died because they understand very clearly what your wishes were.

Planning for My Dying and Funeral

In their book *Children's Letters to God: The New Collection*, Stuart Hample and Eric Marshall included this one:

> Dear God.
> Here's a poem.
> I love you
> Because you give
> Us what we need to live.
> But I wish you

Would tell me why
You made it so
We have to die.

signed "Daniel" (age 8)[15]

Knowing that every single living thing on earth dies may provide little comfort when facing your own death, but it is a fact. Trees die; pets die; the great white rhinoceros has nearly passed into extinction. And we die. Each one of us. But unless you die suddenly in an accident or in a medical emergency, you often have considerable control over this final leg of the journey. Now it may be your turn to deal with your own dying process. And you have to decide how you want to do this.

What follows are a number of items you might want to consider even though you may still have hope that you will survive this challenge. Making plans while you can still think clearly about them is wise. In fact, as we have been saying, planning for the possibility of your death clears the way for you to live life more fully.

Would I Like to Die at Home or a Hospital, and What about Using Hospice?

For many people, dying at home is by far their preference, but it doesn't often happen. Why is that? Probably for a variety of reasons. One primary reason is that as a patient's condition worsens, the family often panics when they see him or her struggling medically. Since doctors rarely make house calls, you will likely be admitted to the hospital if you call your doctor when a crisis arises. When you are stabilized and if an able and willing family member, a visiting nurse, or a home health care provider can provide assistance, you probably will be discharged to your home once again—at least for a time. But if you cannot manage your own physical needs, do not have adequate assistance at home, and cannot afford to hire help, you will need to go to an extended care facility or nursing home.

Hopefully you, as the patient, will know the point at which you don't want any more medical intervention in an attempt to cure your disease. This decision will likely be made when the treatment no longer produces much improvement in your condition and you become more uncomfortable and tired. When you decide to end medical interventions, you can let your family and physician know you want to stop treatments and spend the remainder of your days at home (if at all possible) enjoying what you can. On the other hand, you may not want to make that final decision without the input of your physician. You may then decide to do everything medically possible to keep yourself alive as long as feasible. This decision is ultimately up to you as the dying person.

Your physician may suggest hospice if he or she judges you have six months or less to live, and you do not wish to pursue further curative treatment because you understand that nothing else can be done medically to reverse or retard the disease. The hospice philosophy of palliative care seeks neither to prolong life nor hasten death. It allows death to come naturally. Hospice strives to help you die in as dignified and pain-free manner as possible. Hospice will serve as the triage agent by determining what interventions are best suited to your needs at any particular time. They will not send you to the hospital to prolong your life because you will have signed a form that rejects lifesaving measures. However, you may be hospitalized briefly for symptom management. They will provide regular assessment and intermittent nursing care in your home, in adult foster care or group homes, in nursing homes, or in a full-time hospice inpatient facility. A family member who is available to give twenty-four-hour support is an asset to a hospice care team but usually not a necessity. If you need more care than you can receive at home, you may eventually go to a hospice care center or a nursing home for full-time care until your death. In that case, the hospice R.N. care manager makes ongoing visits and coordinates all your care. The nursing home staff acts as family caregivers might and gives assistance as instructed by hospice. If you remain in your home under hospice care and a medical problem or emergency arises, your family would be instructed to first call the hospice emergency number for assistance rather than phoning your physician or an E-Unit. Hospice then coordinates with your physician the necessary palliative steps for your comfort. If hospitalization is needed for symptom management, the hospice R.N. can consult with your physician and arrange for hospital admittance. For more information on hospice, please see the section "Midnight" as well.

What Do I Want in My Obituary, Life Story, and Ethical Will?

Do you think it sounds morbid to write your own obituary? Actually we suggest you do just that. An obituary is the notice that the funeral director puts into your local newspaper announcing your death. This notice contains basic factual information as suggested in sidebar 14. Since the publication of the obituary is a part of the funeral expense (you often have to pay for it by the number of lines in the notice), you may not want to write a lengthy one, although you still may want to provide more than just factual information. This obituary will be needed

WRITING YOUR OWN OBITUARY   ⑭

In writing your own obituary, you may want to include the following items. You can, of course, personalize it even more if your local newspaper will allow the space.

1. Your full name.

2. Date of your birth and birthplace.

3. Your parents' names.

4. Survivors and their relationship to you (including those who have preceded you in death, e.g., a spouse).

5. Schools (high schools and colleges) you attended and dates of graduation.

6. Military service, if any.

7. Occupation and employment history.

8. Any awards or honors you received.

9. Special accomplishments and memberships that should be noted.

10. The name of the officiating minister, priest, or rabbi that you would prefer.

11. The organization or charity to which memorial gifts can be given.

12. A photograph for publication.

almost immediately following your death for publication in the local newspaper announcing your death and funeral arrangements.

We would also encourage you to consider writing your life story. Some funeral homes are now preparing personalized brochures that contain pictures and highlights of your life that serve as keepsakes for those who attend your funeral. If you have a part in preparing this information, you will be able to give a very personal touch to your life story. It is a way for you to reflect on your life—your roots, education, career, family, passions, and interests. Your immediate family may want to contribute other information on how they perceive and appreciate you, but you can still decide on the primary contents. In fact, only you may accurately know some of the information to include. Writing your life story can be perceived as a gift to your family, and it may be a satisfying activity for you as well. It is a way to pull together the contents of your earthly life and make some final sense of it, putting it into a meaningful story to be passed on from generation to generation.

Finally, another thing for you to write that will be helpful to those you leave behind is often called an "ethical will." You probably have heard of a person writing a letter to a loved one to be read after he or she has died or creating a video to be shown to surviving children and grandchildren as they grow up. Actually those ideas are the springboard for an ethical will.

So what does an ethical will include? It is a document in which you recite for posterity not only a summary of your life, but also what you have learned, what you have valued, and what you have believed, emphasizing the qualities or characteristics you wish to pass on to your descendants. You might share what you regret doing or what you were not able to complete, and what your hopes and dreams are for those who survive you. You can also include a section about the events or special people who were especially influential in teaching you about life (e.g., "From my parents I learned that . . ." Or: "I am so grateful for [name an experience or an event] because [list the "learning"]). If you actually record what you want people to remember about you, your thoughts and feelings will not be lost. Your ethical will then, along with your life story, can become part of your family's genealogical heritage that gets passed on from generation to generation. Once you have reflected on where you derived your values and perspectives, the ethical will is the place where you can intentionally pass them on to your heirs. You may wish to bequeath to a son or daughter one of your "qualities" (such as your deep concern for social justice) or pass along to a spouse one of your passions (such as appreciating sunsets over the ocean). Obviously, you cannot actually "give" these things to your heirs as you might do with your tangible assets. But the ethical will is a means for highlighting your deeper values and interests and letting members of your family know you wish those for them or perhaps can already see them displayed in a particular family member.

You may choose to write a general ethical will to all those you care about. You may ask that it be read at your funeral or printed in the funeral program. Another option is to write a specific ethical will to different categories of people, such as one to your children, one to your grandchildren, one to your parents, your siblings, and so on. If you have certain individuals who have been particularly important in your life, you may choose to write them a personal ethical will. These special people might include your spouse, a child, a parent, a sibling, or a best friend. Even if you are not presently facing a potentially terminal illness, consider the benefits of writing this now. Doing so can help you see the themes and contributions you have made and help you assess where you want to head with the time you have left here on earth. Should you die unexpectedly, your ethical will can be available for your loved ones to hear what you wanted to say about your relationship with them. This is a way to say farewell and tell them how significant they were even when you have no advance warning you might die. As Seniab once said, "We all want to be remembered and everyone leaves something behind."[16] Writing an ethical will is one way by which your family, friends, and future generations can remember who you were. In so doing, you leave them something tangible about yourself.

What about Donating My Organs, Eyes, or Tissues?

You might like to consider donating your organs, eyes, or other tissues upon your death. After all, thousands of people are on waiting lists to receive organs (such as hearts, lungs, livers, kidneys, pancreas, and small intestines) because their organs are failing. Most religions support the idea of giving a gift from one's own body. Check the Internet for more information, perhaps beginning with the sources mentioned in sidebar 15. Organs are not procured until the person has died, when all brain wave activity has come to an end. A person can be an organ donor only if he or she dies from a brain injury. This precludes those dying a cardiac death. Eye and tissue donation, however, are options in many more situations. After doing your research and talking with your family and physician, decide what seems best for you and your loved ones. If you decide to donate your organs, tissues, or eyes for a transplant or for medical research, indicate "yes" on your driver's license or state ID card. But also check on the specific laws in your state to determine how to ensure your donation will occur upon your death. Make certain you also share this information with your family. This donation does not affect your body viewing at the funeral home.

Should There Be an Autopsy after I Die?

An autopsy is a medical procedure by which doctors can often determine the cause and manner of death. In many cases, people decide not to have an autopsy. Char died of ovarian cancer and Rick of a malignant brain tumor. There was no question about the cause of either death, and therefore no autopsy was necessary. On the other hand, Bob's father

---

ORGAN, TISSUE, AND EYE DONATIONS   ⑮

If you are interested in researching organ, tissue, or eye donations, begin with the following sites. They contain a wealth of information and can link you to several other important sites.

Life Source: Located in St. Paul, MN, this organization serves the "upper Midwest." Their web site is well-designed, contains a wealth of information as well as a number of Internet links. You will find them at www.lifesource.org.

United Network for Organ Sharing: This is the "watchdog" appointed by the federal government to oversee all organ procurement organizations and transplant centers. Check them out at www.unos.org.

TransWeb: A good place to start your search with a lot of information. They are at www.transweb.org.

The Association of Organ Procurement Organizations: This private, nonprofit organization functions as the nation's clearinghouse for organ procurement organizations. You will find them at www.aopo.org.

died suddenly of what appeared to be a massive heart attack. The autopsy was a way for the doctors to determine exactly what went wrong, how that condition might be passed on to future generations, and what preventive measures other members of the family might take to avoid this problem in their own lives. So there are two primary reasons to consider having an autopsy. One is to accurately determine the cause of death. Either your physician or the medical examiner will have to sign a death certificate indicating the cause of death. Especially with a sudden or unexpected death, an autopsy is most often necessary, and it is sometimes sanctioned without the family's permission. An autopsy is optional, however, in the case of an extended illness when the cause of death is more likely known and the person has been under medical supervision. When the family and medical personnel do not know how the death occurred, an autopsy is essential. An autopsy can also give the bereaved specific information to relieve any sense of guilt that they could have done more, because in all likelihood they will know that you died from a particular cause. The second reason for an autopsy is that the information is extremely significant if you have surviving biological children. The autopsy can help the children watch for hereditary symptoms and employ preventative measures.

Some people imagine that if they consent to an autopsy, people won't be able to view the body at the funeral home. During an autopsy incisions are made to examine the internal organs, but these incisions are repaired, and the person's body is restored so no one can tell that an autopsy was done. Some family members can't imagine having their loved one examined like this after all they have been through. But remember, dead people can't be "spared" anything, because their bodies no longer feel anything. After you die, your family may need or want to determine the cause or causes of your death, especially if they are concerned about your children's health or if some questions are left unanswered. More often than not your family will have to be content with the doctor's interpretation of what happened if an autopsy isn't done. Let your family know if you are okay with the idea of an autopsy. If you prefer not to have an autopsy done, talk about it with your family, but know that your family or a medical examiner may need to override your wishes based on their assessment or needs at the time of your death.

What about Funerals, Memorials, and Memories?

She doesn't want to talk about her death and funeral. "Just do what you want," she says. "I won't be there anyway." This is a rather typical reaction some people have to the idea of planning their own funeral. Even if you are not facing a potentially terminal illness, we strongly believe everyone ought to have a basic funeral plan. Funerals are both a healthy way to say good-bye and a way to celebrate a life lived. These two components provide an effective ending to one's life and are an essential part of the grieving process for the surviving family and friends.

Use the following questions to help you think about four primary areas in planning your funeral events: (1) the disposition of your physical body, (2) the visitation, (3) the funeral service, and (4) the burial (or final "good-byes").

How Do I Want My Family to Deal with My Body?

What do you want to have happen to your body after you die? Do you want to be six feet under or scattered to the wind? You have the choices of earth burial of your body or cremation. Another option is an anatomical donation of your body.

Traditionally bodies were placed in a casket and either buried in a vault in the ground or placed in a mausoleum. This is still the most common form of interment in the United States. Families prefer, in many cases, to go to the final resting place in a cemetery to remember the person who died.

Cremations, however, are now becoming more popular, with about 30 percent of the population selecting that option. Cremations do not rule out embalming for a visitation or the use of other traditional events of a funeral. Final disposition of the body can include an earth burial of the ashes, entombment, scattering, or keeping the cremains in an urn or container.

Whichever you choose, we firmly believe your family and friends should view your body after you have died. Whether a person decides on cremation or a more traditional burial, for psychological reasons your family members will benefit from seeing your body before final disposition. This act supports one of the primary tasks of grieving, namely, accepting the reality of the death. Seeing your body gives your loved ones an opportunity to concretely remember that you died by firmly planting in their mind this vivid image of you as dead.

If you choose an earth burial, the basic series of events will be: the embalming of your body (regulated by state and federal laws), placing your body in a casket for the visitation and funeral, and then putting the casket in a vault in the ground for the actual burial.

While many laws and regulations surround the embalming of the body, the procedure is relatively straightforward. A licensed mortician preserves the body for the funeral events and burial by removing the blood and other body fluids and replacing them with preserving chemicals.

Many funeral homes allow the family to participate in the physical preparation of the outside of the body if they want to be involved. In some cultures and religious traditions, family members wash the body. They may also dress the body and style the hair. Actually touching the body of the deceased may be scary for some people. On the other hand, these activities reinforce the reality of the death. Helping prepare your body can be the final loving act from your family and serve as an important first step in their grieving process. If you would like them to do that, encourage them to seriously consider this option.

Once the body is embalmed, your family must select a casket if you have not done this ahead of time. We would advise you to do this yourself before your death, if you are able, in consultation with your family members. You should know the range of options available before you select a casket. You may build your own, or if you have access to a computer, you can purchase a casket online from a number of web sites. Some families prefer to do that. However, the vast majority continue to use a funeral home to provide all of their funeral needs. Funeral directors usually have display models of caskets or sections of caskets called quarter panels in their funeral home. They can also show you pictures from catalogs or on a computer. The purchase is an important one. We would encourage you to actually see the caskets on display at your local funeral home if possible. Touch them. Find one that seems to fit you as the dying person.

In recent years, manufacturers have begun to make caskets that can easily be personalized. The inside cover can hold pictures or another design to represent your interests. Caskets are now available in various colors with artistic designs, in steel, copper, bronze, wood, or fiberglass. Some of the choices may be too extreme for you, but you can find almost anything to suit your individual tastes.

The selection of a casket can be one of the most emotional and difficult experiences in planning the funeral because you confront directly the reality that this is where your body will be put to rest. This can be especially problematic for those who are grieving if they hadn't talked about caskets with you before your death. Many people experience a conflict of emotions in wanting to honor the deceased while balancing a host of other factors. Will you keep the cost down, or do you think you honor the deceased person by selecting something expensive and fancy? Is it even okay to talk about cost at such an emotional time? Remember that merchandise selection is not the most important thing; creating a personalized remembrance is. One of the primary benefits of planning ahead is that you not only can select the casket together as a married couple or family without as much emotion as often accompanies the selection process after the death occurs but also can create a service that uniquely fits the person.

Grieving is not less painful depending on whether you buy the most expensive or most economically priced casket, vault, and funeral package. Grief is worked through by doing the "tough stuff." That includes deciding together about your casket. Some people tend to downplay their own worth or value. "Just bury me in a pine box," they say. Others might go the other way and spend nearly all their available resources on the casket since they want to go out in style. Obviously the cost of the casket is a significant factor to consider, since this is usually one of the biggest single expenses of the funeral. When planning your funeral, bear in mind that in cases in which surviving dependent family members are involved, the cost of your funeral likely comes from the same resources they need to live on after you die, unless you had previously established a funeral fund. So make the decision together. Talk about the pros and cons of the casket, the vault, the funeral service, the costs, and what financial resources will remain following your death. Hopefully you can reach a reasonable agreement on these important issues. And be reassured that your loved ones won't remember you only in the casket. They will have a lifetime of memories of the times you spent together.

Funeral homes are required to give you an itemized price list of all the costs associated with the funeral arrangements. Funeral directors can coordinate up to two hundred details, from which you can select those you desire to create funeral events to meet your personal needs. The national average for the cost of a traditional funeral (with a casket and earth burial) in the United States is approximately $6,400.[17] There will probably be a few additional charges for flowers, the minister, and so on.

After selecting the casket, you will need to select a vault into which the casket will be placed for burial in the cemetery. (Different states have different regulations, so check with your funeral director.) The basic decision is if you want a sealed or unsealed vault. The purpose of the vault is to keep the ground from sinking and to seal the casket from the ravages of time, dirt, and moisture. Deciding on the type of vault depends on your values and your understanding of what happens to your body after you die. While preserving the body for the funeral service is important, our perspective is that taking extreme measures to retard the natural decomposition of the body over time is unwarranted and futile.

Cremation is the other option for the disposal of your body after death. When a body is cremated, it is placed in a cremation chamber that uses flame, intense heat, and evaporation to reduce the body to organic bone fragments. The cremains of an average adult weigh between four and eight pounds and resemble coarse sand.

While there may be several legitimate reasons for opting for cremation, we would urge you to make certain that cremation is not used to avoid the pain of grief. The notion that the grieving process will be easier if your body is quickly cremated, thereby keeping people from actually seeing the body, is a myth. Also be aware that your loved ones should not use cremation as a means of trying to keep you near them all the time—as if an urn of ashes can replace a living person. The tough thing about death is that you are separated from your loved ones. With your death you have left this world, and certainly an urn of ashes cannot take your place. Your family will need to do the tough work of grieving, and keeping your ashes in a special place generally does not help decrease the intensity of the grieving process. Some people who initially had the cremains in their home later find it necessary to select an alternate site to help them move further through the grief process.

Cremation is, however, a viable option for a number of reasons. First of all, cremation is almost always less expensive than a traditional burial. The average cost of the actual cremation procedure is $1,200,[18] which is best compared to the cost of a casket in an earth burial. There are other expenses besides the cremation involved in having a funeral. You will be able to avoid some of the cost of a casket and vault, although you may still need to rent or purchase a plastic liner for a casket to use if you are going to follow our recommendation to have a viewing at the visitation prior to cremation. You will also need to purchase an urn or container for the cremains or furnish one yourself. Your cremains can then be buried in a regular cemetery plot, in a national cemetery, or in an urn garden on private or public property, or they can be placed in a columbarium (a structure designed to hold urns) or scattered on private or public property or at sea. Cremation is often recommended by those who are sensitive to the acres of land used by traditional cemeteries. In larger metropolitan areas, cemetery plots are becoming a rare commodity because of the lack of available land. Cremation is also, as we have noted, an option for those who wish to scatter the cremains in favorite places. Do note, however, that many states have regulations regarding where cremains can be scattered. This is especially true for inland waterways.

As we have said before, we believe it is important that those who love you see your body after death. If cremation is your choice for disposition, consider having your funeral director embalm your body for public viewing and a funeral service before cremation. The disposition of the cremains can follow a few days or even weeks after that.

The thought of actually burning the body of a loved one seems to be a major challenge for some people. A few religions, such as Orthodox Judaism, Islam, and Eastern Orthodox Christianity, believe cremation violates their teachings. On the other hand, if a person's religious or worldview is such that a deceased body returns "to the dust," cremation may make sense. In any case, decisions about cremation should be made with as much discussion as possible with close family members.

If you are facing a potentially terminal illness, making decisions about the disposition of your body may be quite emotional. Ultimately the choice is a combination of your wishes and your family's final determination following your death. That is why it is so important to talk this through together to understand each person's perspective. If your family knows your preferences for burial or cremation, hopefully they will honor your wishes. But the only way to ensure that choice is through legal means, particularly if there are conflicts in family relationships.

Should I Plan a Visitation for Family and Friends?

Bob's grandfather was married and widowed twice. When his second wife died at the age of eighty-two, he was getting a little "forgetful." While sitting in the funeral parlor during visitation, Grandpa was so delighted to see all his family and friends again that he was heard to say, "We should do this more often!" Now, of course, the visitation isn't just a place to meet friends. It is not just a family reunion or a social gathering. More importantly, it is a place to confirm the reality of the death, to express our feelings of loss by telling stories about the deceased, to share our memories, our sadness, perhaps to smile, to cry, and to begin to say good-bye to the deceased.

You have also heard us say that one of the main reasons for the visitation is for people to actually see you dead. Obviously an open casket is an important aspect of the visitation for people to begin to accept the reality of your death. It is also a wonderful opportunity to provide your loved ones the chance to pay you their respects and to talk with your immediate family about their connection to you. The visitation offers a never-to-be-repeated time and place to share memories. We suggest you plan the visitation in conjunction with your family's wishes. Share your ideas for the visitation and also listen to your family's thoughts about the amount of time they want for the viewing, how to arrange the receiving line (if they want one), and so on. Your family will likely make the final decisions about these details since they are the ones who will go through the visitation, but having your input would probably be helpful. You may also have some preference about the type of music to be played, the personal articles near the casket, or the placement of a picture board of your life and loves. Consider what clothes you want to wear. Susan's ninety-nine-year-old grandmother bought an outfit well in advance specifically to be worn for her visitation and burial. Selecting your clothing may or may not be important to you. By preplanning the visitation with your family, you can influence the character of the event to fit your own tastes and personality.

What Do I Need to Consider in Planning the Funeral Service?

You have a number of things to think about when planning the actual funeral or memorial service. The difference between a funeral and a memorial service is quite simple: A funeral service is conducted when the body is present. A memorial service is held without a body available. As professionals who have studied grief responses, we strongly recommend a funeral service whenever possible since we believe the experience of saying good-bye to the actual body is a healthy start to the grieving process (even if the body is to be cremated later). That doesn't mean a memorial service has no place. Such a service is especially useful when there is no body (if it was lost in a tragic accident, for example), or when the actual funeral and burial occurred in another place some distance away, or when the extended family wanted a private funeral followed by a public memorial service.

In planning the service, you and your family members have a number of items to consider. What do you want the general order of the service to be? Do you want a printed program for the service? Do you want the program to say something about your life? Do you want to write it yourself? Perhaps you could write a final farewell letter to your family and friends to be printed for all to keep. You might write something to be read at the funeral service or have someone speak on your behalf bringing a message you asked this person to convey. The nice thing about your funeral service is that there are very few rules. It might seem to you that every community or religious tradition has a "right way" to do funerals. Most people follow that way out of custom. But actually you have all the freedom in the world to design your service the way you want it. Just remember the two important themes: provide a meaningful summary or conclusion to your life, and provide comfort for those left behind. Therefore both you and your surviving loved ones certainly need to be part of the planning. Remember that your family will make the final decisions since they will be attending to the final arrangements.

Some basic decisions can be made well before you get too weak to think about the funeral. Use the questions in sidebar 16 to guide your thinking about what you would like included in your funeral events.

EXPRESSING YOUR PREFERENCES FOR THE VISITATION, FUNERAL SERVICE, AND DISPOSITION OF YOUR BODY   ⑯

1. Do you want a period of visitation?

2. Do you want the casket open for viewing?

3. Where would you like the funeral held? At your local church, synagogue, the funeral home, or some other favorite place?

4. Who would you like to have officiate at the service? Your clergyperson or rabbi? A friend or members of the family?

5. What Scripture passages, favorite readings, etc., would you like included? Is there a theme you wish for the homily or message?

6. Do you want a printed program? What will be the general order of the service?

7. Who will provide music (if you want it)? What specific music do you want? Do you want the audience to sing as well?

8. Will someone(s) give a eulogy? Will others read favorite poems, verses of Scripture, or other readings that are meaningful to you? Do you want someone to read something you have written?

9. Will you have pallbearers? How many? Who will they be?

10. Do you want to be buried or cremated? Where will your remains be placed?

Designing your funeral service to reflect your own personality and life can reassure you that your loved ones will be able to honor you in the way you would like. If you have no opinion about some aspects of the service, your family can design those sections to meet their needs knowing that this was fine with you.

In many traditions, the people who have attended the funeral or memorial service also gather for a social time following the service. This gathering time can be an important extension of the service itself. We have often attended funerals at which the officiant invited people to gather for the social time as a means to continue sharing personal stories about the deceased in an informal setting for the benefit of the surviving loved ones.

In some communities this social gathering marks the end of the funeral process. While tea and coffee are being served, the funeral director quietly removes the casket. Perhaps a small contingent of family and close friends might slip away from the gathering after an hour or so to meet at the grave site for a committal service. But this method may not be the most helpful to the grief process. We think the ideal scenario for the funeral events begins with one or two days of visitation. The funeral service, along with a reception, would be held the next day. Then on the day *after* the funeral service, the family and other interested friends could gather at the cemetery for the burial or at the place designated for the disposition of the cremains. This method extends the funeral process over at least three days to allow those who are bereaved more time between events to digest what is happening. Many people who pay their respects at the visitation or funeral service probably will not attend the burial anyway, so you don't have to schedule it for their convenience. The bottom line is that the immediate family and close friends can benefit by not rushing through the funeral process. We realize that sometimes there may be extenuating circumstances making it difficult to hold the funeral events over this period of time. However, remember that spacing the events as much as possible helps the bereaved experience each funeral event individually and offers a little longer absorption time.

How Do I Plan My Burial or the Scattering of My Ashes?

The last step in the funeral process is the burial or scattering and your family's final good-byes to your body. We believe strongly in the importance of the family participating in the actual burial of the body or disposition of the cremated remains. You may find that some funeral homes or pastors may be eager to complete their responsibilities by officiating at the burial immediately after the funeral (even before or during the social gathering). Some may even suggest conducting the committal service at the conclusion of the funeral service rather than going to the cemetery. The intent is often to save everyone the unpleasantness of going out in inclement weather or the inconvenience of traveling to another location. But we believe that participating in the actual burial is an extremely important aspect of the grieving process. The bereaved often experience this as the most difficult part of the entire funeral process. Nonetheless, throwing a shovelful of dirt on the casket or actually scattering the cremains helps those who are grieving experience the harsh reality of death. It is the time for the final good-byes to your body. You may even want to encourage your family to remain behind while the grave is filled and a temporary marker is placed. Or you may want to ask a close friend or family member to remain at the cemetery until the burial is completed so they can share that with your family. In that way your loved ones will know how the entire funeral process went from beginning to end.

If you have chosen cremation and want your cremains placed or scattered at a special location that might involve travel (so it can't be done at the time of the funeral), help your loved ones plan how they can do this in a timely and meaningful way. Part of that planning involves deciding who, among your family and friends, will be involved in this ceremony.

So where do you want to be buried? The options are nearly end-less. If you are older, will you want your body returned to your home of origin to be buried in the family plot? Or if you have retired and live in a retirement community, would you prefer interment there? If you have been married only once and your spouse may likely survive you, the question will be the number of plots to purchase. Are you going to buy plots for yourself and your spouse only, or will you buy plots for your children as well? As with so many other issues associated with your possible death, discuss this with your family. Check out possible burial sites personally if you are able to. If cremation suits your way of thinking, investigate potential sites where you might like your cremains placed or scattered. Then make as many decisions and purchases as you can. Plan ahead. The more decisions you make now, the easier it will be for your family when you eventually die.

If you have been married more than once due to the death of a first spouse, you face special concerns when deciding on a burial site. Next to which deceased spouse will you be buried? Or will you opt for your own plot in another location? As two people who have both been widowed, we have had several discussions about this topic. Both of us had plots reserved for us adjacent to our first spouses at the time of their deaths. The logic in being buried there is that this symbolically preserves the biological origin of our respective children, and they would have one place to visit and maintain for both their parents. On the other hand, our love and commitment to each other is certainly at least equal to our first marriages. We have not "settled" for a second-rate marriage. Our marriage is unique, grand, and special in ways that people who have not been happily married a second time could never imagine! So for us logic would suggest that we be buried next to each other—leaving our first spouses "alone" in their plots. Or we could buy four plots in a row in another cemetery, be buried in the two center plots, and place our first spouses on either side. Or we could opt for cremation, opening up a number of other possibilities. See how com-plicated this can be? Many additional dynamics enter the picture. So our answer is, as we have said so often before, talk about it. Let your preferences be known. If you are not clear about your choice, you have all the more reason to talk it out with your spouse and family. Maybe you will not come up with a clear answer quickly. But can you imagine the conflict that could arise if you didn't say anything about where you want to be buried? If you face a potentially terminal illness, you certainly have a lot of things to think about. This is an important one. Talk about it now.

What about a Monument or Marker?

The other issue you face with respect to burial or cremation is the matter of the monument or marker for your final resting place. Cemeteries frequently have rules about the types allowed, so check with the cemetery office to learn about their policies. You may decide to let your family members select a marker or monument after you have died. On the other hand, choosing one yourself is another good way to face the reality of your own mortality. By selecting the marker or monument yourself, you can customize it with your favorite saying, verse, or symbol.

We alluded to some of the special issues associated with the death of a spouse when it comes to burial plots and markers. Some older couples find a double headstone, one that contains both their names, comforting. Seeing their name as a widowed person etched in stone alongside their departed spouse gives them a sense of connection even though death has separated them. While you are certainly free to make your own decision about having a double or single headstone as a married couple, we would encourage you to consider two things. First, we believe that marriage ends with the death of one of the partners. "Till death do us part" is not only a traditional phrase in a wedding ceremony, it is a fact. The surviving spouse now has the challenge of accepting the reality of the death and eventually moving back into a full and complete life.[19] When all is said and done, each of us dies alone just as we were born alone. Therefore, consider if an individual marker or monument might convey and celebrate your own life most directly. Second, if the surviving spouse is younger, he or she might find it especially uncomfortable (after working through grief) to have his or her name on a marker since he or she most likely has many more years to live, regardless of the possibility of remarriage. We would encourage you to discuss this thoroughly with your spouse when deciding about a marker or headstone.

How Do I Talk about the Tough Stuff?

Throughout this book we have said that you were born into this world alone, and you will die alone. No one else can do either one for you. But that doesn't mean you are not surrounded by scores of caring people. Your journey is something like a relay race. You certainly have to run your own leg of the race by yourself, but many other people have a deeply vested interest in how well you do. We have already discussed the importance of evaluating the relationships you have and ranking them according to their level of significance in your life. We also encouraged you to address the unfinished business you have with others. Talking about your thoughts and feelings regarding end-of-life decisions will help you die more peacefully and will facilitate comfort and support for your family and friends.

A Closer Look at Family Communication

You might think that discussing tough issues is difficult because you have never done something like this before. Now you are at this crucial point in your life. You likely are experiencing all the stress that comes along with a potentially terminal diagnosis. You may not feel very well physically, and now you need to talk about serious things with your partner or a close family member (even though you may never have had "serious" talks with them before). Just remember, bridging the silence by expressing your inner thoughts and feelings is extremely valuable. Deciding to talk about your potential death and mustering up the courage to invite others into a conversation is the most difficult part.

Talking about painful, sad, or hurtful subjects is a real challenge for many people because they are often uncomfortable dealing with their feelings. For example, if you tell your family that you want to talk about how you feel about the possibility of dying, one of your adult children might say, "But, Dad, we don't really *know* you are dying. Don't give up hope; this new treatment might work." People who love you most often want to keep hope alive under all circumstances. If they don't disagree with you directly, they may try to avoid the conversation by changing the subject or even leaving the room. One helpful approach is to ask your family to schedule a specific time to talk with you about some important matters. That way each person can think about what they may want to say, and they can be better prepared for the conversation. Catching them off guard will probably not promote the most healthy or helpful exchange.

Once you begin talking, let your family know that you love them, that you don't want to keep things inside, and that you want to share your concerns openly and honestly. Be forthright about how difficult this may be for you and probably is for them too. Let them also know you see real value in getting your thoughts and feelings out. Talk about what you'd like to have happen if your disease progresses, and ask for their concerns and suggestions. Once you have overcome the initial discomfort and have begun to talk with them, you will likely feel closer, and everyone will have more confidence to talk about their deeper feelings.

On the other hand, you have heard us say that keeping your feelings inside can put distance between you and others. You are holding the other person at arm's length. If you do this, the other person has little idea how you feel or what you think about what is happening. You might feel quite lonely and believe you are a burden to your family. As we have said before, feelings are for sharing. If you want to feel close to others, tell them what is on your mind and heart.

People frequently use the verb "to feel" incorrectly. We say things like "I feel like it's going to rain today" or "I feel like going to the concert tonight." Those statements are thoughts or desires—not feelings. Think about what a "feeling" actually is and how you can communicate that feeling directly. Feelings are described by using feeling words such as *sad, angry, hurt, frustrated, upset, uncomfortable, happy, excited*, and *eager*. There are a multitude of both positive and negative feelings. "Feeling" sentences follow a certain format: "I feel (sad, glad, mad, etc.) about (whatever it is) because (give the reason)." Please notice that after the word "feel" comes a feeling word. A person might tell his or her loved ones: "I *feel upset about* the fact I might not live long enough to attend Melinda's wedding *because* I am getting weaker, and I want to be there for her." Or "I *feel worried about* your mother being left alone after I die *because* she really doesn't understand our finances." Sharing those feelings creates understanding, can give you a sense of reassurance and support, and can give your loved ones a point of reference when they need to make decisions later on because they are aware of your feelings. We all can communicate on two levels: with our thoughts (cognitions) and with our feelings (emotions). We can argue with others about our thoughts and ideas. We can disagree with their opinions, and they with ours. But that doesn't work with feelings. Your feelings are just that—*your* feelings. They are valid in themselves because they belong to you. They are not debatable. No one can disagree with them, because they are not their feelings. Sharing your feelings is like opening a window into your unique soul—what constitutes you as an individual. It is okay if you are the only one in the world who feels a certain way. Your feelings can stand alone, and you do not have to defend them even when others do not feel the same way. So if you want to be genuinely yourself around your family and friends, try sharing your feelings. You will open the door to a better understanding, which will in turn hopefully strengthen the emotional bond between you.

Communicating with Congruence

What we have been discussing involves the principle of congruence—how mentally healthy people strive to handle their thoughts, feelings, and behaviors. The principle is basically this: What a person thinks, how a person feels, and how a person behaves (what is said or done) in a particular situation should all be consistent. Thoughts, feelings, and behaviors have to match each other and make sense together.

> ### CONGRUENCE ⑰
>
> congruence = the act of being honest in order to maintain your integrity
>
> thoughts + feelings = behaviors (what you say or do)

Sidebar 17 helps you visualize what we mean by congruence. What can frequently happen, however, is that we give in to social pressure to behave one way while thinking and feeling another way. For example, one of your family members might want to spend an afternoon alone to talk about a hurtful issue with you—just the two of you. But the whole family shows up to do something together and the original intention is lost. Rather than being congruent, the person who made the initial arrangement stifles his or her original desire and gives in, saying, "Oh, that's okay; I guess everyone wants to be here." Not only does that person lose out, the rest of the group truly believes this was okay with him or her. Feelings get stuffed inside.

People sometimes are not congruent because of low self-esteem. They don't believe what they want or feel is legitimate or matters as much as what other people want or feel. That simply is not true. We are all of *equal* value and worth. Each of us matters to the same degree as others. Congruence will help you say, "My thoughts and feelings are as important to express as anyone else's, and I owe it to myself, as well as to others, to let people know what I think and feel about this matter."

Some people do not want to hurt their loved one's feelings by saying or doing something they think will be hurtful or upsetting. But to avoid saying how you feel is to deny your own importance and worth. Only after you say what you think or feel can you begin to work toward a compromise with others.

Another example of congruence is how you respond to the routine question "How are you doing?" We are often tempted to simply say, "I'm fine," even when that is a far cry from the truth. That is being incongruent. To be able to say, "I'm struggling some now" or "I'm feel-ing sad" (or however you might be feeling) would be congruent. When you express an idea and make clear your feelings associated with that idea, you remain congruent to both the idea and the feelings. To do less is to compromise your integrity, especially if you remain silent when you are misunderstood. This principle of congruence helps cre-ate inner peace and allows you to be genuine and honest with yourself and others. Life is too brief to play games. This is especially true if your life may be cut short by disease. You don't want to give people false messages. It is important that they understand you and how you think and feel about things. Thoughts, feelings, and behaviors work best when they are consistent with each other. That is what congruence is all about.

Forgiving: Why Is This Important If I Am Going to Die Anyway?

When you face a potentially terminal illness, the amount of work you might still have to do to prepare for your possible death may seem overwhelming. However, don't lose heart, because your efforts will pay off by providing you a sense of contentment and peace. One area that may especially need to be revisited is forgiveness. Do you have a clean slate in your relationships with other people? Somewhere along the line you may have either hurt or been hurt by someone else. Perhaps you are waiting for the other person to make the first move to remedy the situation. But now this disease has raised the ante. You have more at stake because time has become a pressing factor. You are not sure you want to wait much longer to set things right.

How did the problem begin? Was it something you said? Or something the other person did? Was trust broken between the two of you? Now may be a good opportunity to heal the relationship. After all, your time may be limited. Perhaps you can do something to make things right. But remember, your feelings belong to you. No one else can make you feel a particular way. Of course, certain situations may trigger feelings, but they are still under your control. Did you know that being angry, bitter, or upset or holding a grudge is harming you? Studies show that keeping those feelings inside you is extremely unhealthy both physically with the development of symptoms or a disease, and emotionally by causing anxiety or depression. Interestingly enough, holding a grudge really does not harm the party you are upset with. Do you know the wonderful benefits of forgiving? Not only will forgiveness decrease your anger, anxiety, and depression, it might help prevent further physical or emotional problems from developing. Remember, though, that forgiveness is a process that takes time. It often begins with a decision to intentionally work through your feelings. This process is valuable because it actually increases a person's self-esteem and emotional stability while promoting inward peace. However, before you can forgive, you must deal with your negative feelings by expressing them to someone verbally, in journal writing, in letter form, or by actually talking with the person involved about the problem and how you feel about it. Most often how we *feel* comes from what we *think* about a certain situation. So reframing your thoughts can be very helpful in eventually changing those feelings so they no longer harm you. Also, making a decision to behave in a way that reflects your integrity can further help feelings change in a more positive direction. Along with addressing the specific emotional and cognitive aspects involved with releasing and reframing negative feelings, most any kind of physical activity such as hitting a pillow with your fist, hitting a golf ball with a club, jogging, or doing hard aerobic exercises can also assist in releasing the stress and tension of the feelings.

Maybe you think that the other person does not deserve to be forgiven. Perhaps he or she is not sorry or has not asked for forgiveness. Perhaps you feel stuck in your thinking because you hold a distorted view of what it means to forgive another person. From a psychological perspective, consider what forgiveness *is not*. Forgiveness is *not* a legal pardon. Forgiving someone does *not* mean you now agree with, condone, or excuse the other person's behavior. Forgiveness does *not* mean you will forget the situation that created the alienation, hurt, or sadness in the first place. *Nor* does forgiveness necessarily re-create the kind of solid, intimate relationship that may have existed before. Frequently forgiveness does *not* include that ideal "making up" that we might like to see. Certainly the most rewarding outcome would be that the two people who were at odds apologize, "fix things," and experience a full reconciliation. But many times only one individual is interested in working things out, and the other party ignores or rebuffs these efforts at resolving the conflict. If that is the case, you can forgive in the sense that you decide to vent and release your anger, hurt, or sadness. "Venting" means working intentionally at getting those emotions out of your system, similar to pulling a splinter out of your toe. The final act is to let the feelings and situations go. Release them like you would a helium balloon that quickly disappears from your sight.

How can you vent your feelings or engage in one-sided forgiveness? One excellent way is to write a letter that may or may not be sent to the other person (depending on the particular circumstances). You might want to write an initial draft to express your raw feelings and thoughts. Then, once the intensity of your emotions has decreased, you can rewrite the letter in a form you can send. Remember the principle of congruence. Write about what has upset you and honestly express your feelings about the problem between you. Use healthy assertive language, which consists of "I" messages rather than words that attack the other person, "you" messages, which are considered aggressive.

Once you have determined your perspective on the conflict, you may be ready to talk directly with the other person. If you decide to do that, the first step is for each person to describe his or her view of the situation. After you have listened to each other without interrupting, you may already have a better understanding of the situation. Misunderstanding is a major part of many disagreements. So are false assumptions. Often one person has no idea what the other person was actually thinking, feeling, or wanting in the conflicted situation and responds based on this distorted viewpoint. Once a dialogue is established, hopefully one or both parties will think and feel differently enough about the situation to open the door for reconciliation.

Sadly, however, even when both persons listen in an attempt to understand each other, the situation is not always cleared up. You may still disagree. Then the challenge is to "agree to disagree" about how each person sees the problem. That agreement might allow the opportunity for some future compromise. But even if neither party is willing to apologize, hopefully you can at least both understand each other's perspective a little better. You might even ask for help from an unbiased third party to further facilitate resolution.

Just remember, if a resolution does occur, returning to a level of closeness similar to what was there before still takes time. *Forgiveness is a process* and therefore usually does not happen immediately. Changing thoughts and feelings into new behaviors is a slow process. The situation almost certainly will not return to exactly how it was before the disagreement happened. But you can develop a "new normal" between the two of you that feels comfortable and workable.

Resolution, or even just developing a better understanding of the conflict, does not always happen. You may have tried to initiate contact with the other person. Maybe you wrote letters, sent cards, or made phone calls, but he or she did not respond. That certainly is sad, but at least you can feel good that you did everything you could to reach out. You have served the ball into the other person's court, so to speak, and now you don't have to respond until they return the ball. You may have to find a way to accept that the ball may never be returned. Try to feel good about the effort you have made, and then forgive the other person as well as yourself for your own sake. Clearing the slate of old emotional injuries is very healthy. A clean slate is a burden lifted!

Letting Yourself off the Hook—Accepting Self-Forgiveness

Sometimes forgiving yourself can be more of a challenge than forgiving another person or asking someone to forgive you. Self-forgiveness is as necessary as forgiving the other person. Maybe you have realized that you should not have said or done what you did. There was no excuse for it. You really messed up the situation. Hopefully you at least agree with the premise that "no one is perfect." Very few arguments or disagreements are caused by only one person. We all contribute to these misunderstandings in one way or another. But making mistakes doesn't actually have anything to do with your inherent value and worth. Getting down on yourself doesn't help the situation, especially when you are already facing the stress of an illness.

So after asking (in some way) forgiveness of the other person, how can you go about forgiving yourself? First, focus on the specific thing or things you did that you now regret. Was it something you did? Or said? Or failed to do? Name the actions as concretely as you can. Then apologize to yourself: "I am truly sorry I said or did that. I normally do not behave that way, but I got so wrapped up in that situation that I reacted very poorly." Remember, you are talking to yourself—yes, talking to yourself is healthy in spite of jokes to the contrary! Once you apologize, accept the apology. You may feel guilty and have a sense of remorse. Acknowledge that you were wrong, and then *let go* of the self-recrimination. These "letting go" and "letting be" elements are very important in forgiveness, especially when facing the possibility of dying. We would encourage you to be open to the grace of forgiveness.

You might also want to do something tangible to symbolize this self-forgiveness. Write a letter to yourself or journal about what happened. Include what you regret, rid yourself of the "if onlys," and reframe the situation. Another helpful activity is to release a helium balloon as a sign you have let the issue go and it has now flown away. You could give a donation to a charity or do something significant for someone else who would appreciate it. Be as creative as you can be. Then start fresh again.

Ira Byock identified five tasks for people who are dying, two of which deal with forgiveness. The five tasks are:

1. To say I forgive you.
2. To ask you to forgive me.
3. To say thank you.
4. To tell you I love you.
5. To say good-bye.[20]

That's a pretty good list to consider. We would add one more: *To forgive yourself.* When people who face a potentially terminal illness carry on living as if a life-altering event isn't occurring and still refuse to talk about unresolved situations, it seems very sad. The ending of our lives reflects a story well told. A good story brings all the drama and tension of the narrative to some conclusion. Even if a final resolution doesn't come as completely as you want, the reader sees at least an attempt to make sense of it all. How much more for a person facing the end of his or her life's story! Mending broken relationships, forgiving others, being forgiven by them, and finding peace within yourself through self-forgiveness are critical ways to experience that contentment and peace you so much want in the final chapter of your life.

Dusk Has Arrived: A Perspective

Life and death are intricately bound together. When you hear a potentially terminal diagnosis from your doctor, the reality of your death comes one step closer. But as death gets closer, life becomes more precious. You probably have little idea how much longer you will live. No one really does. Even though you have received a disturbing diagnosis, you really have no idea what the outcome will be. Because of that, we hope you have taken seriously our suggestions in this section of the book for preparing for the inevitable. Each one of us would do well to ask ourselves the questions that are asked here. You, at least, have the advantage of having had something happen to pique your interest and increase your motivation to consider your own mortality. Use this time to do some hard work. Be prepared for your death. We think you will benefit from it in the long run.

CHRISTIAN MEDITATIONS ON FACING THE POSSIBILITY OF DYING

And the LORD God commanded the man, "You are free to eat from any tree in the garden; but you must not eat from the tree of the knowledge of good and evil, for when you eat of it you will surely die."

Genesis 2:16–17

But now, this is what the LORD says—
  he who created you, O Jacob,
  he who formed you, O Israel:
"Fear not, for I have redeemed you;
I have summoned you by name; you are mine.
When you pass through the waters,
  I will be with you;
and when you pass through the rivers,
  they will not sweep over you.
When you walk through the fire,
  you will not be burned;
  the flames will not set you ablaze.
For I am the LORD, your God,
  the Holy One of Israel, your Savior."

Isaiah 43:1–3

Divine Insurance

> _Then the devil took him to the holy city and had him stand_
> _on the highest point of the temple. "If you are the Son of_
> _God," he said, "throw yourself down. For it is written: 'He_
> _will command his angels concerning you, and they will lift_
> _you up in their hands, so that you will not strike your foot_
> _against a stone.'" Jesus answered him, "It is also written:_
> _'Do not put the Lord your God to the test.'"_

Matthew 4:5–7

How do I trust God when things go bad?

Most people say you shouldn't tempt "fate." They use that phrase when trying to persuade a son not to go skydiving or to keep a daughter from dating someone they don't like. We tempt fate (or so we say) by driving too fast, failing to practice safe sex, drinking bad water, or refusing to take our medications. We tempt fate by taking unnecessary risks.

Christians, however, don't believe in fate—this impersonal prescriptive force that responds with vengeance when we violate its boundaries. Our God, we believe, is a loving, merciful, and gracious God who interacts with us in a personal way.

Here we find Jesus in the wilderness facing a second temptation from Satan. Jesus has already refused turning stones into bread. He will live "on every word that comes from the mouth of God" (Matt. 4:4).

So now sly Satan figures that if Jesus trusts God so much, he should put this trust to the test. The temptation is pretty straightforward: If you are the Son of God, throw yourself down from where we are standing on the highest point of the temple. "But," said Jesus in response, "you don't tempt God" (see Matt. 4:7). You don't do foolish things. You don't take unnecessary risks. You certainly don't try to force God's hand. A Christian saint once said something like, "In becoming a Christian, you don't kiss your brains good-bye."

If you are facing a disease, you likely find yourself in a pretty tough situation. The diagnosis has been made. Your condition may be potentially terminal, and your days on earth may be limited. So what are you going to do now? What is a responsible Christian response? Or what might you do that would put God to the test?

Let's first try to understand why this might have been a temptation for Jesus. Parts of it seem pretty ridiculous, don't they? Who in their right mind would even be tempted to jump off the top of the temple? Obviously something here made Satan think this would tempt Jesus. The key to understanding this situation might be found in the fact that Satan wanted Jesus to test ahead of time something that would ultimately come at the end of his earthly life. So the argument might have gone like this: "If you are the Son of God, if you are truly loved by the Father, of course he won't let anything happen to you. He'll keep you safe. He'll protect you. He won't let you die—surely not his own son!" And Satan even uses the Bible, quoting Psalm 91 to claim that God won't even let Jesus stub his toe. He'll send angels to surround him. Or will he? Before you begin this whole Messiah thing, Satan argues, maybe you should try it out. Give it a kind of "test drive." Let's just see if your Father will keep you safe. Go ahead. Jump. See if his angels swoop down and catch you.

Then Jesus turns to the Bible again, answering, "It is also written: 'Do not put the Lord your God to the test'" (Matt. 4:7). In fact, isn't the idea of putting God to the test pretty absurd? After all, he is God. Isn't one of the main themes of the Bible that God is in charge? We must trust him, follow him, go where he leads. That was pretty much what God was trying to help us understand through the stories of Noah, Abraham, and especially Moses and the Israelites in the wilderness. To put God to the test is to doubt his competence to lead us. We doubt that Noah thought building that boat was a really terrific idea. Yet he did it by faith in spite of all the mocking he received from his neighbors. Abraham hiked all the way up Mt. Moriah with his son and the supplies for an altar fire. He had to trust God so much that he would be willing to actually sacrifice his son on a fire at God's request. Moses, of course, made all kinds of excuses. There was no way he wanted to be the leader of the Israelites. He tried everything he could to get out of the job. But God convinced him, especially with the argument that Moses really didn't have to do anything. He just had to follow orders. He had to trust that God would send the manna, bring water from a rock, and keep their clothes from wearing out.

"Don't tempt the Lord your God," said Jesus. "He's the one in control. He is the leader; I am the follower." That's a tough attitude to develop when facing a life-threatening illness. Yet some of the old clichés really do work in this case, especially "take one day at a time." Jesus' response to Satan was basically, "Sorry. No way. I will die sometime, but not today, and not in this way. God the Father is my leader. I will follow him." So the diagnosis has been made. Perhaps a temptation similar to the one Christ faced now plagues you: Test God; see if he will really come through. But Christ's temptation really teaches us simply to say, "I will die sometime, but not today, and maybe not in this way. That really doesn't ultimately matter. God is my leader. I will follow him."

The other part of this temptation is that Satan wants Jesus to take control of the situation, do it his way. How tempting that is, especially when facing a desperate disease. We both had a lot of experience with this when our respective spouses were being treated for cancer. We wanted to make certain things went well, right down to the time and place of treatments, how the treatments would proceed, and their effectiveness. But we both soon learned that our "control" was only a facade. We were never really in control at all. It was all in God's timing. What Jesus was tempted to do here was violate God's timing, do things out of turn.

One of the real challenges to the Christian's faith when facing a potentially terminal illness is this matter of trust. The challenge is to strike a balance between being confident and hopeful in faith and being realistic about this physical life. How hard we fight against accepting our mortality! How we hate to even consider the fact that life—my life—might end. So our natural tendency is to fight it, or to take control. But Jesus reminds us, "Do not put the Lord your God to the test."

One final word about this passage. Hidden beneath it all was the fact that Jesus could see beyond death. He could be confident that after his mission on earth was completed, he would return to a wonderful eternal life. We need to know that this eternal life he saw has become ours through him. Death may be scary, but it isn't the end. Jesus already went through it. He opened the door for us, and he invites us to walk through. But he wants us to walk one step at a time, following him, because he is our leader. Birth, death, life eternal—these all come in God's time. Don't jump ahead of him. Let him lead you. He won't let you down.

PRAYER: *I find that trusting you, dear Lord, can be very hard at times. I am sometimes tempted to be in a hurry. I want a cure or a miracle. And I know you can heal. But help me trust that healing isn't the only way to face this disease or the end of my life. Help me also see, as Jesus did, life beyond death. Even now, help me see you in both places—here in my life on earth right now and in that life on the other side of the grave. Please give me the patience to trust in you. Amen.*

God's Grand Design for His People

"For I know the plans I have for you," declares the LORD, "plans to prosper you and not to harm you, plans to give you hope and a future."

Jeremiah 29:11

Does God still have a purpose for me when I face the possibility of death?

Deep within us is a passion for life. We need a reason for living, for waking up each morning. If we have no sense of purpose or direction, we have lost the very essence of being human. God knew that from the very beginning. After he finished creating Adam and Eve, he gave them a reason to live. They were to be in charge of the world. "Let them rule over the fish of the sea and the birds of the air, over the livestock, over all the earth, and over all the creatures that move along the ground" (Gen. 1:26). Today we translate that purpose into our careers, into our relationships, or into leisure time activities. Whether we stamp out auto parts in a factory or collect stamps in the quiet of our homes, we need a reason to live every day. Over time, we begin to construct our lives as our career, family and friends, and activities blend into a beautiful symphony of life. Susan often tells the story of how she and Rick thought life was so great during the early years of their marriage. Both were well established in their careers, they had their dream home on a little lake, and they had just begun parenting their young daughter. Life was good. Life was wonderful! Things were going just as they had hoped and planned. But you know her story—how the grand mal seizure ended all that and began an eighteen-year journey

138

through a medical labyrinth until death finally reached down and took Rick's life. Not what either of them had planned, and certainly not what either of them wanted!

Perhaps something has happened in your life that has called your plans into question. Maybe you or a family member or friend received a discouraging medical diagnosis. The future suddenly looks very different than it did before. As you read this meditation, we would encourage you to read the verse above in context. Read Jeremiah 29:1–23. This passage is a letter from the prophet Jeremiah to all the Israelite people whom the Babylonian king Nebuchadnezzar had taken captive. The memory of the long exile in Egypt was still vivid in the minds of the subsequent generations in Israel, and now their attitude was likely "Here we go again!" Just about the time they really were starting to be comfortable again in their homeland, this foreign king ripped their future from them. They wanted to settle in. Build houses. Plant the fields. Worship God. Raise their children. Retire in peace after a long and prosperous life. Sound familiar? These are pretty common plans all of us have regardless of the year or place we live.

Now Jeremiah, the mouthpiece for God, has to explain something to all these captives in a foreign land. So he writes them a letter. Read it carefully. Do you hear the theme? He is saying, "Maybe your plans have been thwarted. Maybe you won't be able to do exactly what you wanted, when you wanted, the way you wanted. But God still has a plan for you." Not only is God promising the final, overarching victory that will eventually come through Jesus Christ on the cross, but he is also saying that in the meantime they should go ahead with their own plans. Maybe they are in Babylon, but the message is "Plant your fields anyway. Build your houses. Have your children marry. Worship God. Seek peace and prosper in the city." Why? Because "I have carried you into exile" (Jer. 29:7), and "[I have] plans to prosper you and not to harm you, plans to give you a hope and a future" (v. 11).

So how is God going to do this? How can he take this new exile of Israel and make the people prosper? That doesn't make sense to the logical mind—any more than it makes sense that a life-threatening disease can give purpose and direction to your life. The prospect of the disease, like Israel's captivity, is the very thing that robs you of your sense of future. In order to make sense of this whole thing, we need to take a step back mentally and spiritually from what is going on. That is really Jeremiah's advice. You may only hear the doctor's reports, see the results of lab tests, or feel the increasing pain within your body. You think *this* is your future. Everything else you had imagined is vanishing quickly. But step back, as Jeremiah encourages you to do, and get a better view of what is going on from God's perspective. He is saying several things to Israel that may apply to you as well.

In the letter he asked Jeremiah to write, God is saying that he has a much broader perspective on the matter than we ever could have. He is saying that the outcome of this seventy years in exile is already determined. While God is *allowing* this exile to happen, he is still in control of all the circumstances—so much so that he is already telling the people that at the end of seventy years "I will come to you and fulfill my gracious promise to bring you back to this place" (Jer. 29:10). God doesn't operate on our schedule. When we make our plans, we usually have a fairly firm idea of when we want things to happen. The promotion should come within the next two years. Then within the next three years we can build our new house. After that our daughter will likely graduate from college and get married. By the time we reach sixty-two or sixty-five, we can retire. We not only make plans, but our plans have a relatively firm timetable assigned to them. God works with a different clock. We must wait for him to act as so beautifully expressed in Psalm 130:5–6: "I wait for the LORD, my soul waits, and in his word I put my hope. My soul waits for the LORD more than watchmen wait for the morning, more than watchmen wait for the morning."

But if we have to wait, what do we do in the meantime? Jeremiah answers that as well. Go right on living! Go ahead and do what you had hoped you would do. So you are in foreign land, he says. Why should that stop you from planting your fields and raising your children? We have talked about trying to maintain a balance between despair and hope when you begin dealing with a potentially terminal disease. We think Jeremiah is giving us a good example of how to do that. Every single day the Israelites knew they were in captivity. In Psalm 137:4 the Israelites lament, "How can we sing the songs of the LORD while in a foreign land?" Yet God is saying through Jeremiah's letter, "Don't give up on your dreams. Don't lay aside your plans too quickly. Plant the crops; water the fields; raise your children." Only now you have to do it in a "foreign" land—under circumstances you would not have chosen. Now you or your loved ones have to continue to embrace life while under the threat of this disease. That takes faith and trust. You have to believe in God's promises. Can you take this one to heart so that you can balance your despair with hope? "'For I know the plans I have for you,' declares the LORD, 'plans to prosper you and not to harm you, plans to give you hope and a future'" (Jer. 29:11).

PRAYER: *Dear Lord, you know how carefully I laid plans for my life. You know as well that I really believed that those plans were what you wanted for me. I really don't understand what happened—not any more than the Israelites could understand another captivity. Quiet my heart. Give me courage to face this trial. Restore a sense of purpose to my life, and let me see what you have planned for me. I find it hard to let go of my own plans. Give me the courage to understand and embrace your plans. Amen.*

The Right Time

There is a time for everything, and a season for every
activity under heaven: a time to be born and a time to die.

Ecclesiastes 3:1–2

Do things always happen at the right time?

On most weekends we bake four loaves of French bread at our home. This fresh, homemade bread is one of the staples of our weekly menu. We either eat it plain or fancy it up with a bit of cheese or oil and spices. We have also learned that baking yeast bread (without a bread machine) means that you need a sense of timing. You knead the bread just so long, let it rise for the proper length of time, let it rise again, and then again, and then bake it. You don't want to take it out too soon because it will be mushy and sticky. But you don't want to overbake it either, or it will be too dry and hard. You need to take it out at the right time.

Time is a natural aspect of human nature. We have a sense (either right or wrong) about timing. Your daughter starts dating, but usually this dating is begun too early. Or you may decide to sell an investment, but you are overly cautious and suddenly realize that you sold too late. Life is in the timing.

The writer (known in Ecclesiastes as "the Teacher") makes the point that there is a time for everything under heaven. A time to plant and a time to reap. A time to laugh and a time to cry. We could say that everything has its season. There is a season, or time, to be born, and there is a time to die. The "time to die" is the tough one. Our sense is that very few people think that their own death, or that of a loved one, is on time. Most often, in our opinion, people die either too soon or too late. They are either too young or they have suffered too long.

How do you know when the time is right? We have to be careful about taking every word of the teacher in Ecclesiastes literally. He is really quite a cynic. Many times he calls life "meaningless" (Eccles. 4:7) or "a chasing after the wind" (v. 16). The cynic especially shows his true colors in Ecclesiastes 6:12, saying, "In the few days of our empty lives, who knows how our days can best be spent? And who can tell what will happen in the future after we are gone?" (NLT). But in the end: "Here is my final conclusion: Fear God and obey his commands, for this is the duty of every person. God will judge us for everything we do, including every secret thing, whether good or bad" (Eccles. 12:13–14 NLT).

Those verses may not sound very comforting if you are suddenly facing the possibility of your own death. On the other hand, many times we begin to think like this cynic under those circumstances. Questions pour out of us: "What good was my life? What difference does it make anyway? I thought I was going to live a longer and happier life. Why can't God just let me live a few more years?" Bitterness may creep in. Cynicism begins to take over. "Is this all there is? You mean I will never really get to retire (or see my daughter or son married, or take my grandchildren with me to Florida on vacation)?"

Timing! The battle is engaged! My sense of timing competes with God's. He sets the seasons. He put the planets in orbit around the sun. He causes the earth's rotations to create hours, days, weeks, and months. From the very beginning (even before he created us) God made time, pointing out that "there was evening and there was morning—the first day" (Gen. 1:3).

The teacher of Ecclesiastes speaks the truth in the verses that follow his famous quotation about "a time to die."

> God has made everything beautiful for its own time. He has planted eternity in the human heart, but even so, people cannot see the whole scope of God's work from beginning to end. So I concluded that there is nothing better for people than to be happy and to enjoy themselves as long as they can. And people should eat and drink and enjoy the fruits of their labor, for these are gifts from God.
>
> Ecclesiastes 4:11–13 NLT

One of the older creeds of the Protestant church says that our purpose in life is "to glorify God and to enjoy him forever."[21] One of the spiritual lessons we have learned following the deaths of our first spouses is to embrace and celebrate each day as a gift from God. "This is the day the LORD has made; let us rejoice and be glad in it" (Ps. 118:24). The writer of the book of Hebrews advises us to "fix our eyes on Jesus, the author and perfecter of our faith" (Heb. 12:2) in order to live with a single focus.

When our lives are moving along rather normally and we are in our routine, our tendency may be to plan ahead—so much so that we delay doing or saying the important things today. We think we can always do that tomorrow. But Christians are people of the present. We live each day in the grace of God. Today is the time God has given you. What will you do with the next twenty-four hours? Maybe things will change for the worse next week or next month. Perhaps the blood counts or lab reports from your routine physical exam will be the harbinger of gloomy days ahead. But today is the day God has given you. This is the time to rest in him. There is a season for everything. What season are you in right now?

PRAYER: *I confess, dear Lord, that I watch the clock closely—especially now that I sense a threat to my life. Will this be the end of it? Will you give me more years to live? How many might that be? My timing is not the same as yours. Help me understand you as the one who created time, as the one who controls time, as the one who is timeless. Thank you for today. Help me be content with it. I want to trust you one day at a time. Help me start with today. Amen.*

What Went Wrong?

As for you, you were dead in your transgressions and sins,
in which you used to live when you followed the ways of
this world and of the ruler of the kingdom of the air, the
spirit who is now at work in those who are disobedient.
All of us also lived among them at one time, gratifying the
cravings of our sinful nature and following its desires and
thoughts. Like the rest, we were by nature objects of wrath.

Ephesians 2:1–3

Where did evil and death come from?

od said to Adam and Eve, "You are free to eat from any tree in the garden; but you must not eat from the tree of the knowledge of good and evil, for when you eat of it you will surely die" (Gen. 2:16–17). These words were among the first God spoke to Adam and Eve in the Garden of Eden. Were they a warning or a curse? It makes a difference what you think. If you see the words as a curse, you might have a picture of an angry, judgmental God threatening damnation to anyone who doesn't obey him. If you see a warning, you could see a loving, benevolent God who cares so much for us that he doesn't want anything to go wrong. So which one do you think it is?

Actually, the issue goes a little deeper. Facing the prospect of your own potential death, you almost inevitably also have to face the question of how God can be good at the same time that bad things happen. For most of us, the dilemma is like this: God is presented in the Bible (and in most of our churches) as an all-powerful, all-knowing, all-loving

145

God. That leaves us with the impression that if he wanted to, he could fix any bad situation (immediately!). But we also know that bad things happen to us, such as disease, divorce, or other forms of distress. Bad things happen to everyone, religious or not. In our world we constantly hear about war, poverty, disease, prejudice, and injustice. We see that this world can be a pretty tough place to live. So we read books like *When Bad Things Happen to Good People*[22] or *Affliction*.[23]

Nearly all the world's religions struggle with this issue—certainly the struggle is felt in the Jewish, Muslim, and Christian faiths alike. It's not just a Christian problem. How do we explain why a loving, powerful, and all-knowing God lets bad things happen?

Answers are plentiful, though they don't all agree with each other. The approach we take comes from a professor Bob had in seminary several decades ago. "Imagine," this professor would say, "that God was the sun and we were the earth. Earth is nourished and warmed by the sun. Life is abundant and good as long as the earth stays in its proper orbit around the sun. But when Adam and Eve disobeyed, it was as if the earth decided to do one of two things. The first possibility was that the earth decided to leave its orbit and attack the sun. Desiring to take the sun's place, the earth runs an assault on the sun's position. In response, the sun cries out, 'Don't come any closer! If you do, you will surely die! You cannot withstand the heat and the fire that I generate. You weren't made to be exposed to these. If you come closer, you will burn up. That's just the way it is.' But in spite of the sun's pleading, the earth disobeys and, of course, is burned in a consuming fire."

Or the other option, according to this professor, is that the earth decides to leave its orbit and go away from the sun, to head the other direction. Again the sun calls out to the earth, "Don't do that. You need to remain close. The farther you get away from me, the colder and darker it will become. If you go too far, it will be so cold, so very bitterly cold, you will freeze. You will enter the outer darkness where there is no life." But again the earth disobeys and leaves the warmth of the sun. The outer darkness consumes the earth, and it is no more.

God isn't a mean, vindictive God who delights in punishing those who disobey him. On the contrary, he desires that everyone would be saved (1 Tim. 2:4). However, he also created us as humans with freedom of choice. So his desire is that we would believe and follow him, but that doesn't always happen. Adam and Eve ate of the forbidden tree (Gen. 3:1–7). People resisted Jesus (John 6:66). He wept over Jerusalem because they wouldn't believe (Luke 13:34–35).

Because Adam and Eve did rebel against God by disobeying his command not to eat of the tree of the knowledge of good and evil, all of us face the consequences of their poor choice. When they fell into sin, three things happened almost immediately. The battle between the devil and the human race began; the natural, loving relationship between a woman and a man was turned on its head; and work (the joyful tending of God's garden) became a punishment of hard labor ending in nothing less than death (Gen. 3:14–19).

God set in motion a natural relationship that must exist between him and his creation—especially between him and his image bearers. He is the Creator; we are his creatures. As long as the right relationship is maintained and honored, life is ultimately good, complete, and rewarding in its final outcome. That was what Jesus had in mind when he said that if anyone is in him, they have life eternal. One of the truly amazing things about the Christian faith is that while it takes death very seriously, death is also not a threat or the final answer. For those who are in Christ, life is eternal. Sure, we have to pass through physical death. That part we don't look forward to. But on the other side, we will continue in a perfect way the wonderful, life-sustaining relationship with God that he created at the very beginning. Even when we want to attack God and take over his throne or run away from him into the darkness of our soul, Christ keeps us in the right orbit. In him we have life, and that abundantly (John 10:10).

PRAYER: *You are a mighty, powerful God who set the stars and planets in their orbits. You created everything in its proper place. But I am realizing through what is happening within my own body that we, as human beings, have gone away from our orbit with you. Give me security in Christ. As I face an uncertain journey, keep my faith strong and vibrant. Most of all, dear God, keep me in the right relationship with Jesus Christ, in whose name I pray. Amen.*

Day 17

Death Is Gain

For to me, to live is Christ and to die is gain.

Philippians 1:21

Do I have to see death as a good thing?

t first blush we think that most anyone who hears they may be dying must be terrified at the thought. That is understandable. We have literally spent our entire lives building relationships, making contributions to society, loving people, and doing good for ourselves and others. Why would we want to sever all those wonderful ties we have made—especially to trade them for something we know so little about?

Christians really do not know very much about heaven. The Bible does give us some pictures, but most of what the Bible says about life after death falls into one of two categories. The statements are either highly metaphorical—that is, they are like fantasy pictures for which many of us have a hard time finding an earthly counterpart, such as streets paved in gold, streams of crystal, precious jewels in crowns, and strange beasts singing in a heavenly choir. Or the statements focus on Christ, the Lamb of God who has been raised victorious and is now seated in a place of authority over all the cosmos. Surrounding him are people from all the tribes and nations of the earth, along with the elders of Israel, angels, and the believers from all of time.

But the Bible doesn't say much, if anything, about day-to-day living in this celestial home. For someone who loves a good steak, enjoys the music of Tchaikovsky, and gets a thrill on water skis, those descriptions of heaven don't offer a lot of hope. We even joke that there won't be any golf in heaven since golf is based on the premise of imperfection—a matter of making fewer mistakes than the other player, or fewer than you made yourself last week—and heaven is a perfect place.

Most of us have learned to love this life a lot. Even if we don't love it, we still don't want to give it up because it is the only one we have and really understand. We don't know anything else. That's where the apostle Paul steps in with an entirely different approach to this matter of death. In Philippians 1:20–26 Paul is discussing with his dear friends in Philippi the quandary he now faces. Paul is getting older. He is in Rome, under house arrest. Over the years he has been beaten, shipwrecked, stoned, and nearly killed for the sake of the gospel. He is now eager to go home. By this he means that he is eager to die! "I desire to depart and be with Christ, which is better by far," he writes (Phil. 1:23). After all, years earlier Paul wrote to the Roman church that death had lost its power. "We are more than conquerors," he declared, "through him who loved us. For I am convinced that neither death nor life . . . will be able to separate us from the love of God that is in Christ Jesus our Lord" (Rom. 8:37–39).

Paul is providing a model for us as we come to the point in our lives at which we must face our own mortality. Of course we know we will all die. But some of us know that it will probably happen sooner rather than later. The doctors have told us so. We pray for the miracle. We ask for healing. But we also confront the reality that in a month or a year, our breathing and heartbeat may stop, and we will die. Can you in any way find yourself agreeing with Paul that to die would be better?

Of course, Paul feels the tension just like you probably do. He doesn't want to leave his family and friends. He doesn't want to abandon the work he has done in all those churches. If it were up to him, he would most likely stay on this earth a lot longer. "If I am to go on living in the body, this will mean fruitful labor for me," he says (Phil. 1:22). But he is torn. "What shall I choose? I do not know! I am torn between the two" (Phil. 1:22–23). So what makes the prospect of dying so appealing? It comes down to something quite simple and spiritual: He loves Jesus more than anything else. Maybe you have said that you love Jesus too. Maybe you have said it all your life. But the prospect of death puts it to the test. Don't misunderstand. Loving Jesus does not mean you cannot or should not love all those other important people and things in your life. Paul loved them too. That was his struggle. But in the end, his desire to be with Christ wins the day.

Remember some of the conversations Jesus had with his disciples when he started his ministry? He talked about storing up treasures in heaven, not on earth (Matt. 6:19–21). His words were very direct when he said, "Anyone who loves his father or mother more than me is not worthy of me; anyone who loves his son or daughter more than me is not worthy of me" (Matt. 10:37). He commanded the rich young ruler to sell everything he had, give it to the poor, and come follow him (Matt. 19:21). None of these passages mean that we should not love our parents or children or enjoy certain comforts of this world. The point is clear, however, that these things are all temporary. They belong to this world, which is passing away. Christ alone is eternal. As our foundation we must find our comfort and strength in him.

The difficult thing is saying good-bye to someone who can touch you, hug you, and make you smile. How do you say good-bye to someone who will eat steak or go skiing or enjoy the concert with you? Somehow our faith in Christ must now become that real, that tangible. No longer a routine prayer or a habit of worship, no longer a rescue squad for when we get into trouble or need a quick fix for something that has gone wrong—now our relationship with Christ must become a true love affair, a deep desire to be near to God. We need a yearning to be in his presence, even if that means saying good-bye to the rest of this world. Perhaps that is why we should read the book of Revelation as a love letter rather than a prophecy of literal things that might happen. This new eternal life with Christ is going to be so much greater, so much more enjoyable, so much more fulfilling than anything we could imagine here that the only way the Bible can talk about it is in fantasy terms. Now our focus is to be on the Lamb of God, who is at the center of everything—including, hopefully, your life. If he is at the center of your life, then you can likely understand Paul a little better. If I go on living on this earth, great! I can continue to be an ambassador for Christ in all I do. "For to me, to live is Christ" (Phil. 1:21)! But if I die, then it is pure gain. Then I will be with my Savior forever. But it is a struggle. No one, not even Paul, said it would be easy.

PRAYER: *Dear God, some days I pray that when I wake this entire threat to my life will suddenly vanish. I like it here on earth. I've had my problems; this life isn't perfect. But it is still good. It's all I really know right now. O God, I am not sure I want to exchange it for something I can't see. Yet deep in my heart, you know I want to be with you. It's just that saying good-bye would be so very hard to do. Help me develop the contentment of Paul—a contentment to work for you on this earth as long as you want me to. Then, but only then, take me home to you. Amen.*

How Great Is God?

And he did not do many miracles there because of their lack of faith.

Matthew 13:58

If God is all powerful, why doesn't he always answer our prayers by healing us?

We all want a miracle. When faced with a life-threatening illness, one of the normal reactions of Christians is to say that "God can heal." He certainly can. We believe this because the Bible tells so many stories of the healings Jesus performed. Why not us? So we muster our forces, we storm heaven with our prayers, and we wait for a miracle. As we wait we do remember that Christ didn't heal everyone. We also know that we have no inherent right to expect a miracle. But then we think *Why not? Why wouldn't God want to heal?* So we pray even harder.

The danger, of course, is that when a miracle doesn't happen and the healing doesn't come, we begin to question our faith. Or someone else does through comments such as "Maybe you haven't prayed hard enough" or "Maybe we should organize more prayer warriors to help you in your prayers." These comments are based on the assumption that prayer is like dollar bills and miracles are things we can buy. The more prayer we "spend" or the more faith we have, the more likely we can "buy" the miracle. Obviously this is not what God intended. Miracles and answers to prayer are all within God's domain. He decides what he wants to do for each one of us and when he will do it. But we often

151

still face the trauma of wondering if our faith is strong enough or our prayers good enough.

This meditation and the next two address the issues of faith, prayer, and healing. The focus of this meditation is the question "If God is all powerful, why doesn't he always answer our prayers for healing?" If we really love the Lord, why doesn't he take care of us with his almighty power?

Let's examine, for a minute, why Jesus did miracles of healing. Was his purpose to establish a standard operating procedure to use whenever anyone is sick or afflicted? We think not. Jesus' miracles were actually signs that he really was the promised Messiah. When John the Baptist inquired about Jesus' identity, Christ sent a message back saying, "The blind see, the lame walk, the lepers are cured" (see Matt. 11:4–6). Miracles of healing were one of the signs of his coming kingdom.

The other side of this equation is the matter of faith's connection to healing. The Matthew 13:58 passage is often understood from some English translations to mean that he *could not* do many miracles because of their lack of faith. That is not really what the verse says. It simply reads that he *did not* do many miracles because of their lack of faith. The distinction is subtle but important. Yes, faith is important for a miracle to happen. When faith is not present, Christ will not often heal. But faith is not sufficient to *cause* a miracle. Jesus did not cure everyone, even though many may have had faith. He performed miracles when and where the witness of his power would help people understand who he was. Actually, if God answered every prayer for healing, we would live in a perfect world. There would be no more sickness, pain, or even death anymore. But do you know what? That is actually the miracle Jesus performed on the cross at Calvary for all of us. He died once for all of us, not so that we will necessarily experience a miracle here with physical illness, but rather so that we will have an *eternal* miracle. His resurrection made possible for us a perfect world for eternity.

Death is a frightening thought, and if you are facing it you certainly may want a miracle. Remember, though, that even a miracle for healing now only avoids for a moment the inevitability of your own death. While we don't want to minimize your desire for healing, we also want you to remember the bigger miracle—the miracle that Christ performed in creating a new world beyond this death, a world in which all this disease, pain, and suffering is gone. That is the heart of the message of his resurrection and his healing power.

PRAYER: *A miracle sounds so good to me, Holy Father. I know you have the power to heal. I've been sick before, and I returned to health. You were the healer then. Please consider my request for healing now! But also work in my heart to accept the fact that healing from a physical disease is not the greatest thing you do. The greatest gift to me was done through your Son, Jesus. Help me accept the weakness of my body knowing that you provide strength for my soul. Help me, dear Lord, understand that healing comes with Christ's return and the advent of heaven. In the meantime, walk closely with me day by day, for Jesus' sake. Amen.*

Centurion Faith

The centurion heard of Jesus and sent some elders of the Jews to him, asking him to come and heal his servant. . . . So Jesus went with them. He was not far from the house when the centurion sent friends to say to him: "Lord, don't trouble yourself, for I do not deserve to have you come under my roof. That is why I did not even consider myself worthy to come to you. But say the word, and my servant will be healed. For I myself am a man under authority, with soldiers under me. I tell this one, 'Go,' and he goes; and that one, 'Come,' and he comes. I say to my servant, 'Do this,' and he does it." When Jesus heard this, he was amazed at him, and turning to the crowd following him, he said, "I tell you, I have not found such great faith even in Israel." Then the men who had been sent returned to the house and found the servant well.

Luke 7:3, 6–10

Doesn't the Bible teach that God heals us if we have enough faith?

"centurion" is like a sergeant in the army. In this case the man was in a position of high command in the Roman army. He wasn't a Jew; he wasn't part of the crowd that followed Jesus; he had no reason even to be interested in this prophet from Nazareth—except, of course, that he had heard some amazing things about Jesus' power and miraculous healing of the sick.

And his servant was very sick, nearly dying. But here's where the story gets interesting. Unlike so many others who were sick who personally took the trouble to journey to Jesus' feet, this centurion sent some friends to Jesus on his behalf. Their job was to carry this man's instructions. He basically said, "Look, I am a man of authority. I can tell people what to do, and they do it. I also recognize that you, Jesus, are a person of authority. All you need to do is say the word and my servant will be healed." And Jesus did it, because, as he said, "I have not found such great faith even in Israel" (Luke 7:9).

We said in the last meditation that the quantity of faith isn't the deciding factor in whether or not Jesus will do a miracle. Now Jesus is measuring the quantity of this man's faith in comparison to Israel. Doesn't this contradict what we said before? Not really. Look again at the passage. What is the focus of the centurion's faith? We think the key to this story is the word "authority," not the word "healing." The Israelites were having a hard time accepting Jesus as an authority. Remember how they said that "nothing good could come from Nazareth" (John 1:46) and that "a prophet has no honor in his own country" (John 4:44)? And now here is a Roman soldier who immediately recognizes the authority Christ has over the world.

In facing the possibility that you might die, perhaps your struggle isn't so much for healing as it is for control. Who has the authority to make decisions about your life? Christians recognize that this authority belongs to God. That's why Jesus himself, in the Garden of Gethsemane, prayed fervently that he might find a way to avoid crucifixion. But he concluded his prayer, "Yet not as I will, but as you will" (Matt. 26:39). The authority to make those decisions rested squarely with God the Father, as was made clear at the end of Christ's life. In introducing his "Great Commission," Christ made it clear that "all authority in heaven and on earth" now belongs to him (Matt. 28:18). He is in control of everything, including sickness and disease.

That was a hard lesson for both of us to learn as we took care of our dying spouses. Susan's first husband, Rick, had his brain's right frontal lobe totally removed eight years prior to his death and for those years faced severe challenges to both his mental and physical capacities. Bob watched his first wife, Char, slowly erode to about ninety-five pounds before she died of ovarian cancer. Both of us wanted a miracle. But both of us ultimately also understood what it meant that God was in control. He would work his will in our lives. We had to learn the very hard lesson that not only could we not control the circumstances of our lives; we also could not (and, of course, should not) attempt to control God himself. We could tell him what we wanted, but finally we had to yield to his judgment and his control.

Accepting God's total control over our situations is not easy. Most of us want to keep on living and being healthy so much that we might give anything to be healthy again. But remember, the Bible is very silent about all those who had been healed previously by Christ. Do we assume that they never got sick again? Do you think that after Jesus raised Lazarus from the grave, Lazarus never died again? We must assume that Lazarus did die again, and those whom Christ healed likely got sick again. The healing wasn't a permanent thing, but what God offers us in Christ is far more permanent and wonderful than just physical healing. He offers a completely new life—an eternal life. Dying is not fun. Saying good-bye to others is not easy. You may not die at this point in your life. You really don't know what is going to happen. But isn't this a good time to settle the issue of who is in control? To reinforce the idea that we rest fully in God's will, plant the words of James in your mind and heart as you work through your diagnosis. James writes:

> Now listen, you who say, "Today or tomorrow we will go to this or that city, spend a year there, carry on business and make money." Why, you do not even know what will happen tomorrow. . . . Instead, you ought to say, "If it is the Lord's will, we will live and do this or that."

James 4:13–15

Jesus also instructed us in the Lord's Prayer to pray one of the hardest prayers: "Your will be done" (Matt. 6:10). That's difficult to say when death may be knocking on your door! But faith, like the centurion, ultimately believes that Christ has the authority. He will make the decision. Then we need to trust that his will is for our best, even if it doesn't appear that way at the present. Our Lord is in control. And ultimately we will be healed for all eternity.

PRAYER: *Almighty God, King of the world and of my life, why do I sometimes become so impatient? Why do I want to control my situation instead of trusting you as the Commander of my life? My life isn't very easy right now. My future really seems to be in question. Build my faith so that, like this Roman centurion, I will recognize and accept your authority over my life. May I rest fully within your control today. I know that your control ultimately will lead me home to be with you for all eternity. Amen.*

He Heals All Our Diseases

Jesus went throughout Galilee, teaching in their synagogues, preaching the good news of the kingdom, and healing every disease and sickness among the people.

Matthew 4:23

But he was pierced for our transgressions, he was crushed for our iniquities; the punishment that brought us peace was upon him, and by his wounds we are healed.

Isaiah 53:5

How does God's healing actually happen?

 e have always liked the passage from Isaiah 53. Of course, this passage is a direct prophecy for Good Friday and Easter, when Christ's suffering and death would bring peace and healing. But what is healing? Bob remembers really struggling with this passage when he was a young boy. At the age of fourteen, he contracted rheumatic fever. He was confined to bed for ten weeks and couldn't even get up to go to the bathroom. He had just professed his faith in Christ at church—now this! No, it wasn't life threatening, but it certainly made him wonder about the faith he had just embraced while he struggled to get better for those many weeks.

Then we come to the stories about Jesus healing that we so easily remember. Can you picture Jesus right now, walking among the sick, the lame, the lepers? With a wave of his hand here and a touch of his finger there, people are cured!

This is the third meditation in a series that deals with faith and healing. To this point, we have tried to make it clear that God, through Christ, does have the ability to heal—even today in North America and elsewhere. We also stated that faith is generally a necessary component of healing, at least as it was presented in the Bible. But we also tried to demonstrate that faith alone does not guarantee healing. To heal or not heal is still God's decision and under his control.

We have mainly talked about healing as if it primarily means healing a physical ailment. We have also been talking about healing an individual person—a sick one, a leper, or a blind person. So we identify with that situation when we hear the diagnosis of the doctor. I'm sick. I might die. Me! Perhaps soon! And I want to claim this promise of healing for myself.

But remember, Jesus performed his miracles of healing for a specific purpose, namely, to demonstrate the power of his coming kingdom. He did not perform miracles simply to dispense medical favors to those who were special to him. He did miracles for a purpose that went far beyond an individual person. He did them for the world—a world sick with sin.

Healing has a far deeper and more pervasive meaning in the Bible than just the healing of one person's illness. Jesus is going to heal the sickness of the world, a sickness that came into the world through sin and would not leave until he conquered it through death itself. You might want to remember that as you begin to face the possibility of your own death. Maybe the healing that God is promising is not a personal, individual miracle but a participation in the great healing that Christ accomplished on the cross of Calvary. The apostle Paul reminds us that we must "share in his sufferings" if we are to participate in his resurrection (Phil. 3:10–11). Facing death is a terrible experience to go through. Dying can be extremely frightening. But the Bible says two basic things about this death: First, there is no other way for us to get to the real eternal life promised us in Christ. Death is the doorway, the secret passageway to new life. And second, once you die physically, you will never have to do it again. Life will be perfect again as it was at the very beginning of creation. You will then be healed—completely and forever.

PRAYER: *Dear Lord Jesus, I confess with Isaiah that it is by your wounds I am healed. But I also realize that this doesn't necessarily mean you will*

remove my cancer, or strengthen my heart, or take this disease from my body—at least not on this earth. Help me learn to live with this medical condition and even, if it is your will, to die by it. Kindle in my heart the confidence, however, that this disease, like all illness, is a passing thing and that I will someday be completely healed when I join you in the beauty of heaven. Amen.

What If I Had Done Things Differently?

"Lord," Martha said to Jesus, "if you had been here, my brother would not have died."

John 11:21

What do I do about my regrets?

The death of Lazarus is an especially poignant story of the special relationship Jesus had with one family. It seems that Jesus was a rather regular visitor to their home. Mary and Martha, as different as night and day, both had a loving and devoted relationship to Jesus. They truly believed he was the Messiah, sent to redeem the people of Israel. Lazarus was their faithful brother, also highly devoted to Christ.

But one day they received the word from the doctor. "I am so sorry to tell you this. But based on the results of the tests we've run, I am afraid that Lazarus is extremely ill. We're going to have to admit him to the critical care unit. We're not sure what we can do. Maybe he'll pull through, but we can't guarantee it."

When you hear that kind of news, what do you do? For one thing, you call for help. "Someone has to be able to help us," you say. If Jesus were your friend, a regular visitor to your home, wouldn't you do exactly the same thing these sisters did? Looking at each other through tearstained eyes, they both may have said almost simultaneously, "Let's call Jesus!"

Of course! Isn't that what we all do? We pray, we plead, we bargain and beg. But since the sisters lived near Jesus and he sometimes walked the dusty road that came right by their house, wouldn't it be so much easier just to have Jesus come over? Send word! Right now! Hurry! Let Jesus know that Lazarus is seriously ill and that he should come right away.

When we struggle with traumatic situations, we want someone there who can help. Even in our faith we often want a friend, a spiritual mentor, or a pastor to come and pray with us. But deep down what we really want is to get in touch with Jesus. Send him word that my loved one is sick and might die. Let him know so he can come and prevent this whole horrible thing from happening.

So the word went to Jesus. And here we find one of the most puzzling verses in the New Testament. Hearing that his close friend was dying and knowing the sisters so desperately wanted him there, "he stayed where he was two more days" (John 11:6). He waited. He waited on purpose! Only when the two days were over did he make the twelve-mile trek over to Bethany to learn that Lazarus had died and was already in his tomb. Mary and Martha, hands sore from wringing them in anxiety and grief, finally see Jesus coming. What a conflict of emotions!

"Where have you been?"

"What have you been doing?"

"Didn't you get our message?"

"Were you ignoring us?"

"Wasn't it clear to you that Lazarus might die?"

And then the key phrase. They both said it. "If only you had come when we called you, this thing wouldn't have happened" (see John 11:21, 32). *If only!* How often have you said that in the past few days or months? If only I had gotten tested earlier! If only I hadn't smoked so much! If only my husband hadn't worked so many hours in such a stressful job! If only my wife had taken time for a mammogram!

Mary and Martha are making two assumptions in their accusation of "if only." The first is that they can control and direct their own fortunes or destinies. Their desire—their command!—that Jesus come right away and their subsequent anger over his delay both stem from the assumption that they knew what was best in that situation. But while Christians are responsible to make clear and proper decisions, the Christian believer also knows that we are not the masters of our personal destiny. The Bible teaches us that God is a God of providence—a God who watches over us and is indeed in control.

But knowing that God is in control reveals the other assumption. We often assume that God will opt for the least painful road. We assume that physical comfort or a temporary answer to our predicament here on earth is of ultimate value. We assume that pain is one of our worst enemies. We need to be careful not to look at God through rose-colored glasses. Something bigger is going on in the lives of Mary, Martha, and Lazarus than just a man getting sick and dying. We need to remember that death came because of sin, because of humanity's failure to live faithfully in God's presence. Mary and Martha were correct in thinking that Jesus could have prevented Lazarus's death. They knew Jesus had the power to cure disease. What they had not yet learned was that the power of God exercised through Christ was greater not only than disease but also than death itself. Jesus told his disciples, "Lazarus is dead, and for your sake I am glad I was not there, so that you may believe" (John 11:14–15). Believe what? Believe that death itself is not the end! Believe that death is not troublesome to God! He can raise a dead man, but better yet, he conquered death once and for all. Jesus wanted them to believe, as he would say almost immediately, that he is "the resurrection and the life. He who believes in me will live, even though he dies" (John 11:25).

Jesus then goes to Lazarus's grave. He weeps, for he genuinely feels grief over death. But then, with a bold voice, he calls Lazarus out of the grave. Within a week of that event, Jesus himself would hang on a cross. He would die. He would be buried. He wanted this loving family, his disciples, and us to remember his power over the death of Lazarus. He wanted them to have confidence that he would also rise from the dead.

Having that kind of faith is hard when you are facing potential death or experiencing deep grief. That kind of faith is even harder when you live with regrets, with the "if onlys" of Mary and Martha. Through this event Jesus encourages us to be a people of hope—not necessarily of a hope for an earthly solution to our problem but of a hope that can look beyond this world to the real world of eternal life.

Can't you hear Jesus talking to the sisters? "Come, Mary. Come, Martha. Lazarus is not dead. He is asleep. Don't say 'if only.' I am the resurrection and the life. Whoever believes in me will never die. Do you believe this?"

PRAYER: *Lord, I don't know how many times I have wondered about what I might have done to prevent this situation. If I had done something differently, would I be facing this challenge now? Then I must also confess, dear Lord, that I might be tempted like Mary and Martha to wonder what you might have done differently. What if you had intervened sooner or*

with more power? Help me understand a little more clearly your message to Lazarus's sisters—that death is not a scary thing for you. You are the resurrection and the life. Help me overcome my fear of death so I can enjoy my life while I am still here. But also help me focus my eyes heavenward without being held back by earthly fears. I know that death is no problem for you. Amen.

Wasting Away?

We are hard pressed on every side, but not crushed;
perplexed, but not in despair; persecuted, but not
abandoned; struck down, but not destroyed. We always
carry around in our body the death of Jesus, so that
the life of Jesus may also be revealed in our body. . . .
Therefore we do not lose heart. Though outwardly we are
wasting away, yet inwardly we are being renewed day by
day. For our light and momentary troubles are achieving
for us an eternal glory that far outweighs them all.

2 Corinthians 4:8–10, 16

How do I keep from despair when my body is wasting away?

North American culture places a high value on appearance. Advertisements bombard us with solicitations for exercise machines, the latest fashions, in vogue hairstyles, and sharp-looking automobiles. All of this is to entice us to look good. Not every disease makes itself evident by changing our appearance, but many of them do. Chemotherapy can weaken us, make our face pale, or cause us to lose our hair. Other diseases may make us shake, slow down our walk, or reduce our stamina to the point at which we are obviously suffering. We realize that our body is beginning to waste away. Something is eating at it from the inside. We haven't given up hope that we can conquer this enemy within, but others may look at us and immediately be aware of the battle we are waging.

The apostle Paul eloquently expresses similar feelings in this passage. His challenge came from persecution, opposition, and even the thing he called "a thorn in my flesh" (2 Cor. 12:7). We don't know what Paul looked like. But the description he gives in the passage for this meditation suggests that he likely was not the epitome of good health. His body may have been bent over by the weight of his ministry. His face may have contained deep lines of stress and concern. His back was certainly scarred from beatings received at the hands of persecutors.

Losing strength or having our appearance change isn't something we often accept very easily. We grieve the loss of function. Even under normal circumstances we finally have to accept as we age that we aren't as strong or handsome or beautiful as we once may have been. Now this, a disease that seems to be eating away at us! We don't want to lose our dignity.

Paul reminds us of a very basic principle: While the world may look on the outside, God looks on the heart. Our bodies may be wasting away, but he renews us inwardly day by day. We are actually carrying around in our body "the death of Jesus" (2 Cor. 4:10). This wasting away is a sad and unavoidable reminder that the bodies we have in this world will not last for eternity. We will all die. Death doesn't come just at the end of our life; in a very real way, we begin our journey toward death the day we are born. This, says Paul, is a constant reminder of why Christ himself finally had to die for us.

The good news, however, is that this wasting away also reminds us that in Christ we can have a new life and a new body. Even as we carry in our bodies a sign of the temporary nature of this life, our body also serves as a reminder of new life in Christ. Precisely because our present body will not last forever, the body itself becomes a promise of something new, beautiful, and eternal. An eternal glory waits for us, and whether or not we are actually facing the prospect of death right now, we believe as Christians that at our resurrection we will be renewed into the image of Christ and enjoy a new body that is far more magnificent than our present one.

So Paul also suggests that we change our mental focus. "Though outwardly we are wasting away, yet inwardly we are being renewed day by day" (2 Cor. 4:16). You might be offended or put off by Paul calling things like Parkinson's disease, multiple sclerosis, congestive heart failure, Alzheimer's disease, or even cancer a "light and momentary trouble" (v. 17). But that is what he is talking about. Actually he is saying that *any* trouble or trial we are facing in this life is nothing compared to the glory we will experience in Christ. Haven't we said something like that at the funeral of a loved one who has preceded us in death? Don't we sometimes remark (or at least think), "Well, at least he is in a better place now—a place where he is free from all this pain and sorrow and suffering"? If we say that about others, why wouldn't that attitude also apply to us as we begin to experience more and more the wasting away of this body and move toward acquiring our new heavenly body?

Our bodies will not last forever because of the curse of sin. As a result of the fall into sin, God said that from dust we came; to dust we return. But not permanently. Christ arose with a new body. The wasting away of our body can be a sure and certain sign that, as we cast off this earthly body, Christ is preparing for us a new, eternal body. "Therefore," says Paul, "we do not lose heart" (v. 16).

PRAYER: *Eternal God, you are the one who sits beyond this world and who has, through your Son, Jesus, conquered death. I know the real possibility, dear Lord, that I will die sometime soon. I know we will all die, but this disease may be the occasion of my death. Some days I feel like my body is wasting away. Even if it is normal aging, I am more aware than ever before that this body won't last forever. Make my transition to my resurrected body a bearable one. Don't let me lose heart on what may be the final journey of this life. Stay near me in the fullness of your glory. Amen.*

Rotten Produce

Not only so, but we also rejoice in our sufferings, because we know that suffering produces perseverance; perseverance, character; and character, hope. And hope does not disappoint us, because God has poured out his love into our hearts by the Holy Spirit, whom he has given us.

Romans 5:3–5

What can I realistically hope for?

When Bob was in high school, he worked for a summer as the produce manager in a small corner grocery store. He learned quickly how to find and order the best cabbage and kale, carrots and cauliflower, bananas and beets. But he also learned about the opposite of fresh produce when the unsold products rather quickly deteriorated and began to rot. The bananas weren't so bad. They just turned from yellow to brown and then to black. They did get mushy, but there was nothing terribly offensive about them. Not like carrots! Rotten carrots wasted away into a stinky, slimy mess. You could smell a rotten carrot a hundred yards away.

We've been talking about our bodies "wasting away." Sometimes we might think that our bodies are becoming like day-old (or even older) produce slowly losing its freshness, color, and texture. Eventually we know that the day of our freshness has passed, like very old fruits and vegetables, and it's all downhill from here.

What Bob never really put together when he was produce manager is that the word *produce* can be either a noun or a verb. As a noun, the word typically refers to the grocery store stuff—like the radishes, celery, and rutabagas. But as a verb, the word *produce* refers to the process of making something. We can take a variety of different types of *produce* (such as lettuce, tomatoes, cucumbers, and onions) and *produce* a salad. Perhaps farmers first started calling their vegetables "produce" since they were the stuff they "produced" on their farm.

But let's move back into a spiritual frame of reference. Paul has the audacity to suggest that we should rejoice in our sufferings because of what they produce. That idea can be hard to comprehend! Maybe you can accept your suffering, or at least tolerate it. But to rejoice in it? That seems to be asking too much!

But hear again what Paul is saying. He develops a golden chain of Christian logic. Suffering, he says, produces perseverance, which in turn produces character, which then produces hope. Hope is what ties us directly to the strength and power of God through his Holy Spirit! That hope does not disappoint us. In a sense, Paul is listing the ingredients for a spiritual salad. Mix the following ingredients, he seems to be saying. Take a bit of suffering, combine it with developing perseverance and character, and you will get a wonderfully satisfying dose of hope. Isn't that what we really want or need when we face illness or disease? Isn't hope the one thing we really want in life?

Between suffering and hope lie two important Christian virtues. Perseverance means that your faith has deepened to the point at which you are willing and able to see the matter through to the end. Winston Churchill in his now famous speech of October 29, 1941 said to his former students in Harrow, England, when reflecting on the war: "Never give in—never, never, never, never, in nothing great or small. . . ."[24] The difference between Churchill and Paul, however, is that Churchill was assuming that the soldiers (and citizens) would have to reach deep down inside themselves for the courage and strength to persevere in the battle. Paul invites us to reach down deep into Christ's strength and power (not ours!) for this perseverance.

This type of perseverance results in character, according to Paul. By "character" he means a balanced personality—the ability to accept all the circumstances of life. A person of character has a depth to his or her personality, a flexibility of spirit, and a sense of purpose in life. This is another way to talk about the type of maturity that Christians are to seek by following their Master. Jesus never said being a Christian would be easy. You may be experiencing that in a direct and personal way more now than ever before. But Paul is holding out a golden chain that will lead you to hope. Once you have that hope, you will have something that will never disappoint you precisely because it has been poured into your heart by the Holy Spirit.

The role of the Holy Spirit in giving us hope is made all the more clear in Ephesians 1:13–14, where Paul says that this Holy Spirit is a "deposit," or a down payment, on all the promises God has made to us. The Holy Spirit in our hearts is a reminder that all the rest of the promises God has made to us will come true. You may be suffering now. But if you press through that suffering, learn perseverance, and develop that Christian character, you will know the Spirit's hope all the more richly. And that hope will not disappoint you.

PRAYER: *God of all hope, as I face this trial of disease in my life, give me the ultimate hope that you will never forsake me and will eventually lead me home. I praise you for the encouragement of Paul's words. Help me develop my character and learn perseverance. I know I can do this only through the Holy Spirit whom you have given me as a down payment of all your promises. I am counting on you, Lord, to see me through this difficulty. I need your hope so that I won't be disappointed with the way this may all end—perhaps in my death rather than my healing. My hope is in you, Lord. Amen.*

Trials and Temptations

*Dear brothers and sisters, whenever trouble comes your
way, let it be an opportunity for joy. For when your faith is
tested, your endurance has a chance to grow.*

James 1:2–3 NLT

*And remember, no one who wants to do wrong should
ever say, "God is tempting me." God is never tempted to do
wrong, and he never tempts anyone else either.*

James 1:13 NLT

Should I be happy because I have this potentially terminal illness?

The apostle James picks up on the theme of perseverance
introduced in the previous meditation. He is saying basically the same thing Paul did—the testing of our faith
produces perseverance. Paul, of course, went on to add that testing also
produces character and hope. James, however, is addressing another
issue we often face with trials and problems in our lives. Many Christians
struggle with the question, Why did God let this happen to me? After all,
isn't God all powerful? Isn't he also loving and merciful? If he is both of
these things, then why does he let bad things, such as a disease, afflict
my life? After all, if you are a parent, don't you do everything you can
within your power to protect your children from harm?

We must admit that this issue is a deep mystery for Christians—at least
if we approach it as if God thinks and behaves the way we, as human
beings, think and behave. So the question is, what role does God play
in the fact that I am sick and might well die? Or to put it another way,

do I have the right to expect that God will muster all his forces to fight this disease or situation in my life?

I suppose there are a number of logical answers to this question. Some people may answer this dilemma by saying that God really does not intervene in our lives in cases like this. Certainly he may be all powerful, they might argue, but once sin entered the world, God more or less washed his hands of the matter—at least as far as individual lives and predicaments are concerned. He does provide salvation; he has created a new heaven and a new earth where disease will be no more. But as far as this world is concerned, this approach simply says that God is letting the sin and evil of the world run its own natural course.

Others may answer in quite the opposite way. They say that God is in fact the one who has designed all of this, including sickness and disease. Somehow in his plan, he makes sure that we suffer in this world so that we might love him more and depend on him daily. The whole thing is part of his plan, his grand scheme. This view, of course, makes God responsible not only for all the good in the world but also for the evil.

James is, we believe, inviting us to consider a middle ground, a third option. In the first text listed above, James is repeating what we have been talking about in the two previous meditations. Like Paul, James is saying that a real spiritual benefit can come from suffering. These bad things can have good results. Paul stated this most clearly by saying that God can take these evil things and turn them to our profit. Remember the wonderful testimony of Joseph after his brothers consorted together, sold him into slavery in Egypt, and thought he was gone forever? Many years later, when famine forced Jacob and his sons to flee to Egypt in order to survive, they ran into Joseph face-to-face. Joseph was now Pharoah's right-hand man! Joseph later made this observation about what his brothers did to him: "You intended to harm me, but God intended it for good" (Gen. 50:20). That testimony holds a key to understanding the mystery of God's role in evil.

Another clue to this mystery is in the second passage we listed from James. Many English versions use the word *temptation* in these verses, but the original language of the Bible does not make a clear distinction between *trial* and *temptation*. James is in essence saying, "Don't make God the culprit. Don't accuse God of being the one who caused this all to happen." The Bible is quite clear that all the "bad" stuff we face really comes as a result of humanity's rebellion against God, represented by the story of Adam and Eve violating God's command in the Garden of Eden. That's where evil came from. We can't blame God for that.

What also is clear, however, is that any situation we think is bad, evil, tempting, or a trial is still under God's final control. He didn't cause it, but he also doesn't walk away from it. God allows bad things like illness to happen, and he uses them. It's like God is saying, "Since this bad stuff has happened, let me see how I can make it turn out for good." In plenty of stories in the Bible, that is exactly what God does with evil. Think about Job or the persecutions of the early church. We already mentioned Joseph in Egypt, but add to that the trials Paul faced on his missionary journeys.

Perhaps it finally comes down to our eyesight—our spiritual eyesight. We can see only so far. Certainly we can't see into the future as far and as clearly as God can. He knows the rest of the story. We can only guess how it will turn out. But sufferings and trials propel us ever closer to the heart of God, who can lift us up in his arms. From there we can see the future a little more clearly. Remember, Isaiah 40:28–31 says that God gives power to the faint and in the Lord we are able to mount up with wings like eagles. Just like a parent who puts a child on his or her shoulders to see farther down the parade, so God is able through faith and hope to give us the assurance that "in all things God works for the good of those who love him, who have been called according to his purpose" (Rom. 8:28).

None of us knows what will happen tomorrow. James makes that point clearly in his short letter. He reminds us that we should say "if it is the Lord's will" every time we make our plans (James 4:13–15). Now that this trial, your diagnosed disease, has come into your life and made you more aware of the possibility of dying, isn't it time to let God pick you up, place you on his shoulders or lift you up on eagle's wings, and help you have confidence in him? He is the one who is faithful. He will not leave you nor forsake you. That much is certain on your uncertain journey. The journey may be rough. You may not know the road ahead. But remember, the way is certain with God. In the end, whether we continue to live or die, we have confidence that we are the Lord's.

PRAYER: *Eternal Father, I turn my life over to you as I face this uncertain future. I am often confused by what is happening to me. I even sometimes have a hard time understanding why you let this happen. But then I realize that everyone faces their own trials. Everyone will have to go through what I am potentially facing—death. Pick me up spiritually. Even if my body may get weaker, make my spirit that much stronger. If you will, place me on your shoulders so I can see the future a little more clearly. No matter what happens, keep me close to you in this life, in my death, and for all eternity. Amen.*

THREE

Midnight

The Day Has Ended

Midnight.
Darkness has come,
No time to do more.
The day has ended.
Though life brought satisfaction,
Still regrets at what hoped would be.
Did I do my part? Contribute?
Wrap up the day.
Hug them close. Say good-bye.
Rest now. Feel at peace.
Smile at loved ones. At myself too.
This present adventure over.
What lies ahead?
Let go, soar beyond.
Apprehension. Excitement.
Sadness. Joy.
This day ends. The stars come out.
That's not all. A new day begins.
Eternity.

S. Zonnebelt-Smeenge and R. De Vries

I run to death, and death meets me as fast;
And all my pleasures are as yesterday.
This is my play's last scene, here heavens appoint
My pilgrimage's last mile; and my race,
Idly yet quickly run, hath this last pace,
My span's last inch, my minute's latest point.

John Donne

THE MENTAL HEALTH PERSPECTIVE ON FACING DEATH

Walking the Final Leg

You never know for sure when death will strike. Even for people who are healthy, death could occur within the next few minutes. Life is indeed very fragile. On the other hand, you may have lived for a while now sensing the approach of your death. The disease has continued to eat away at your body. Muscles have lost their strength. You begin to realize that your options are becoming limited.

August was hot and humid in Michigan. Char, Bob's first wife, was three and a half years into her battle with cancer. She was losing ground steadily as her lungs filled with fluid. At first she thought the fluid buildup was because of the heat. The doctors drained her lungs several times. By early September, the doctor ordered a chemical searing of the outer covering of the lung to prevent further fluid buildup. Bob was the one to confront the doctor: "You don't do this procedure on someone you think is going to live very long, do you?" "No," the doctor replied. "I suspect, then," said Bob, "that she isn't going to live much longer, maybe only another six or eight weeks." "You're probably right," was his reply. She died seven weeks later.

The neurologist made a home visit to Rick in early October, two and a half weeks before his death. He had managed Rick's medical treatment for eighteen years. Susan and Rick discussed his estimate of the time Rick might have left. The bottom line was "not long at all." Rick's health was failing. The steroids were losing their effectiveness. There was nothing more to do other than keep him comfortable. Final good-byes were said by many people who loved Rick as his body slowly shut down. He died quietly with his hand in Susan's.

The span of time between when we both knew death was imminent for our first spouses and when they actually died was agonizing, yet it was also an extremely precious time. It was filled with many hugs, kisses, tears, and conversations. Both of us took the opportunity to talk with them further about what dying might be like for them. They also wanted to tell us again what they hoped life would be like for us after they died. We were blessed with spouses who were willing and still able to communicate, at least to some degree, close to the end of their lives.

This section will likely be read by both the person who is dying and by those who love and care for that individual. We are writing it with the dying person foremost in our minds. We want to walk the final leg of the journey with you. But we know that people who love you will also be walking alongside you. They can benefit from knowing what to expect as you are dying, and once you have died from knowing how they can begin to grieve the reality of your absence.

The Difference between Dusk and Midnight

Throughout this book we have used the metaphors of daylight, dusk, and midnight to designate the movement from health through a potentially terminal diagnosis to imminent death. We now move from the shadows of dusk into the darkness of the night—midnight has arrived. All reasonable options have been exhausted, and your body no longer responds to any further treatment. The end of your attempts to cure or preserve your life has come. Medicine does eventually fail. Nothing can ultimately save any of us from death. At times it appears that persons in the medical field could acknowledge more openly the limitations of their healing ability and make earlier referrals to and be supportive of palliative care options. If your medical care provider hasn't helped you in making the shift, you may need to take the initiative to change your focus from trying to beat the disease to making your transition into death as peaceful, pain free, and emotionally rich as you can.

Deciding you want no further curative medical treatments is part of what midnight is all about. You admit that you will undoubtedly die and no longer actively pursue medical attempts to reverse the progression of your disease. We refer to that as a palliative care philosophy. Palliative care can be defined as "the active total care of patients whose disease is not responsive to curative treatment. Control of pain, of other symptoms, and of psychological, social, and spiritual problems is paramount. The goal of palliative care is achievement of the best possible quality of life for patients and families."[25]

The world-renowned movement in palliative care known as hospice originated in England and began in the United States in Connecticut in 1974 as a grassroots effort to provide compassionate care for patients at the end of their life with the focus of "living until you die." Hospice organizations understand dying as a part of the normal life cycle and work to support the dying person and the family by providing physical care and oversight of medical management either in the person's home or in other facilities (see sidebar 18).

GETTING IN TOUCH WITH HOSPICE   ⑱

If you wish to learn more about hospice, we encourage you to begin with the **National Hospice and Palliative Care Organization**. Contact them:

NHPCO
1700 Diagonal Road, Ste #625
Alexandria, VA 22314
Voice: (703) 837-1500
Fax: (703) 827-1233
Web: www.nhpco.org

Their web site contains a wealth of information, including a search engine to find a hospice in your vicinity and a full catalog of resources.

Hospice Net is another excellent web site (www.hospicenet.org) that provides excellent information for patients, children, caregivers, and the bereaved.

The Hospice Foundation of America is primarily dedicated to serving those who work in the hospice movement. However, under "Resources" there is free access to over fifty organizations that deal with various illnesses.

Hospice provides a supportive environment to help families learn how to deal with their loved one's progressive physical symptoms. Without that assistance many families eventually have a difficult time coping with the end-of-life care for their loved one and finally place him or her in a nursing care facility. Research indicates that most people prefer to die at home, yet only 25 percent of Americans died at home in 2001, with 50 percent dying in a hospital and 25 percent dying in a nursing facility. For those patients who died under hospice care, 52 percent died at home, 22 percent in a nursing facility, 10 percent in a hospital, and 8 percent in a hospice facility.[26] Hospice enables patients and families to develop a supportive environment in their home to help deal with their loved one's progressive physical symptoms. When home care is no longer possible, the patient can be transferred to a nursing facility, a hospice inpatient facility, or another treatment option and still remain under the hospice team's care. Hospice care is limited to those people who are expected to live six months or less if the illness (whether cancer or some other terminal disease) runs its normal course. Of course, this time frame is often difficult to determine precisely. Predictions of longevity are especially difficult for patients with chronic illnesses such as some types of heart or lung problems or neurological diseases. Some hospices would like to change that regulation so that a person can receive palliative care if needed and desired before the six month period immediately preceding one's death. However, benefit rules under most health insurance programs and Medicare restrict longer use unless the prognostic time line is found to be in error and the person simply lives beyond what is expected. In that case, the physician will simply need to verify that the disease remains a terminal one. Hospice is covered under Medicare or Medicaid, as well as some private health insurances, often at a minimal cost or no charge to the patient. If you choose to use hospice, you will have a medically knowledgeable team including your physician, an R.N. care manager, nurses, a social worker, spiritual counselor, home health aides, physical and occupational and speech therapists, dieticians, and volunteers who will provide for your needs. Services such as nursing care, medical equipment and supplies, outpatient drugs for symptom management and pain relief, and physician's care are also covered.

As the dying person, you need to look realistically at whether or not you and your family want to utilize hospice to assist with the planning and coordination of your end-of-life care. We think there are definite benefits to hospice care even if right now you believe you have adequate support within your own family. Hospice can facilitate communication with your doctor for pain relief and other symptom management. Hospice care involves little or no cost to your family, often unlike arranging care through an independent health agency or hiring individual help and paying for medication and some medical supplies out of pocket. We recommend that you at least request that your area hospice conduct an evaluation of your particular circumstances. A doctor's order is required to initiate the evaluation for hospice care. Hospice can tell you what services they provide in your area. If your community has more than one hospice organization, check on the specific benefits each provides and compare which one best suits your family's needs. Hospice provides four levels of care including routine, continuous, inpatient, and respite care.

Family members of a dying person should be aware that sometimes dying patients may not want hospice involved, perhaps because their focus is narrowing and they are less aware of what is really happening. They sometimes overestimate what their family members can realistically do to provide for their care. As the family, you will need to remember you will be the ones providing the care to your loved one, and you need to know your limits as well as your strengths. When the dying person resists hospice care, we challenge you to be assertive and tell her or him you feel more comfortable checking out all the options. Then have someone from a hospice agency do an evaluation of your dying loved one's particular situation. The hospice staff person who does the initial assessment will be trained to discuss with the patient the benefits of using the hospice program. If you choose to use hospice and you don't like it, you can discontinue it at any time. If you choose to manage care without the assistance of hospice, you have at least explored hospice as an option, collected the information, and made contact in the event that the need arises later in the dying process.

One Last Chance to Make Final Arrangements

We are people who live in the day. We like the light. Daylight is a productive time, and sometimes we try to cram so much in that we frustrate ourselves with high, often unrealistic expectations. Many times when people hear a diagnosis that could be terminal, they think they still have plenty of time to do everything they need to. They believe a better time will come to plan their final exit. After all, there *will* be more time. Let's not do it now. There's no hurry. Does that sound familiar? You may be saying: "What does it hurt? I'll wait until I feel like it." But many times the "right time" doesn't come until it's really too late to think clearly or have the energy to do much—or it doesn't come at all.

We hear from many families that they never made final arrangements or talked specifically about some of the important aspects of dying with their loved one. Everyone involved may have a hard time facing the reality that their loved one is not going to get better this time as they may have done in the past with other close calls or illnesses. Even when the person is obviously weaker and has more limited function, people resist talking about death (even if they privately sense the end is near). This, as we have said before, creates distance between people because the dying person and family both undoubtedly know that the time left is short. Most dying individuals and their loved ones are relieved when the silence is finally broken. Then no one is left out of the loop about what will happen as the end of the person's life approaches.

So how do you break down the walls of silence surrounding the topic of dying? If you are a family member and want to find out what your dying loved one thinks and feels about his or her failing health, here are a few suggestions for how to start the conversation. Using an assertive approach, you could say, "I would really appreciate hearing what you are thinking about the seriousness of your condition." Or, "Would you be willing to talk with me about how you feel, because your health seems to be slipping away?" Or, "It would be helpful for me if you would be willing to share your views about dying. How do you feel about the possibility that you might die from this illness?" You will undoubtedly need courage to ask these types of questions of your dying loved one, because confronting unpleasant issues is often difficult.

If you are the person dying and your family resists talking about the seriousness of your condition, you can say, "It would be helpful for me if you would be willing to listen to me talk about my approaching death with you." Or, "Could I read you the ethical will I've written about my life and our relationship together? I'd like you to hear it before I die."

There are also many ways for either the dying person or family to open a conversation if the other party is resistant to the idea of talking about what is occurring. You might try saying, "It would give me a lot of comfort when I am (or you are) no longer here to have talked about what is going on in your mind and heart right now. It will be hard for me to die (or have you die) without having a conversation about these things." If the answer is still "no," you can at least ask the person to give your request more thought and then check back later to see if he or she is then willing to honor your wishes to have a conversation. Whatever the answer, you will know you tried to talk about the "hard stuff" even if the other person was not willing. Then you won't have to wonder if the other person just didn't know how to initiate a conversation about dying.

There are two specific questions to discuss regarding arrangements once you acknowledge your impending death. This is the time for one more review to ensure your affairs are all in their final order and your life can conclude peacefully knowing that everything is done that needs to be.

Question #1: Are Legal, Financial, and End-of-Life Decisions in Place for Your Death?

One very important area to revisit one more time is your legal and financial matters. In each section of this book we have examined these legal instruments from different perspectives. You may want to reread the portions in the first two sections that cover other aspects of these legal documents. By now everyone close to you should know you have a will or a will and trust and have appointed a Durable Power of Attorney to manage your affairs. Let your family know who will be carrying out your wishes once you can no longer manage for yourself. Begin to include your agent under the Durable Power of Attorney in making decisions about your finances (in consultation with you) even though you may still be able to yourself. That way the person has ample time to ask questions and discuss how you would like things managed when you can no longer be consulted. Give that person a complete picture of your current bills, debts, and financial holdings. This may be similar to what Susan experienced when the neurosurgeon told Rick the day prior to brain surgery that he needed to "get his affairs in order." She quickly gathered their important papers for a last-minute update with Rick on their financial picture in case he died during surgery or was mentally unable to handle finances again. She then continued to manage their finances throughout the course of his illness and death. Perhaps you have just learned you have a very fast-growing tumor and "may not last out the month." That will require some speedy planning depending on how much of this you have done in the past. You may have already lined up all your financial and legal affairs. Now you need to recheck them to ensure all your loved ones are aware of what you want them to know about your legal and financial status.

Your family will benefit from knowing that you have taken care of your financial matters and that you are confident the person named as the Durable Power of Attorney will follow the mandates in your will and trust. Telling your family at least that much answers some of their potential concerns, even if you want them to know nothing else. If you have a surviving spouse, you may want to let your immediate family know that he or she will inherit everything you owned jointly (if that is indeed the case). If your spouse died before you, then your family may want to know how and in what proportions your estate will be distributed. You may have heard stories of conflicts and estranged relationships developing following the death of a family member. Those sad tales often happen because the dying person didn't have the courage to tell his or her loved ones they weren't inheriting what they were promised or expected or that the funds simply weren't there anymore. Remarriage can complicate matters all the more. For example, a parent may have died and the surviving biological children expected to receive their father's estate only to discover that his second wife actually received the majority of it. Perhaps stepchildren may have even received a portion of it along with the biological heirs. Talking about this with your family may be difficult, but hearing your explanation is better than never understanding why the decision was made the way it was. Telling others how you want your estate divided can give you a profound sense of relief and will give your survivors confidence that they understand and are following your wishes.

With respect to the Power of Attorney for Health Care, review your document to ensure you have not changed your mind about the life-sustaining measures you may or may not want. You may benefit from reviewing those parts of the first sections that discuss this area in more detail. Make certain that the person whom you have appointed as Durable Power of Attorney for Health Care clearly understands your directives. Also discuss this thoroughly with your family so there will be no confusion if and when your directives need to be implemented, since that will undoubtedly be a very emotional time for everyone.

Whatever your situation, don't put these matters off for another day. Be prepared for the unpredictable. You can have peace of mind knowing you have all the bases covered by clarifying your desires now.

Question #2: What Are Your Priorities for Your Last Few Months or Weeks?

We have been talking mostly about your legal and financial dealings as well as the health care decisions that arise near the end of your life. Hopefully you have already made funeral and burial (or cremation) arrangements. Turn to the first and second sections of this book to review the basic information and options in considering these issues as well. If you have not made these arrangements before, do so immediately! If you have already made these plans, review them now to ensure they still represent what you really want to have happen.

We also want to encourage you to give the same level of attention to talking with your family about a number of other "final wishes." These include those things you would still really like to do before you die. They may include taking a last trip, attending a reunion (perhaps even requesting one be organized), or engaging in a few of your best-loved activities. Some of these may no longer be realistic. Now is a good time to think of those things you still want to and can do. You might want to get all the grandchildren together one last time or visit your favorite beach or park. You could ask a family member to arrange a small gathering of your family and closest friends to celebrate your life and say good-bye. Many people have only a small window of opportunity still available to do something like that. As your disease progresses, it seems that doing this sort of thing becomes almost impossible. Do it while you can.

You may not have much time to talk about your "final wishes." Your disease may progress so rapidly that by the time everyone realizes what is happening, you may be too sick or weak to do much of anything. About four months prior to Rick's death, both Susan and Rick observed a decrease in motor function and with testing realized that his brain tumor had changed from a slow-growing astrocytoma into a more rapid form of cancer. They knew then he might not have much time or energy left for extensive "final wishes." Steroids were prescribed to help forestall the swelling of Rick's brain, and his physician approved hospice to assist with his care. The focus on curing the disease changed quite rapidly to a palliative approach as they now realized that Rick would die soon. Susan and Rick still had time to talk about his thoughts and feelings about dying and adjust plans now that they knew Rick had little time left. They contacted people whom he had not seen for a while to let them know his death was near. As a result, one of his grad school friends whom he had not seen in years came from out of state for a visit. Rick was also able to spend special time with his family knowing they would have to say good-bye to each other soon.

Susan knew that Rick still wanted to go to their favorite spot in Pentwater, Michigan, for a final summer weekend with Susan's parents and some out-of-state friends. That annual event had always been meaningful for their family. That weekend, approximately one and a half months before his death, would be the final block of time Rick would spend with their daughter, Sarah, before she left in the fall for an out-of-state university. His final wish was to create some special memories for both of them by spending time together. Two or three weeks before he died, Rick also managed to attend a play and a football game—two other experiences he wanted to have one more time with Susan and their friends. He actually didn't have much energy for either of those events and dozed some of the time, but he was still able to experience the ambiance of these activities and was grateful he could do them. During his eighteen-year battle with cancer, Rick and Susan's motto was to do everything they could do together until he was no longer able to. Rick wanted to live life fully until he couldn't anymore. And he certainly did that in every imaginable way! You may be perfectly content to live your final days or weeks without any major changes in your normal routine. But we would urge you to at least think about what else you may want to do and who you may want to see. Let others know of your impending death and give them an opportunity to contact you.

Two different sets of interests are part of this prioritizing process. Obviously, as the person dying, you have the dominant voice since your life will be the one ending soon, and your family will undoubtedly want to help in any way possible to meet your wishes. You may want to do some things that you can no longer do physically. Susan recalls that Rick thought he could still take one more trip to California, but she realized he was not physically able to do that. Bob remembers that the week before Char died, she wanted to get out of bed but didn't even have the strength to lift up her arm. Talk about which of your final desires can be met. The fact that you have talked about your last wishes may be comforting to both you and your family.

The other set of interests is that of your family members. Encourage your family to be candid about what they may like to do with you during your final days. Try to make that happen as well. We have met family members who regret passing up an opportunity to simply talk with their dying loved one, much less do one last meaningful activity together. Regret is sad, especially when it could have been avoided.

Taking time to be by yourself during this last leg of the journey is also important. Maybe you haven't learned how to relish being alone, but this is healthy and necessary, especially at this point in your life. If you have reserved time for reflection throughout your diagnosis and dying process as we have been suggesting, you won't be uncomfortable with this recommendation. But regardless, consider where you are headed shortly. You are about to embark on something you have never done before—the act of dying. Your physical body will soon be dead. This will certainly be a trip far more extensive than any you have taken before. Remember how you would plan, make a list, and pack for your vacations? True, you can't take any belongings with you on this trip. But preparation for dying needs even more forethought than any vacation. Think about what will happen when you breathe your last breath. Prepare your heart and soul by making peace with yourself and your God. If you believe in an afterlife, spend time thinking about where you are headed. Be sure you are "right" with God, whatever that may mean to you. Pray. Ask for forgiveness. Meditate. Read Scripture. Listen to sacred music. Get ready! And let your family know you are ready.

Getting the Emotional Support You Need When You Need It: Visits from Others

One of the most frequently expressed wishes of dying people is to have their family close at hand as their condition weakens and they prepare to die. It can be reassuring to know your loved ones are nearby to visit with you as a way to show their caring and support. Generally, family members are very intent on being available, as their schedule permits, when you need or want them. Just remember, however, you have to be clear about what you would like and from whom. Bart, who was dying of lung cancer, actually had his wife schedule visits for his family and friends while he was still strong enough to talk. She would call to tell a friend or family member that Bart wanted to see her or him at least one more time at a particular time if that worked for both of them. That way when he became too weak to carry on a conversation, he and every one of his loved ones had the wonderful memory of their last talk together. You might also want to plan a visitation schedule. So speak up about who you would like to have visit. Talk about what time of the day and for how long you may want to see certain people. You will need to do this sooner rather than later. Some people want to wait for a "right" time, which never arrives. Don't plan on having time at the very end. One visit is usually sufficient for those who are not your closest or most intimate family or friends. The visit itself provides an opportunity to say good-bye and bring closure to your relationship with them by sharing feelings with each other. If you wind up having more time, you can still have them visit again, but a second visit is no longer critical for either party. As your energy wanes, your focus may narrow to a few select friends or family members. There is often a direct correlation between your increased discomfort as your disease progresses and your decreased level of alertness, ability to communicate, and tolerance for visits.

Undoubtedly you would really like to have certain people available as you end your life. Talk with them about what you want. Let them know if you would like them to pray with you, read favorite Bible passages or other literature selections, play certain music, or sing to you. Both you and your family want you to be comfortable and to help meet your needs as best they can. Remember we are not only talking about physical needs. All human beings also have emotional, social, psychological, and spiritual needs that require attention, particularly when a person is in the process of dying.

A primary concern dying people often voice is that they don't want to become a burden to others as they become increasingly sick. Yet the people closest to you will want to be around if at all possible as your condition worsens. You have likely been there for them when they needed you. Hopefully you had a history of healthy, balanced, "give and take" relationships with your loved ones. Now it's your turn to take their offers of caring. Interestingly, this circle of care completes itself and can be very satisfying for the people who love you. Let them do for you what you can no longer do for yourself. It is their final gift to you. We have already talked about your value and worth. Having healthy self-esteem will help you acknowledge your own significance and be able to accept others' expressions of caring graciously. Life often does have a way of coming full circle.

Will Your Family Actually Provide for Your Care?

One important thing to discuss with your family is how (if at all) they will function as caregivers when the need arises. We are not talking here about your family just being around to keep you company. We are talking about how and in what ways your family can and wants to actively participate in providing for your physical and medical care. First you will need to decide what you need for your physical care. Then you can determine your family's ability and desire to meet those needs. Once you have talked about this with them, you can determine if you also need to hire supplemental care, enlist the services of a hospice provider, or at some point move to a residential treatment facility. You may be in a situation in which you actually do not want your family to provide any of your physical care, so supplemental help is all the more important. Hopefully your family will respect your wishes if you can make other realistic arrangements. On the other hand, you may want your family's caregiving assistance, but they may not be able or willing to give it. Your family might feel you expect everything to revolve around what you want, even to the point of expecting them to take time off from work to provide for your care. As much as your family may want to help you, they may not be financially or functionally able to do so. By "functionally" we mean they may have other responsibilities that cannot be left unattended, such as child care or work needs. Geographic distance may be an issue, or perhaps they cannot provide physical or emotional support. Unfortunately, life doesn't usually wait for us to get through caring for a dying loved one before the pressures and expectations of normal life resurface. You and your family members both have legitimate needs and wants that require consideration. Everyone involved will likely feel the pressure to maintain the difficult balance between being with you and attending to their own responsibilities. If you need more care than your family can provide even with additional help from hospice or a private health service, you might investigate a residential hospice facility or an extended care facility as you become more dependent on others for your care.

If your family is able and willing to function as your primary caregivers, both you and they may realize the benefits of spending this large amount of time together. It can help make your relationship even closer and help you both develop a sense of peace even in the midst of your discomfort. While providing care is often very difficult, most family members feel a sense of satisfaction knowing they did what they could for you. They may feel relieved that you did not have to go to a nursing home or extended care facility but could remain in your familiar environment.

It is often a difficult decision and a stressful time for you as the dying person and your family to make a realistic decision about who can provide the necessary care. Hopefully your family will know they acted responsibly toward you (particularly if you are a parent, spouse, or child) in that they did what they could to be helpful regardless of what they were actually providing for your physical care. You and your family may benefit from a greater sense of cohesion by understanding each other better and working together in making a decision that can be supportive of your care.

Most people who spend time with you as you die experience personal growth in the process. The experience of coming face-to-face with someone who is dying can be rewarding. They often have an opportunity to discuss with you various aspects of your life and your perspectives in more detail. They can hear from you what you valued most in this life. Being with our dying partners gave both of us not only a sense of satisfaction in doing everything we could for them but also a greater understanding and peace about our own potential deaths. To have been so close to someone in the dying process often removes some of the mystery and anxiety about what it is like to die. In a real sense, as you die you can teach the rest of us a great deal about dying and death by letting others observe and walk alongside you on your final earthly journey.

Who Do I Want with Me during My Final Days?

The people you would like to have around probably can't be available twenty-four hours a day, seven days a week. Even if death is near, no one can predict the exact time you might die. You may have heard of a family member sitting almost continuously with their dying loved one but finally leaving to grab a sandwich or stepping out of the room to stretch his or her legs—and just then death steals in. The dying person and family members need to understand that although they can do some things to ensure that family will be around, no one can guarantee that any one particular person will be present at the actual time of your death. Your family could devise a visitation schedule so that at least one family member can be with you around the clock if you have a large enough family to do this.

Many of us have probably painted a rather idyllic picture of having our loved ones gathered around the bedside holding our hand as we die. In this fantasy we would still be alert enough to be able to say the last good-byes and then peacefully shut our eyes and die. But this doesn't happen as often as dying people or their loved ones may want.

Even if you do not make a twenty-four-hour visitation schedule, you may want your children and close family around you as you die. Make a plan so someone can notify them as the time approaches. If you are married, you may want only your spouse with you at the moment of your death. In that case, let your partner clearly know your wish so that he or she will not call in other family members as that time draws near. Remember, this is your death and you get to decide (as much as possible) how you would like things done when the time comes. Hopefully you will be sensitive to other people's feelings in making your choices, but your family will know they helped fulfill your "final wishes."

Communicating in These Last Months, Weeks, and Days

Nearing the end of your life is, no doubt, very difficult for you and your family. We have certainly stressed the importance of your (and your family's) ability to talk openly about everything that is going on. Bringing up the subject of dying may be difficult. At some point in your illness, unless you die suddenly of a heart attack or stroke or go into a coma, you will realize that you are going downhill rather quickly and the time has come to talk candidly about the fact that the end is getting very near. This would certainly be the time for final good-byes as well as the time to discuss how others might keep you comfortable in your final days. Ideally you will have already talked with your family about what you would like done when you are no longer able to communicate those wishes directly.

Your family members must realize that even if you can no longer respond either verbally or nonverbally, you will still likely hear what they are saying. Encourage them to talk with you even if it seems one-sided. This may be awkward for them at first, but help them imagine they are the one who is dying. They might be able to sense how frustrating it would be to know that the people you love were standing at the bedside but were no longer talking with you or were even discussing your situation in the third person. We have heard of situations in which families were talking among themselves about funeral arrangements in the same room as their dying family member. That kind of conversation seems inappropriate and insensitive for the dying person to have to hear. The family probably wasn't aware that hearing is the last sense to go as a person dies. You can't be certain when the dying person is no longer able to hear conversations. Let your family know you would like them to talk *to you* (not about you!) as if you were fully conscious until you have died. If you are aware of what they are saying, you will sense their comfort and reassuring support. Even if you cannot hear them, they will still benefit by putting their feelings for you into words one more time. They will be paying attention to you and not just sitting there quietly watching you or talking about something else that doesn't include you.

We want to say a word or two directly to the family who is with their dying loved one. As family, you may not have the courage or desire to give permission for your loved one to die. Or you actually may not know how you feel about this. To say to someone that you are okay with their dying when you feel so fragile and scared about facing life without him or her is tremendously difficult. We have been in that position ourselves, and it can be heart wrenching. But we have good reason to believe that telling them you are ready to say good-bye and they don't have to hang on any longer for your sake actually helps them with the final transition. Perhaps you have also heard of a dying person who tries to remain alive until a certain person can arrive. When that person finally arrives and speaks to the dying person, he or she is then ready to let go and dies. This seems to indicate that sometimes a dying person may be able to exercise a degree of control over the actual timing of death. Particularly when people are closely attached to one another, the dying person may cling to this world thinking that his or her loved one is not ready to have them leave. This final good-bye is often so difficult for the family to say. If the dying person could regain quality in his or her life, the family would wish them back in a heartbeat. Probably the person who is dying would want that too. Unfortunately that is usually not the situation. By then the dying individual undoubtedly has little functioning ability left. Very few families would want him or her back with the severe physical or mental limitations they had near the time of death. In fact, most family members would readily admit it wouldn't be good to have their loved one return in the condition he or she was in as they were dying. The quality of one's life seems to us to be more important than the length of one's life. Most of us would like to have both quality and quantity in our life if we possibly could, but that is not possible when a person is dying. When death is imminent, it is so helpful to release the dying person by lovingly saying good-bye.

Now It's Time for Life Closure: Letting Go and Dying a "Good" Death

We have talked throughout this book about summarizing your life, but the closer you get to actually dying, the more you realize your earthly journey is really coming to an end. We have encouraged you to finalize your legal and financial matters, to reconcile all significant relationships, and to stay open to receiving your family and friends' love and caring while dying. Hopefully you now have a sense of completion in the relationships you held dear while healthy. You may now realize more fully the finality of your time on earth but also see more clearly what life has taught you. The time is approaching to let go.

This whole idea of "letting go" is difficult to understand. When we are healthy, accepting the possibility of our own death is hard to do. As humans we want to hang on to our lives, even if we believe in an eternal life. But accepting the fact that you will now die means you have to "let go" of all that holds you here. This is known as *disengaging*. Disengaging is an extremely painful, heart-wrenching, and grief-filled process, because at death you separate from those you love. Now you begin to realize that your life with your family is ending soon. You may withdraw into yourself. You may not want to watch television or listen to the news. You may be less concerned about all the social news visitors talk about when they come to see you. You may even be less interested in other people, especially those who were on the outer fringes of your life. In your own mind you may be remembering your life, contemplating where you are going, and musing on how you feel about this direction. Yet to others, you may often seem to be sleeping because you may just lie in your bed quietly with your eyes shut. Your family may be troubled when they see this happening. Family members might even feel hurt or rejected because they assume you are no longer interested in the normal affairs of their lives. But in fact your focus as the person dying normally becomes more inwardly directed. You are embarking on a journey on which no one else will be accompanying you. And so as you become weaker you may not be interested in talking as much about this earthly life you are leaving.

You may be quite anxious about what lies ahead, because dying is a new and unknown experience. The unknown causes anxiety for most of us. That is where your personal faith comes in. Your personality also affects your reaction to dying. If you were keen on trying new things during your life and are in intense pain now, you may be more open to this entirely new experience ahead of you when you die. On the other hand, you may not believe in an afterlife but simply believe that death is the final end for you. In that case, accepting your life's ending may be more difficult, or you may simply have the stoic attitude that "this is all there is." Your life was good, and now the end has come. Nevertheless, this experience of dying may elicit some feelings of ambivalence and precipitate a reexamination of your beliefs. The question "Is there something beyond this life?" often pushes itself to the forefront of people's minds as they approach death—along with a corresponding response of "I sure hope so!" and, if they are religious, "It's what I believe!"

Have you heard the phrase "dying the good death"? As we "let go," almost everyone wants at least to die this "good" death. But many people are confused by the adjective *good* associated with the word *death*. Death doesn't seem good, so what does this mean? One way to think about a "good" death is that you don't experience undue pain or suffering in the process. Everything possible should be done to increase your comfort during the dying process so you are now able to quietly say farewell to your family in relative comfort. A second way to define "good" is to know your wishes about treatment and care have been honored. As the patient, you still have the power to choose viable treatment options. Making those decisions while you are still able preserves your dignity. Being allowed to function both physically and mentally in an independent manner until you are no longer able to do so is an important part of dying a "good" death. It is important for you to do what you still can and want to do for yourself, even though others may want to do those things for you. A third aspect of a "good" death is to know your final wishes will be respected regarding how and where you want to die and how the disposition of your body will occur. You may want to die at home with your family at the bedside, with as many family issues settled as possible, and with a clear sense of meaning and purpose to your life. Dying that way would be a "good" death.

The "good" death is what both the medical profession and your family also want for you. You should understand that your worth is not based on how much normal function you have left. The time may come when you have no control over bodily elimination or you are no longer mobile. This does not make you less valuable. If you have read *Tuesdays with Morrie*,[27] you may remember that Morrie Schwartz knew that someday someone would have to wipe him because he could no longer take care of his own elimination needs. He had to come to terms with the "nitty-gritty" realities of dying. Unless death is sudden, people generally lose physical functioning in the process of dying. Don't confuse that with your dignity or life's value. You still are extremely significant in and of yourself and to those who love you, and you can still achieve the qualities of dying a "good" death.

On occasion a dying person may consider either suicide or euthanasia as a way to take the situation into his or her own hands. Maybe the pain is intolerable, the physical weakness is unacceptable, or patience is waning as the body slowly deteriorates prior to death. Of course, these situations are very difficult to handle. But if you are considering this, we would urge you to think about three things. First, in this book we have often drawn the parallel between death and birth. Both are natural processes that follow their own timing. We believe taking your own life makes as little sense as a mother deciding in her fifth month to give birth to her child because she can no longer endure the pregnancy. Second, most mental health professionals and medical personnel recognize that suicide is not a rational choice under any circumstance, even when temporarily facing one of life's major difficulties. Professionals do whatever they can to intervene when someone becomes actively suicidal. Why should that be any different at the end of one's life? Third, if you are coming from a religious perspective, most religions acknowledge that God is in control and therefore the one who ultimately allows death to occur—we are not in control of the timing of our death. However, we can control to some extent the way we go about managing the dying process by the choices we make. We believe that dying a "good" death means a person would allow their life to run its natural course. Pain medication and other palliative treatments can generally make the dying process comfortable and nearly pain free.

This actual dying process does not always go smoothly, however. At one time or another the pain medication may not be strong enough, the oxygen not delivered promptly, or a medical person may not be as compassionate as they could be. Having those things happen near the end of your life can remain a challenge for your loved ones to accept even after you die. Following your funeral your family may have to deal with their feelings about how they (and others) handled the last-minute complications or challenges during your dying process and immediately following your death. If that is the case, family members will need time to work through their feelings about all these issues. Reassure your family that you have confidence they will handle your dying experience the best way they can at the time. We cannot plan for every eventuality. Life and death aren't that tidy and predictable. Only hindsight can give us a clear picture of how the situation actually worked out. Hopefully your family can deal with any guilt or regret they may have and eventually reframe the situation and place it in the past.

For Loved Ones: The Aftermath of Letting Go

We want to say another word directly to the family and friends of the person who is dying. We all die when it is our time. For those who believe in an afterlife, death can be a joyous transition for your loved one to go to his or her heavenly home for all eternity. This new life is often understood as a place with no more pain, sadness, or suffering. The problem for those left behind is that the grieving process following a loved one's death is a painful, yet necessary, individual journey. The intense pain of grief comes precisely because a loving attachment to the deceased person was forcibly broken at death. So if you had a meaningful relationship with the person who died, you *will* hurt. That is the price you pay for loving someone. During the time your loved one was dying, this process of separation was undoubtedly difficult for her or him as well. However, most religions that believe in an afterlife also suggest that there is no awareness of painful things in heaven. It would follow then that once the person has died and his or her soul or spirit has transcended this world, they no longer experience the sadness of the separation. One way to look at eternity is as a place that is timeless, no longer bound by the constraints of our earthly time. In that case a dying person would experience no time lag between his or her death and the end of the world, a time when, according to the Christian faith, all people will be gathered together. No matter what your beliefs about death and heaven, we encourage you to consider that when your loved one dies a physical death here and leaves this broken world, he or she no longer experiences the pain and grief of leaving you and other loved ones behind. If you have more spiritual or faith questions, we would advise you to seek pastoral counseling to clarify these issues.

The Physical Aspects of Dying: The Last Few Weeks and Days

Predicting how long you might have left to live is difficult, almost impossible. Progressive and gradual changes occur within the body as vital functions slowly shut down during the dying process. Family members often think that death must be imminent because you are no longer eating or drinking for the last few days. However, that is not likely the case. A person can go for three weeks or more without food or fluids, depending on their previous hydration and nutrition levels. You might be surprised how long some people can survive without any nutritional intake. Because your family may notice the changes we discuss in this section, they may expect you to die soon. But death can take longer and be more elusive than expected. If you have ever watched someone die, you probably have a deeper appreciation of the phrase *"process* of dying."

Whether you are the one dying or a member of the family, you may know very little about what to expect will happen near the end of life. This section is written to help you understand some of the common physiological changes that occur in a dying person's body as various bodily functions shut down. However, remember that even though there may be some common patterns, no two deaths are alike. Each individual is unique, and that includes how you will die as well.

We will begin by discussing the inevitable changes in appetite and thirst that occur as a person gets closer to death. Susan knows from her work as an R.N. that families have a difficult time seeing their loved one no longer asking for food or drink. This often gradually begins a few months prior to death and increases within the last few weeks of life.

Often the family tries to coax the dying person to eat or drink more. We all know that a person loses strength and eventually will not survive if he or she doesn't eat or drink. Most families don't want death to come, as much as they probably know their loved one is in the final phase of life. So they insist that their loved one has to eat! But remember, because bodily systems begin to shut down, the body doesn't need nutrition or fluids anymore. The body is no longer trying to maintain its normal functions. The person may even say he or she isn't hungry and nothing tastes good. Usually the taste for meat is the first thing to go, followed by other foods that are hard to digest. Cravings may also come and go. Trying to force a dying person to eat or drink something they don't want goes against this natural closure of bodily systems. As a matter of fact, evidence suggests that a terminal patient who dies after fluids and food have been discontinued experiences a more peaceful death because food deprivation increases an endorphin that has a pain-reducing effect on the body. As family, you can certainly ask your loved one if they want to eat or drink something but don't induce guilt or apply pressure if they don't want anything. Take "no" as a valid answer. Ultimately you need to accept that no one will be able to prolong your loved one's life.

As the dying person decreases food and fluid intake, the family can relieve his or her dry mouth and lips or the unpleasant taste in his or her mouth resulting from no intake by applying glycerin swabs or petroleum jelly to the lips, giving ice chips if the person can still swallow, and washing the person's face and mouth with a cool cloth.

The dying person may also experience nausea and vomiting. These are often side effects of the pain medications. Usually an additional medication can be prescribed to relieve the nausea and vomiting.

Loss of control of one's bowels and bladder can be quite disturbing to the dying person and awkward for the family. If alert, he or she may be uncomfortable having someone else clean up the results of incontinence. Protective pads on the bed itself or a diaper can be used for the incontinence problems. That will help keep the dying person clean and dry and reassure the family that their loved one is as comfortable as possible. It will also alleviate anxiety for the dying person in thinking that he or she is making a mess for the caregivers. As death comes even closer, the person will probably have fewer to no elimination needs because his or her intake is decreasing and the kidneys and intestinal tract are shutting down.

The family may notice other changes as well. As a person gets closer to death, his or her body temperature fluctuates between being cold and running a fever, accompanied with feelings of clamminess, perspiration, or both. Extremities become cooler or actually cold to touch. The skin color will probably change to appear cyanotic, or bluish.

That is because body systems are shutting down and the circulation is not functioning well. Blood pressure gradually decreases. The pulse often becomes irregular and thready (weak or difficult to detect) and seems to either become more rapid (greater than one hundred beats per minute) or decrease to zero. Breathing also alters near the end of life. Respirations often become distressing with shortness or gasping of breath (dyspnea) accompanied by more rapid or labored breathing. With dyspnea the person probably experiences what is called air hunger—the inability to get enough oxygen. In that case a person may seem panicky or anxious. Medications can help relax the person and alleviate these breathing problems. Sometimes oxygen is also beneficial. People often have Cheyne-Stokes breathing as they near death. This consists of periods of rapid, labored breathing alternating with apnea, which are spaces of time during which the person doesn't breathe at all for up to forty-five seconds. It almost seems like the dying person is forgetting to breathe. Many times a dying individual has fluid in his or her lungs, sounds congested, and may cough but not be able to handle the secretions. The noise from the congestion, almost like a snore, is known as a death rattle. Repositioning the person on one side or the other may be helpful. If the secretions are reachable with suctioning, the nursing staff may be able to use this procedure to make the person more comfortable. Within the last few hours before death, a "fish out of water" type of breathing may develop. This image is used because the person's breathing behavior mirrors the motions of a fish out of water. Generally no pain is associated with this phenomena, but the dying person does appear to be exhausted, which may be difficult for loved ones to watch.

Changes in cognitive function may also occur as death approaches. Frequently the dying person becomes disoriented, confused, or comatose close to the end of life, and therefore meaningful conversation is often no longer possible. Sleeping becomes the primary activity, and the dying person has difficulty keeping his or her eyes open. The person often can still be awakened if not comatose, but sleep actually increases to conserve energy as the body begins to shut down. Some people believe the dying person experiences an enhanced awareness of the spiritual realm awaiting them through visitations from a deceased loved one, or Jesus, and so on, as they prepare for the transition from this life to the next.

At times, restlessness, delirium, picking at bedding or clothing, or a general agitation may develop because of a lack of oxygen in the blood. This can be treated with medication. Occasionally a dying person is quite alert right up until the last breath and can still communicate with his or her family. This is a gift, but one that doesn't happen frequently. More often than not, the family stands by the bedside without any response from their loved one. Generally when near death a person no longer responds to their environment. However, as we have said previously, the dying person can likely still hear conversations even though he or she may be comatose.

One other phenomenon bears mentioning: The dying person may experience a surge of energy, or the "last hurrah," as some refer to it, a few days to a few hours before death. What typically happens is that the dying individual wakens from a comatose state and appears oriented and alert. The person may be hungry, get up and sit in a chair, and have a meaningful conversation with others around him or her. This can last a few hours and might actually give the family a sense of hope that the dying person's condition may be improving. However, the person will probably return to a comatose state after a few hours and die within a few days or hours of the energy surge. This "last hurrah" seems like his or her final good-bye to this world.

While none of these signs and symptoms of approaching death are easy to watch, this is the way an anticipated death usually occurs. But if you are the family waiting at the bedside, you can know what to expect and can recognize these signs and behaviors as normal. What you witness as a caregiver or family member is probably not the way your dying loved one experiences it because as their body shuts down, their focus and level of awareness changes. So try to remember when the time comes that while you may see your loved one as perhaps uncomfortable or having some difficulty, his or her actual experience may be far more comfortable than it appears. It is also reassuring to check with medical personnel to verify what is normal in the dying process and that nothing else needs to be done for your loved one.

Will I Suffer? Pain and Symptom Management

One of the aspects of a "good" death we talked about earlier is to be either pain free or have only minimal discomfort when dying. No one wants to suffer unbearable pain, certainly not at the end of their life. Some people fear that as they are dying they will experience horrendous pain and not be able to tell anyone about it because they can no longer talk. They fear they may be in a coma, be confused due to medications, have dementia, or have some other motor impairment. An anxiety for the dying person is that he or she may be helplessly trapped in his or her body and left to writhe in pain without others knowing about it.

Pain is a very subjective experience. If a person with a terminal diagnosis can no longer communicate, most medical personnel agree that the use of pain medication is warranted. In fact, medical personnel usually act as though pain may be present unless they are confident that is not the case. Medical staff often consult with family members who know the dying person well and are more familiar with his or her nonverbal behavior to determine when more pain medication is needed. If you as the dying person have any concern about this matter, talk with your family while you are still able about your fears of being in pain when you may not be able to communicate much. Some dying individuals and their family devise a system such as rating the pain on a scale of one to five. The dying person can use a hand signal to indicate the level of his or her pain in the event verbal communication is no longer possible. With all the medications available today, no one needs to be in unbearable pain as they are dying.

The Bedside Vigil

A dying person often asks that specific family members be present at the time of their death, and most families want to be there as well. Yet you as a family member may have some anxiety about actually watching someone die because you fear the unknown or don't want to watch someone who has been an important part of your life slip away. Naming your specific fears helps, whether it is the fear of actually watching the dying process; the fear of not being able to manage the situation if help is needed; the fear that the person will die while alone with you as the only family member present; the fear of having to watch your loved one suffer; or the fear that you won't know what to do when the person actually dies. Talk with appropriate medical staff to get answers to help alleviate these fears. Remember, all you really need to do as the family is provide a loving, supportive presence for your dying loved one.

A Light, a Person's Image, or Some Other Visualization from "Beyond"

Some people have had a "near-death experience," which simply means they were resuscitated and brought back to life after their heart stopped. They report experiences such as being in a tunnel heading toward a bright light and feeling peaceful. As family members, you may hear your dying loved one say something like that as he or she is dying. Not every death has this kind of experience, but some dying people report an enticing, peaceful sensation; seeing a vision or a bright, calming light; or seeing and talking with a person who has already died. They might even say they saw or talked with a figure they describe as God or Jesus.

Of course, we have no way to be certain what they actually saw, especially when factoring in the dying person's pain medication regime. However, most individuals who are in the process of dying seem less involved in this world and more focused on what dying is all about—letting go of this life and moving beyond it—as they get closer to death. Our prevailing hypothesis is that something pleasant or reassuring draws the dying person's interest from this world to the next and is helpful for him or her on the journey. We believe those of us left behind can be quite confident that the transition was a peaceful one for those who died.

Recognizing When Your Loved One Has Died

If you have never been present when someone died, you may be concerned about what will actually happen. What does dying actually look like? Throughout this entire book we have been talking about preparing for this one final moment, the very last breath. Watching someone die can be a traumatic and emotionally disturbing event. The impact can be reduced by knowing what you can expect to see when a person has died. You will observe a number of concrete signs including the following: The person will give no verbal or behavioral response; the jaw may fall open; the pupils will be fixed with open, the eyes appearing glassy;

WHAT A DYING OR DECEASED PERSON LOOKS LIKE   ⑲

AS A PERSON DIES:	AT THE TIME OF DEATH ITSELF:
• Often (but not always) the person will be sleeping or unconscious.	• Jaw falls open.
• Body temperature will begin to fluctuate between cold and a fever.	• Eyes open and appear glassy.
• Feet and hands will become cooler (down to room temperature).	• Skin color turns waxen.
• Skin will begin to turn bluish.	• Urine and stool may be released.
• Blood pressure will decrease.	• No verbal or behavioral response.
• Pulse rate will either increase or drop very low.	• Heart stops beating.
• The person may gasp for breath.	• No breathing.
• There may be a rattling sound in the lungs.	• No pulse or blood pressure.

the heart will no longer beat; breathing will stop; the skin will begin to look waxen and pale as the blood flow stops; the blood pressure will drop to zero; the body will become cool and extremities turn a bluish or purple color; and there may be a release of urine and stool (see sidebar 19 for a summary of signs of death).

If you are with your loved one when he or she dies in a hospital or some other medical setting, put on the call light to notify the medical staff. When they arrive, they will confirm the death and then offer you time with your loved one. If you are at home using hospice services, call the emergency hospice number. If you want time alone with your loved one or want other family members to gather with you, simply let the hospice nurse on call know when you would like assistance or that you will call back when you are ready for someone to come. If you are at home without having used a hospice or home health care service, call the attending physician for directions on what you should do next. If your loved one has been under medical care, the doctor may tell you to call the funeral home when you are ready to do so. If there is any question about the nature of the death, your physician may instruct you to call an ambulance or the police and have your loved one taken to the emergency room where the cause of death can often be determined through an autopsy. If the deceased person has not been in contact with a medical doctor recently, the medical examiner may need to be involved.

If hospice is involved, the R.N. on call will come to your home and verify the death as well as prepare your loved one's body for the funeral staff or assist you if you want to be personally involved. Many times the nurse, along with family members, will want to give the person a light sponge bath, especially if secretions or elimination were released at the time of death. You can also put clean clothes on him or her before others come on the scene. Stiffness of the body (rigor mortis) usually begins to set in about three to six hours after the person dies, so most funeral homes find it best to work with your loved one's body for positioning within that time frame. If your loved one's body will be embalmed for a visitation, it is a good idea to call the funeral staff relatively soon after the death (or hospice will do that for you) and check with them about when you wish them to come to remove your loved one's body to prepare it for the visitation. It is important to clarify this with them so as not to feel rushed in spending time with the deceased as a family before the funeral staff arrives.

Having said all of this, we want to emphasize that it is very important to spend time with your loved one *after* he or she dies. Don't feel hurried or pressured. You have adequate time to be with your deceased loved one and other family members. Sitting by, hugging, holding, or laying next to the person can actually be a wonderful experience and can create memories for later on. You don't have to be afraid of a dead body. Touch and hug him or her. Crying and spending time with the person alone or together with the family may be a special time of honoring and remembering. Perhaps you want to say a special prayer, read a favorite passage, sing a favorite hymn, or recall fond memories of that person with those you love gathered around the bedside.

When Char died, all of the previously mentioned signs occurred. At 11:15 on a Sunday morning, she gasped her last breath. The family all knew instantly she had died. For the next thirty minutes they quietly sat at her bedside, shared some precious memories, and prayed together. When everyone was ready, Bob called the funeral director with whom they had made arrangements. Those thirty minutes together were a wonderful, peaceful time before the hectic pace of the visitation and funeral began.

Susan waited anxiously for their daughter, Sarah, and Susan's parents to come from the airport. Sarah was flying home for a surprise celebration for her father's forty-eighth birthday the following day and to spend a final time together with him. When Susan heard that Sarah was on her way home, she told Rick to try to hold on a little longer. He seemed to work at breathing all afternoon, but finally exhaustion seemed to overtake him and he couldn't hold on any longer. Before they arrived, Rick died with Susan alone at his bedside. It was a quiet, peaceful passing. Susan spent time crying and holding him until Sarah and Susan's parents arrived. After adjusting somewhat to the news of Rick's death, they all had some individual as well as family time with him. Rick's parents also came over following his death. Being with Rick as a family helped them all begin to concretely realize he had died.

Once family members who wanted to be present at the time of death see their deceased loved one and you are all ready, one of the family members can contact the funeral home, or you can ask a medical person (if available) to do that for you. At that point be prepared to have the funeral staff take your loved one to the mortuary, where they will prepare the body according to your and your family's wishes. The removal of the body can be a very emotional experience. Susan remembers how difficult it was to watch Rick being carried out on a stretcher with his entire body wrapped in a sheet and realize he would never again be in their home—their normal shared environment.

The Funeral Staff Comes to Take the Body—Then What?

When the funeral personnel arrive, they will usually arrange a suitable time later in the day or the next morning (if the death occurs in the evening) for the immediate family to make final funeral arrangements. We suggest that you talk about who will go to the funeral home for that purpose. With every death there is a primary griever who needs to be the one who will make the final decisions about the funeral events. By a primary griever, we mean the very next of kin. In the case of a spousal death, it would be the surviving spouse; in the case of the death of a child, it would be the parents. If a parent dies with no surviving spouse, the primary grievers would be the children. That doesn't mean that other family members' input wouldn't be appreciated. However, we are suggesting that the family actually identify who the primary griever is so everyone knows who will make the final decisions. This person can also ask a few other family members to go to the funeral home to add their perspective if that seems appropriate. If the deceased had already pre-arranged the funeral, very little likely needs to be decided if the family is in agreement, and so the meeting at the funeral home serves primarily as a final verification of the deceased's and family's wishes.

When talking with the funeral home staff, remember that the funeral is designed for several purposes: to honor the wishes of the deceased, to meet the needs of the grievers, and to confront the reality of death. Hopefully you will have discussed the funeral arrangements with your loved one before his or her death. If not, make the best choices you can, perhaps discussing the options with other family members and the funeral staff.

There are few "shoulds" or "have to's" to follow. However, we would encourage you to keep in mind a few principles as you make your final choices. First, the evidence clearly supports the importance of seeing the deceased after the death (if possible). Do not worry that if you do this you will remember your loved one only as dead and not in any other situation. That is simply untrue. Our minds are much too intricate to fixate on only one visual memory, so you will recall all the other past images of that person as well. The second principle to consider is to space the funeral events (visitation times, the funeral service, and the burial or scattering) over a period of time, giving as much time as possible in between events. This will give those who grieve time to experience, express, and reflect on their thoughts and feelings. Even though our society likes things done "quick and easy," facing painful things is really most helpful on the grief journey. Otherwise, whatever you try to avoid by making things easy winds up having more power than what would have been the healthier choice. Giving yourself enough time to digest what is happening may be more painful and take longer, but it will help keep funeral events from becoming a blur for those who are bereaved.

We suggested earlier that the funeral events not only summarize and celebrate the deceased's life but also benefit the bereaved. The funeral marks the first step on the grief journey. Before then, grieving was focused on the loss of bodily function or other changes experienced by the dying person. Until the person is actually dead, you as family still have some form of relationship with him or her. That is why acknowledging the death is so important. The acknowledgment helps you begin to experience life without your loved one. It helps the bereaved begin to accept the reality of their loved one's death, to express some of the emotions involved, and to review some of the significant memories of the life they lived with the deceased. As you make the final arrangements, use your judgment on what you think would best honor your loved one and help you begin to digest the death and remember his or her life.

What Happens to Those Left Behind? Introducing the Grief Journey

We think it only fitting to briefly address the needs of the bereaved here because when a loved one dies, the bereaved often feels like the one who died was fortunate to not have to go on with life and experience this devastating grief. To think about living without your loved one is very difficult. You undoubtedly feel intense pain and a myriad of other emotions because you loved and were attached to that person who has now died. So in some ways, grieving is a tribute to and evidence of the significance that person had in your life.

It is important to realize that grief is a *normal* response to your loss of a loved one that affects you physically, emotionally, cognitively, spiritually, and behaviorally. Significant changes occur in the ways you now think, feel, and behave; they may be very different from what is typical or normal for you. Most all of the responses of grief fall into the acceptable range. You need to realize that under most circumstances (unless you are actively suicidal) you are not abnormal or "going crazy" but rather experiencing normal grief.

You may have heard people say, "Just give grief time and you will eventually feel better." Time is a necessary ingredient in the healing process, but it is only one aspect of effective grieving. In addition to taking time, grief requires intentional work to achieve a healthy outcome. Much like someone getting medical help to set a broken leg so that it might heal properly, you must take action to move through grief. The intentional work of grief can be summarized as five tasks that involve specific behaviors (things to do to help yourself work through grief). **The five tasks facing you as a bereaved person are:**

Task 1: Recognize and accept that your loved one has died and is unable to return. Although this task may sound obvious at first, head knowledge is not the only acceptance that needs to take place. You may have a difficult time accepting the emotional reality of your loved one's death and facing the harsh truth that the person is not coming back. Accepting the reality of a death emotionally can often take six to twelve months, and then usually only if you have intentionally worked at the process by putting yourself in situations that evoked painful emotions because of the death of your loved one.

Task 2: Experience all of the emotions associated with the death of your loved one. That includes experiencing all the occasions and special days that you now need to face without that person. If you attempt to suppress emotions by stuffing them inside, you will only have them come to expression later in more physically and emotionally detrimental ways. You eventually will achieve a healthier state by giving full expression to all the emotions (such as anger, sadness, guilt, regret, and relief) that you experience, as long as the expression is not destructive to you or others.

Task 3: Identify, summarize, and find a place to store the memories of your loved one in ways that will honor those memories and make room for you to eventually move on to a new chapter in your life. This means dealing with all the belongings, memorabilia, and pictures by sorting through them, writing or journaling about them, going to places you used to visit together, and recalling both the positive and negative aspects of your relationship. Resolution of grief *never* means forgetting your loved one. Memories are precious possessions that eventually need to be placed in your past. You are then free to live life fully in the present and to remember your deceased loved one only when you choose.

Task 4: Identify who you are now, independent of your prior connection with your deceased loved one. Basically you are an individual—that is how you were born and that is how you will die. As a result of the strong connection with those you love, the separation and resulting readjustments when a person dies are painful and difficult. In order to truly live a full and complete life again following the death of your loved one, you must discover or rediscover who you are *individually* and independent of the relationship you had with the deceased.

Task 5: Reinvest in life as an individual without your deceased loved one. You must learn to accept that all of life is marked by change. Each day calls for a new form of investment. You have experienced a deep trauma, but eventually this can be seen as an opportunity to reevaluate your present life pattern and begin again in a new and fresh way.

You might wish to consider a number of other things to better understand the grieving process. For example, the grieving process usually takes a *minimum* of one year to experience all the "firsts." The grief process may take as long as two or three or even four years, but the intensity of the emotional pain should gradually decrease during that period of time. Important decisions should not be made too quickly, because you will feel differently about things as you move through the grief process. There is great wisdom in the advice to wait *at least* one year before making any major changes or moving on with your life.

Having had some warning or advance notice that your loved one was going to die does *not* reduce the intensity of the grief or pain. Anticipating the death may have helped motivate you to do some planning with your loved one (such as concerning financial, funeral, and relationship matters), which might eventually serve to make the grief process less cumbersome or complicated. Nonetheless, this is the first time your loved one is no longer present, and the pain of that loss is every bit as intense as in the case of an unexpected death.

Know as well that comparisons with other people who may also be grieving are unhelpful and unhealthy. Grieving is an individual journey that is affected by many factors, including your personality and that of the deceased, the type of relationship you had with the deceased, and the present circumstances of your life (age, family structures, finances, health, employment, children, and so on). You are unique and so was your relationship with the deceased.

Grief work is designed to help you move *through* your grief. Hopefully you will not grieve for the rest of your life. On the contrary, you can "resolve" your grief and move again into a happy and satisfying life. "Resolution" means, by our definition, that the emotional pain of the death no longer controls your day-to-day activities (although you can recall your earlier pain) and you are able once again to develop a perspective on your life that is positive and future oriented. Moments may still arise that trigger a temporary resurgence of emotional response to the death of your loved one in a similar way that emotions are associated with other past events in your life. Resolved grief, however, means that you have been able to construct a new "normal" lifestyle that is fulfilling and purposeful without holding on to and without forgetting your deceased loved one.

So when your loved one dies, the grief journey begins in the sense that you now grieve the *total* loss of that deceased person because he or she is now absent from your life in every way except in your memories. The analogy of a journey is an appropriate one because you will not end up where you started. This journey is a process that takes much time and work. However, we want you who have been or will soon be thrown into the state of grieving to recognize that although you will always remember your loved one, you can eventually get to the other side of grief—a place where you won't feel the intense pain or longing you once felt. You will be able to see the joy that life can again hold for you. This may seem impossible to believe right now. But after your loved one dies, the reality will eventually dawn that you did not die. Your loved one did. The memories you hold dear can be retrieved whenever you wish. You can always cherish the time you spent with your deceased loved one. You may forever be grateful for the ways that special person enhanced your life and for what you have become because of your relationship to him or her. And for all your hard work in getting through your grief, you will recognize the ways you have grown and how you have created a new normal without your loved one. Grief helps you become a new version of yourself with an enhanced purpose and direction in your life!

CHRISTIAN MEDITATIONS ON FACING DEATH

Do not let your hearts be troubled. Trust in God; trust also in me. In my Father's house are many rooms; if it were not so, I would have told you. I am going there to prepare a place for you. And if I go and prepare a place for you, I will come back and take you to be with me that you also may be where I am.

John 14:1–3

For the Lord himself will come down from heaven, with a loud command, with the voice of the archangel and the trumpet call of God, and the dead in Christ will rise first. After that, we who are still alive and are left will be caught up together with them in the clouds to meet the Lord in the air. And so we will be with the Lord forever. Therefore encourage each other with these words.

1 Thessalonians 4:16–18

And I heard a loud voice from the throne saying, "Now the dwelling of God is with [his people], and he will live with them. They will be his people, and God himself will be with them and be their God. He will wipe every tear from their eyes. There will be no more death or mourning or crying or pain, for the old order of things has passed away."

Revelation 21:3–4

Bowing Low

Again, the devil took him to a very high mountain and showed him all the kingdoms of the world and their splendor. "All this I will give you," he said, "if you will bow down and worship me." Jesus said to him, "Away from me, Satan! For it is written: 'Worship the Lord your God, and serve him only.'"

Matthew 4:8–10

Why is it so hard to let go of this life?

*A*s we begin this third section of meditations, we return to the temptations of Jesus. We have considered each of these temptations in the light of a situation you might presently be in with respect to your health. The "Daylight" section addressed the issue of life and death from the perspective of someone who was healthy. The "Dusk" section addressed that issue from the perspective of someone who had reason to be concerned more immediately about dying because of a potentially terminal illness. This third section now looks death in the face, when you are reasonably convinced that your death (or that of a loved one) is fairly imminent. That means you are facing a potentially difficult and traumatic experience. You likely have to make more choices than ever, many of them major ones and nearly all of them dealing with the quality and the extent of the life you may yet have to live.

The third temptation of Jesus has something profound to say about that situation. As with the other temptations, Satan poses an alternative to Christ. In this case as they are standing on top of a high peak where they could survey the entire world together, Satan proposes to Jesus what appears to be a quick way to become king of all the world. The choice is simple: either engage in a moment of genuflection at Satan's feet or endure the horrific suffering of death by crucifixion. Jesus is offered an easy way out. Either way he would be king, or at least that was what Satan wanted him to believe. But of course we know that if something sounds too good to be true, it probably isn't true! Jesus knew that too. He makes his choice. He would not yield to Satan's temptation. It is written: "Worship the Lord your God, and serve him only."

What does this have to do with accepting the possible nearness of death? If you have heard the diagnosis from the doctor, or have already contracted for hospice services, or maybe just know deep inside your soul that your days are limited, accepting that reality is not easy. Maybe, you think, there is an easier way. Maybe a miracle. Or this might just be a bad dream that isn't really happening. Add to that the encouragement of well-meaning family and friends telling you to keep on fighting. "Don't give up." "Maybe there's something that can still be done." Maybe there still *is* something that can be done, but at some point you need to face reality. It may be time for the end to come.

Like a child who doesn't want the merry-go-round ride to end, our human nature seems to cling to life. We're tempted to do almost anything to put off death, to avoid it, or to ignore it. No one can really tell you when you need to finally accept the fact that death is near. Some people seem to be able to do it sooner than others. But notice something unusual about Jesus' response in this temptation. In the first two temptations, Jesus carried on a conversation with Satan—a type of debate. They both quoted Scripture. They bantered back and forth. But in both cases, Jesus prevailed by the power of his argument. But in his response to this third temptation, you can sense Jesus' passion. Perhaps it was anger rising in his soul because Satan was pressing in on him; maybe it was part of his human fear of what really lay ahead of him as he marched to the cross. Whatever the cause, Jesus lashes out at Satan: "Get away from me, Satan! I don't want to hear any more of this."

Doctors, nurses, family, and friends want you to survive. So do you. They will likely keep telling you that you can make it. Or else they might simply avoid the subject altogether with talk of the weather, football, or the recipe they tried last night. Regardless of what they do, they are tempting you to avoid facing the reality that you will likely die—perhaps soon. And you now have a choice. The temptation is to play along. Pretend that everything is still going to work out and the miracle will happen. Or you can say, "No! My time is coming. I have a journey to complete that I cannot avoid." You are probably pretty scared. After all, you have never done this before! Remember, Jesus was afraid too. Don't forget that scene in the Garden of Gethsemane in which he was struggling deeply in prayer. Sweat, like great drops of blood, was coming from his forehead. He wrestled with his Father: "Father, if you are willing, take this cup from me; yet not my will, but yours be done" (Luke 22:42).

You see, it is okay to continue to pray for a miracle. To ask for relief. To hope for a cure. But remember how Jesus concluded his prayer: "Not my will, but yours be done." He really already knew the answer. There was no other way. The cross was only twenty-four hours away. He would accept the reality of what was happening. It wasn't easy. But it was the only way.

No one ever said that coming to the end of your earthly life would be easy—especially if you still have a clear mind and are aware of what is going on. But you may sense you are getting weaker. The pain may be increasing. You heard the discouraging reports from the doctors. And you know, deep down, that the time is coming for your transition.

But remember how this temptation ends. Jesus doesn't even talk to Satan about kingdoms or ruling the nations. He basically says that only one thing is important in his life on earth, and that is serving his Father. That is the key to a successful and happy life and a good death. The well-known passage of Romans 8 emphasizes that neither death nor life shall ever be able to separate us from the love of God that is in Christ Jesus our Lord (Rom. 8:35–39).

Accepting the inevitable is sometimes hard to do. Perhaps a final focus on Jesus himself, however, may make it a little easier. Jesus had to choose the hard way of the cross (rather than give a quick nod to Satan) so that this eternal reward would be available to all of us. He endured the cross and suffered its shame for the joy and power of the resurrection that lay beyond. And because of that, we also have something wonderful to look forward to on the other side of death.

PRAYER: *Lord, I am amazed at how Jesus could stand up to Satan's temptations! So many times I have wished there would be an easy way out of my predicament. Yet Jesus was so patient, so solid in his conviction. May I have that strength as well, especially now that I am coming to realize and accept the fact that my earthly journey is going to end, maybe soon. Help me understand that the only "easy" way to do this is in Christ your Son, who went through death first so that we could have eternity to look forward to. Please help me with every step of this final earthly journey. Amen.*

Praying for the Miracle

In those days Hezekiah became ill and was at the point
of death. The prophet Isaiah son of Amoz went to him
and said, "This is what the LORD says: Put your house in
order, because you are going to die; you will not recover."
Hezekiah turned his face to the wall and prayed to the
LORD. . . . And Hezekiah wept bitterly. Before Isaiah had
left the middle court, the word of the LORD came to him:
". . . I have heard your prayer and seen your tears; I will
heal you. . . . I will add fifteen years to your life."

2 Kings 20:1–6

Do my prayers for healing really make a difference?

he story of Hezekiah is a fascinating one. He is one of the
many kings of God's Old Testament people. By the time
he comes on the scene, the nation of Israel has already
been divided into two separate countries. The half nation he now rules is
being challenged by their enemy Assyria. When Hezekiah became king,
he was only twenty-five years old. He remained king for twenty-nine
years and did many things to restore faithfulness to God's people. He
repaired and reopened the temple that had been shut down during the
prior king's reign. "He held fast to the LORD and did not cease to follow
him; he kept the commands the LORD had given Moses. And the LORD
was with him; he was successful in whatever he undertook" (2 Kings
18:6–7).

211

Wouldn't you like those words said of you? Isn't it true that Christians try to follow Christ, try to be faithful to him? Don't we pray that God will be with us in all that we do? But can we also say that we are "successful" in whatever we undertake to do? Well, before you begin to think that King Hezekiah was a "saint"—perfect in every way—we need to look more closely at his life and reign. His story is told in three different places in the Old Testament. You'll find it in 2 Kings 18–20 as well as in 2 Chronicles 29–32. And Isaiah also retells the story of Hezekiah's illness in his prophecy (Isaiah 32). If you read those accounts carefully, you will find that Hezekiah was no different than most of us—he was a believer who tried to be faithful to God, but he wasn't perfect. As a matter of fact, he made deals with his enemies, and (in the story that follows his healing) he was pretty proud. When Hezekiah was terminally ill, he prayed for a miracle. When God gave him the miracle, "Hezekiah's heart was proud and he did not respond to the kindness shown him" (2 Chron. 32:25). Hezekiah did repent of his pride later on.

Hezekiah's illness is the featured scene in the drama of his life. Pastors, theologians, and Christian believers have mused over this situation for centuries trying to understand a truly fundamental question: Can a person's prayer actually change God's mind? The story seems pretty straightforward. God tells Hezekiah to get his house in order because he is going to die. "You will not recover," God says (2 Kings 20:1). Sounds pretty direct, unequivocal, and certain! But then Hezekiah "turned his face to the wall"—a Jewish custom for prayer—and pleaded, almost argued, with God (2 Kings 20:2). In essence he says, "Look, Lord. I've been faithful to you all my life. I tried to run this nation in a way that pleases you. I restored the temple. I got rid of all the evil practices of the prior kings. This just doesn't seem fair!" You can read the actual words of Hezekiah in Isaiah 38, where he laments, "In the prime of my life must I go through the gates of death and be robbed of the rest of my years?" (Isa. 38:10).

Perhaps those words sound familiar. Isn't that somewhat like the feelings you might have, especially when the time has come for you to "put your house in order" and your death seems to be nearly inevitable? How often have you turned your face to the wall, cried out to God, reminded him of your desire to be faithful, and pleaded with him for healing?

But God does hear the prayers of his people! He certainly heard Hezekiah's prayer. He restored his health and promised him fifteen more years of life. When you are in the throes of pain, confronted by the inescapable march of death toward you, the question of whether God changed his mind or planned it all as part of some grand design is really an academic question. The fact is that Hezekiah pleaded, and God answered. Hezekiah would reign as king in Judah for another fifteen years. Prayer does work! God truly listens!

Another fifteen years likely sounded like a lot of time to Hezekiah. If you could count on fifteen more years, you would have time enough to see your children (or grandchildren) grow up. You would have time to really get your "house in order," especially financially, or travel to those places you wanted to visit. Hezekiah did go on to accomplish a number of other things. He built villages for people to live in as they harvested the bumper crops the nation had planted. He engineered an aqueduct to bring water into the city of Jerusalem. But do you know what happened at the end of those fifteen years? Hezekiah died. "Hezekiah rested with his fathers and was buried on the hill where the tombs of David's descendants are" (2 Chron. 32:33).

Perhaps the toughest question posed by this story is *not* "Does God answer prayers?" That question is really pretty easy—of course he does! He may not always answer our prayers in exactly the same way we prayed he would. But he hears us, listens to us, and responds to us as our sovereign, loving God. The tougher question you must ask yourself is "Why would I want to live longer than this?" Don't let the question startle you. The answer is not as obvious as you might think. Certainly our knee-jerk reaction is, "Of course I'd want to live longer!" But consider the question from another angle. When one of our friends was dying of cancer several years ago, he was often puzzled by people wondering why he didn't pray for a miracle of healing. Why didn't he ask for another fifteen years? Friends would press him, saying, "Don't you ever ask yourself the question 'Why me?'" His response was always straightforward. "No, I always say, 'Why *not* me?'" In essence he was saying, "Why should I expect any special favors? My life is in God's hands. My life on this earth is temporary. If I die at the age of fifty, will my life be less full, complete, or rich than if I die at eighty-five?" Of course, a longer life may seem to us to be fuller and richer from our earthly perspective. But our life is still earthly—with the mixture of joy and pain that has marked our lives up to this point.

Hezekiah certainly did some good things with his extra fifteen years. But the story does have a rather depressing (or realistic!) ending. His son Manasseh succeeded him as king. Manasseh was only twelve years old at the time—which meant that he had been born during those extra fifteen years. And Manasseh ruled for fifty-five years! But "he did evil in the eyes of the LORD, following the detestable practices of the nations the LORD had driven out before the Israelites" (2 Chron. 33:2). In other words, he undid everything good his father had done. Fifteen years on earth really didn't make much difference in the long run. Sin still reared its ugly head. Until this world ends, we will be fighting brokenness and evil. There will be disease—even if you were healed once. As a matter of fact, most of us have been healed many times: every time we had a cold, the flu, gallbladder surgery, or any other medical problem. We were healed! But finally, each one of us has to face the final disease (or traumatic accident) that will take us from this life to the next. Fortunately, God does answer our prayers, but he answers them in a way that is most helpful to us. For some reason he judged that fifteen more years would be a good thing for Hezekiah. This same God judged that another fifteen years would not be a good thing for our friend dying of cancer. That is what the Bible really means when it encourages us to pray, "Your will be done on earth as it is in heaven" (Matt. 6:10). There is something more beautiful beyond this life, and death is the only entrance to it. As these meditations progress in the coming days, we hope you will see the beauty and grandeur of what is to come and how in comparison this world becomes less important and significant.

PRAYER: *Dear Lord, I want so desperately to pray the prayer of Hezekiah. A real part of me does not want to let go of this life. And I truly believe that you have the power to change my circumstance, to cure me of this disease, and to give me a longer life. But also help me understand that a healing now is only a temporary fix for my predicament. I know that I will eventually have to die. Even if I do continue to pray for the miracle, work a miracle of grace within my heart by helping me accept the fact that someday—perhaps soon—I too will die. Amen.*

Grave Thoughts

*But someone may ask, "How are the dead raised? With
what kind of body will they come?" How foolish! What
you sow does not come to life unless it dies. . . . So will
it be with the resurrection of the dead. The body that is
sown is perishable, it is raised imperishable; it is sown in
dishonor, it is raised in glory; it is sown in weakness, it
is raised in power; it is sown a natural body, it is raised
a spiritual body. If there is a natural body, there is also a
spiritual body.*

1 Corinthians 15:35–36, 42–44

If my body dies, am I dead?

We don't like to talk about it. As a matter of fact, we usually do everything we can to avoid it. Death! It seems so final, so irrevocable, so sad. And it is! Death began already in the Garden of Eden when Adam and Eve ate of the fruit of the tree, for God had warned them: "You must not eat from the tree of the knowledge of good and evil, for when you eat of it you will surely die" (Gen. 2:17). The apostle Paul underscores the reality of death by saying that "the last enemy to be destroyed is death" (1 Cor. 15:26). When Paul was writing to the church in Corinth, many of the Corinthians thought that Christ would return in their lifetime. They didn't expect they would have to wait very long. But now some of their loved ones were dying. Not only was persecution hitting the church, but others were simply dying of old age. Now they wanted Paul to help them understand a little better what was happening. They even wondered if Christ really did rise from the dead! Maybe this was all a sham, a fake.

To this Paul boldly proclaimed that Christ has, indeed, been raised from the dead. Not only was he raised, he was the "firstfruits" of all of us—that is, he was the first one to do this so that the rest of us can also experience this resurrection (2 Cor. 15:20). But the persistent question, then, is this: What happens to this body when I die? After all, my body is my life. It is the only one I have ever had, and I cannot imagine my *self* existing without this body!

Here is where we run into one of the mysteries of the Christian faith. Paul has to use an analogy to explain what is happening: seeds. Think about planting a seed. The new plant cannot sprout and grow unless something happens first. That something is death—the death of the original seed. It has to fall to the ground and "die" before something new can grow from it. In the same way, Paul argues, the death of our body is like planting the seed. Unless this body dies, we cannot experience our new glorified body like the one Christ had. Let's look at this a little closer.

First, Paul is telling us, the bodies that you and I have had all our lives on this earth will die. They are fragile and weak. They eventually wear out and die. Each one of us has been sick many times throughout our lives. At some point one of those diseases (or some accident) is going to end your life in this body. No matter what physicians might attempt to do to our bodies, the best of them know that their work is ultimately a futile effort. Genesis 3:19 says that God made us from the dust of the ground, and to that dust we will return. Death is real. It cannot be covered up or ignored; it certainly will not go away. We will all die.

But let's take a look at a second issue. If my body dies, does that mean I, as a person, have died? Not at all, according to Paul. Even though the body may be destroyed, you go on living. All those who believe in Christ will experience the joys of heaven. Some Christian traditions believe that the soul is kept somewhere else until the return of Christ. Others believe that the soul goes immediately to be with God. Still others believe that our final entrance into heaven to be with Christ depends on additional prayers and intercessions from those on earth. The important issue here, however, is that we are going to be with Christ—and we will be there with a new, spiritual body.

Do you know what an oxymoron is? It is a combination of two words that seem to be opposite of each other—phrases such as "jumbo shrimp" or "icy hot." The term "spiritual body" sounds like an oxymoron. We almost always think of those two terms as being opposite each other. Either something is spiritual (which means nonphysical), or it is physical (which means it is not spiritual). The old body that dies like a seed is described as perishable, dishonorable, weak, and natural. But the new body is imperishable, glorious, and powerful. It is a spiritual body.

The reason for this change is quite simple, according to Paul. "I declare to you," he writes, "that flesh and blood cannot inherit the kingdom of God, nor does the perishable inherit the imperishable" (1 Cor. 15:50). This earthly body has to die in order for us to experience eternal life in our new body. This new body is a gift from God. Look closely at what Paul is saying: "Listen, I tell you a mystery: We will not all sleep, but we will all be changed—in a flash, in the twinkling of an eye, at the last trumpet. For the trumpet will sound, the dead will be raised imperishable, and we will be changed" (1 Cor. 15:51–52). And with that, "death has been swallowed up in victory" (1 Cor. 15:54).

The formation of this spiritual body has one other consequence for those who have died: They have left behind all the circumstances and situations of this life. In some ways, this is good news. All the bad stuff of this world ends when we die and inherit this glorious spiritual body.

But the good stuff of this world ends as well. A lot of the relationships and experiences that we have come to enjoy and treasure come to an end. That's why those who remain behind grieve. But that is also why we need to say our final good-byes. Matthew 22:30 gives one indication of the radical difference between this world and the next as Jesus reminds us that in heaven people will not marry. The implication is that all the normal relationships we have on earth will be redefined and reconfigured. In some sense, we may not like that thought very much while here on earth. After all, we love our families, spouses, and friends very much and can't imagine that whatever form relationships will take in heaven, they will be greatly superior.

But this passage is also saying that we will finally be able to see it all. We will stand in a place where it will all make sense. We will experience a life that never ends. Our earthly life is just a short prelude to the real life we will have in Christ. "Death," declares Paul, "has been swallowed up in victory. . . . Thanks be to God! He gives us the victory through our Lord Jesus Christ" (1 Cor. 15:54, 57).

Paul is reminding us that both processes are necessary: the putting off of the old and the putting on of the new. As the time gets closer for the seed of your body to be planted in the ground, you may be overwhelmed with the emotions of saying good-bye to this life. Don't lose sight of the fact that unless this seed falls to the ground, new life cannot come. Death is the only portal into heaven. It is not an easy road. But Christ not only walked that road before us, he opened the door so the gate stands wide open. He now waits with open arms for all who believe in him.

PRAYER: *Dear Lord, talking about seeds dying in order to sprout into new life sounds poetic on one level, but I must admit that the thought still scares me. I never thought of myself as a seed. The idea of being buried is overwhelming. I realize more and more that I am going to places I have never traveled before. As this body of mine decays and returns to the earth, protect me as I go through this transition. I hate to say good-bye to this body, but I also know it is wearing out. I don't want to leave my loved ones. I wonder what my new spiritual body will look like, what it will be able to do, and who I will know. Please help me be patient and trust you as I go through this transition—help me trust that this new life of eternity will be a spectacular place to which this earthly life can never compare. Amen.*

The Grand Parade at Christ's Return

And now, brothers and sisters, I want you to know what will happen to the Christians who have died so you will not be full of sorrow like people who have no hope. For since we believe that Jesus died and was raised to life again, we also believe that when Jesus comes, God will bring back with Jesus all the Christians who have died. I can tell you this directly from the Lord: We who are still living when the Lord returns will not rise to meet him ahead of those who are in their graves.

1 Thessalonians 4:13–15 NLT

What happens if I have already died when Christ returns? What is the hope for those still here?

Just like the Christians in Corinth whom you read about in the previous meditation, the believers in Thessalonica were concerned about what would happen after they died. While the Corinthians were concerned about what happened to the body, this group of Christians was more concerned about who might get to heaven first and who might not get there at all. It wasn't a selfish concern. They weren't vying for being first in line. Quite the contrary. Parents, spouses, siblings, and children had died. As these dear Christians thought and prayed about the return of Christ, they didn't want their deceased loved ones to miss out on the spectacular return of their king. They likely remembered the parable of the five wise and five foolish maidens—the foolish ones missed the wedding because they were somewhere else when the bridegroom came by (Matt. 25:1–13). The members of this early church in Thessalonica were now worried that if their loved ones were buried, they might not be able to experience the exhilaration of Christ's return.

In answer to their concern, Paul spells out the order of the triumphant parade of Christ's return. First, he shows that this victorious parade actually begins back at Golgotha—at the cross of Jesus. Then it moves to the empty Easter tomb. We believe that Jesus died and rose again. The death and resurrection of Christ are the key elements for the entire story. Anyone concerned about death, life after death, or the return of Christ must begin their journey at the cross and empty tomb.

Then the actual parade begins. As Christ promised the disciples (and us), he will return: "I will come back and take you to be with me that you also may be where I am" (John 14:3). But when he returns, he will *not* be coming alone. We are not talking about another solitary baby born of a virgin in a manger somewhere in the Middle East. We are talking about an entire entourage parading out of heaven back to this earth. "God will bring with Jesus those who have fallen asleep in him" (1 Thess. 4:14). Whether you are the person presently approaching the end of your life on earth or a loving family member or friend, we would encourage you to picture this heavenly parade. When Christ does come back, he will be accompanied by the multitude of people who have already died. They are now adorned in their "spiritual bodies," and these saints in the Lord have come with him to witness the final return. Paul assures us that as they are descending from heaven, anyone else who is still alive when this grand event occurs will join them for the grand reunion.

The result of this knowledge is that we are not to grieve like others who have no hope. We would also encourage you to read the word *grieve* as referring to all the losses you have had, are experiencing, and will yet experience. Grief isn't limited to the one event called death. We grieve the loss of many things. As the health of each of our spouses slowly deteriorated, we grieved the fact that they could no longer walk on their own, that they needed help with personal hygiene, that they were no longer able to enjoy sexual intimacy, or that they could no longer even talk. The loss of each of these things, and many more, is a grief moment.

Please be careful not to read this passage as if it suggests that Christians do not or should not grieve. That is not at all what Paul is saying. Grief is common to Christians. We do not escape it. We do not go *around* the valley of the shadow of death; we go *through* it. The point in this passage, however, is that we have a companion traveling with us. That companion is Christian hope—the hearty confidence that the grave is not the last word. Christ will return, along with this heavenly parade. The new heaven and the new earth will be set in place. Eternal joy will return. Peace will come.

But the lament comes before the peace. You are encouraged to lament—to weep and complain to God about the situation you or your loved one may be in right now. Lament is the unbridled outpouring of emotions over the tragedy you are experiencing. So many of the Psalms are filled with the laments of God's people. When we are angry with God or feel that he is distant from us or that he does not hear or respond to our pleas, the Psalms help give expression to those laments.

We must take death seriously. Death is the end of life as we know it on earth. Death is also the end of the relationships we know and experience on this earth. We must learn to say good-bye. If you know someone who is dying, the time will come when you have to accept the fact that he or she has died. Their life will become a treasured memory, but they will no longer be present here.

This doesn't mean that those of us who continue on this earth will never feel joy, satisfaction, or peace again. Think of this death transition as a form of Sabbath—a beginning again. The real meaning of Sabbath in the Bible isn't limited to rest but also focuses on the new beginning that follows that rest. Not all new beginnings are ones we really want. Many of them are forced on us. Death does that. But we grieve with hope—hope that God still has something good in mind for us.

This also means, however, that we need to develop a different kind of eyesight. We need a spiritual eyesight to see beyond the grave to the staging area of the grand end-of-time parade that will be led by Christ himself. We can't actually see it now the same way we might watch a local parade form at the beginning of the parade route. But we can see it with the eyes of hope. The apostle Paul wrote elsewhere, "For if you already have something, you don't need to hope for it. But if we look forward to something we don't have yet, we must wait patiently and confidently" (Rom. 8:24–25 NLT).

Patience. That is the toughest thing for many of us. It is hard to wait, especially when we are getting weaker or when we watch the health of the one we love slowly deteriorate. But the grand parade is forming. Christ is preparing for his return. Even if we die (or someone we love does), we will *all* be there for this last grand event on earth.

PRAYER: *Dear Lord, please save a place for me in that grand parade. I know the day will come when your Son will return in all his glory leading this grand procession behind him. Even if I should die soon, give me the assurance that all of us who love you will participate in this triumphant procession. In the meantime, keep me steady. Help me draw near to you in my hour of need. Stay close for Jesus' sake. Amen.*

Facing the Judge

In this way, love is made complete among us so that we will have confidence on the day of judgment, because in this world we are like him.

1 John 4:17

What will it be like for a Christian to face the final judgment?

hat do you think is worse—a fear of dying or a fear of God as the judge? Maybe you have both fears. Being afraid of dying is understandable, at least in the same way we might fear anything else unknown. Going into a dark, abandoned house with the wind blowing and doors creaking can make the bravest heart quiver.

But what about this business of being afraid of God? Those of us who are more seasoned in life may have learned early on that God is righteous and angry with wrongdoing. That would instill some concern about having to stand before him on judgment day. Others of us have heard, perhaps for our entire lives, that God is love; he is merciful, kind, and overwhelmingly gracious. Yet as we begin to approach the end of this earthly journey and recognize that we may actually be in his presence soon, we might also become afraid. We realize that we have sinned, so how might he judge us?

Perhaps you are afraid in the same way you might be a little frightened to meet someone of world-class importance. The pope, shall we say. Or the president of your country. Or one of your heroes. Your palms get a little sweaty, your face flushes, and a twitch develops around your eye. You are excited, but you are also scared.

Another reason you might be a little afraid is because you feel guilty. That's probably true for many of us. After all, none of us have lived a perfect life. It doesn't matter what church tradition you come from; none of us are perfect even as we get nearer to the end of our lives. Most of us recognize that we are not what we should be. And God is the judge! Now we think we really have cause to be afraid. After all, we know deep inside we are guilty. We know we have done unkind and sinful things throughout our entire life that may have offended God. Now we have to appear before him.

A relatively popular view of the entrance into heaven is, of course, that of entering a gated city. Stories (some meant to be humorous) talk about Saint Peter meeting us at the door and ushering us through the pearly gates. Choirs sing songs about wanting to see Jesus after we have wandered around seeing everyone else first.[28] But most of us can probably recall stories (perhaps even from our religious education) of being ushered up to the judge's bench where God is seated. Before him is a book in which he has written down all the nasty and sinful things we have done throughout our lives. We imagine him peering over the top half of his reading glasses and saying in an ominous tone, "I've been waiting for you." Then he reads out loud the list of all the sins we ever committed—all of them, from our birth to our death.

We shudder at the thought. Of course we would be afraid if that is how it will happen. But we really believe this image is false. You know who will meet us? Jesus! He will be the first one to greet us. He will put his white robe of holiness around our shoulders. He'll take us by the arm and say in an excited, welcoming tone, "I've been waiting for you! Look, here is the place I have prepared for you. Come, enter the joy of your Lord!"

But, you say, what about the judge? Oh yes, the judge—God himself. Of course, you must pass by the judge—the one who sits on the throne and who passes judgment on the entire heaven and earth. But remember, we said that Jesus will take us by the arm and lead us into heaven. Our picture also includes this scene: On the way toward the place that Christ has prepared for us, we pass right by the judge's bench. My life's book is laid before God the Father, and as he sees me coming he opens the book to page one. But then he notices that the only word written there is *Jesus*. He smiles as he looks up. Christ, my Savior, looks back at him. "It's okay," he says, "she's with me."

We know of no better assurance and comfort when passing from this life to the next than to know we belong to Christ. One of the pillar statements of faith arising from the Reformation asks, "What is your only comfort in life and in death?" The answer is:

> That I am not my own but belong—body and soul, in life and in death—to my faithful Savior Jesus Christ. He has fully paid for all my sins with his precious blood, and has set me free from the tyranny of the devil. He also watches over me in such a way that not a hair can fall from my head without the will of my Father in heaven. In fact, all things must work together for my salvation. Because I belong to him, Christ, by his Holy Spirit, assures me of eternal life and makes me whole-heartedly willing and ready from now on to live for him.[29]

Believe this. Believe in Christ, and he will see you through the judgment. You have nothing to fear.

PRAYER: *Righteous and holy Father, thank you for your Son, Jesus, who will be waiting for me with open arms. I know that my life has not been perfect. I've done quite a few things that have likely offended you and others. Especially as I near the end of my life, I am more keenly aware of some things I regret or would like to do over again. But now I know I don't have to make those things right with you—Jesus did that. Give me the grace of Christ to make things right with others as best I can and then to die in your peace. Amen.*

Good-bye, My Loved Ones, Good-Bye

*The company of the prophets at Jericho went up to Elisha
and asked him, "Do you know that the LORD is going
to take your master from you today?" "Yes, I know,"
he replied, "but do not speak of it."... When they had
crossed, Elijah said to Elisha, "Tell me, what can I do for
you before I am taken from you?" "Let me inherit a double
portion of your spirit," Elisha replied.*

2 Kings 2:5, 9

*Dear brothers and sisters, I close my letter with these last
words: Rejoice. Change your ways. Encourage each other.
Live in harmony and peace. Then the God of love and
peace will be with you.*

2 Corinthians 13:11 NLT

How do Christians say good-bye to their loved ones?

*S*aying good-bye is hard to do, especially when you know you
likely will not see the other person for a good long time, or
maybe ever again. Perhaps you've been at airports or bus
stations where people cling to each other in tears as they part—shouting last-minute promises to each other about calling soon, or writing,
or keeping in touch. But the plane takes off or the bus leaves, and they
stand there alone. Their loved one is gone.

Even before we have to say good-bye, we may try to avoid the topic the way Elisha did when he learned that his mentor and master Elijah was going to leave. Perhaps you know the story. Elijah was a brave prophet of God during the days of Israel. As he was nearing the end of his life, he trained Elisha to take over his ministry. God had warned Elijah that his days on earth were coming to a close. Unlike the rest of us, Elijah would be immediately taken up into heaven in a chariot of fire. He told all the prophets in his school what was going to happen. When they ran to Elisha to tell him, Elisha put them off by saying, "Do not speak of it" (2 Kings 2:3).

Then Elijah and Elisha began their journey together, both knowing this would be the last walk they would take as companions. Elijah broke the silence. "Tell me, what can I do for you before I am taken from you?" (2 Kings 2:9).

What a good question! Have you asked that of your loved ones—the ones you might be leaving behind? Elijah, the one who was to leave, initiated the conversation. It's often like that. If anyone is going to start talking about the days, weeks, and months ahead, you are likely the one. Others will tend to say, "Don't talk about it." But Elijah wanted to. He wanted to say good-bye, and he wanted to do it in a way that would help Elisha.

Once Elijah broached the subject, Elisha was not timid. "Let me inherit a double portion of your spirit," he said (v. 9). In other words, give me a blessing! I want something of your character to live on in my life. One of the beautiful things about the stories in the Old Testament is the theme of one generation blessing the next. The older generation lays hands on the younger generation and blesses those who come behind.

If you would do something like that for your family and friends, at least three things could be accomplished. First, you could bequeath something special of yourself to others. Throughout your years you have gained wisdom and developed the qualities of your character—now it is the time to pass them on to others. Call your loved ones to your bedside. Lay your hands on their heads. Pray for them. Pray that the blessings you have received in your life may now live on in theirs. Give them the benediction of Paul quoted above: that the God of love and peace will be with them.

A second thing will happen when you bless those you will leave behind: reconciliation. Unless you are very unusual, perfect harmony probably doesn't exist between you and your loved ones. This is the time to set the record straight. Clean the slate. Let them know that just as Christ has forgiven us, we can forgive each other. Saying "I'm sorry" makes saying good-bye a lot easier.

Doing those two things clears the way for the third: You can engender a sense of hope and a future for those who follow after you. You don't bless someone who doesn't have a future! On the other hand, the blessing is a symbol of the fact that God's grace will continue from one generation to the next. You may be taking your leave of them, but just as Elijah threw his mantle over Elisha's shoulders and passed on the blessing of the future, so now your time has come. Think about what you can say to those who love you that will make their memory of you sweet, that will help them on their grief journey after you are gone, and that will nurture those Christian virtues that you hold so dear. This may be written or spoken in the form of an ethical will.

Elijah was able to pass on his blessing on the last day he walked this earth. That is unusual. Most of us who die from a disease slowly lose our capacity either to think clearly, or to have the energy to talk, or even to stay conscious. This may be a good time for you to consider how you will bless others. If confined to bed, you may call them to your bedside one by one. If you are still able to be more active, you might want to consider having a family gathering or a life celebration while you are still physically able. Some of your family or friends may resist. Remember, Elisha didn't even want to talk about it. But Elijah did. Saying good-bye is important. Your family and friends will thank you after you do it. Give them your blessing. Let them know that it is now time to say good-bye.

PRAYER: *Dear Lord, I really do have some things I'd like to say to my family and friends. I'd really like to talk with them about what is going on inside of me. I want them to know my fears, my regrets, my sorrows. But I also want them to know I love them, care deeply for them, and truly hope that after I die they will be able to live a full and rich life. I also want them to know I am eager to meet you, my Lord, face to face. That's hard to imagine, but I know it will happen. Give me the strength Elijah had in order to talk about these important things with those whom I love. Amen.*

Preludes and Postludes

I know that my Redeemer lives, and that in the end he
will stand upon the earth. And after my skin has been
destroyed, yet in my flesh I will see God; I myself will see
him with my own eyes—I, and not another. How my heart
yearns within me!

Job 19:25–27

How do I balance my desire to hang on to life with letting go for what is to come?

he book of Job has all the qualities of a great drama. If it weren't in the Bible, you might think someone like John Steinbeck or Ernest Hemingway wrote the story. The first act opens with this perfectly healthy, fit, God-fearing man minding his own business. He loves his family, is a successful rancher, and conducts his business in a virtuous manner. As a matter of fact, he's so good that we find God bragging about him. The drama really begins in the heavens with a scene showing a conversation between God and Satan. Satan comes walking into the presence of God, and with some curiosity, God asks, "Satan, where have you been?" "Just roaming around the earth seeing what's going on," replies Satan. Then God draws attention to Job. "Have you considered my servant Job? There is no one on earth like him; he is blameless and upright, a man who fears God and shuns evil" (Job 1:6–8). Here you have the greatest setup in history. The contest is set: Satan versus God. And Job becomes the pawn. Satan charges that Job's righteousness is just a ploy to gain more of God's blessing.

God disputes the fact. "Go ahead—take it all away from him. You just watch," God argues, "he'll stay faithful to me. Just don't lay a hand on him" (see Job 1:9–12).

You likely know the rest of the story. Job gets afflicted in a myriad of ways, but he stays faithful to God. Finally God allows Satan to even afflict Job directly as long as he doesn't take Job's life. Job winds up on the ash heap behind the house. His friends try to make Job believe that he has committed some great sin to warrant this treatment from God. His wife tells him to just "curse God and die!" (Job 2:9). Of course, Job argues with God, but he also remains faithful. He pleads with God and questions his own integrity, but ultimately pulls through the trial. The story ends almost like a fairy tale: "The LORD blessed the latter part of Job's life more than the first. . . . After this, Job lived a hundred and forty years; he saw his children and their children to the fourth generation. And so he died, old and full of years" (Job 42:12, 16–17).

There is a drama, a spiritual war of terrorism, that goes on beyond our own personal lives. This drama plays itself out on a cosmic scale. Whether or not you actually believe in a real being called Satan is not the issue. What we need to recognize is that the force of evil is still resisting our heavenly Father's design—but only under his supervision! God has a plan, a grand drama that is working its way out. Job lived thousands of years ago, well before the time of Christ. He had no knowledge of the work of Christ on the cross. What he did know was that Jehovah God would be faithful to him.

But notice as well that Job didn't sit on the ash heap singing praise and worship songs as if his suffering was something he should be enjoying. He cursed the day he was born (Job 3:3–10). He saw himself as a laughingstock among his friends because God wasn't answering his pleas for help (Job 12:4–5). He lost confidence in seeing any of his hopes and dreams for the future fulfilled (Job 17:11–13).

But as Job felt himself slipping closer to the grave, we find one of the most beautiful passages in Scripture.

> I know that my Redeemer lives,
>   and that in the end he will stand upon the earth.
> And after my skin has been destroyed,
>   yet in my flesh I will see God;
> I myself will see him
>   with my own eyes—I, and not another.
> How my heart yearns within me!

> Job 19:25–27

This life is a prelude—like the music that begins the concert or the worship service. This life, with all of its joy and all of its sorrow, is what leads the way into something greater and more magnificent. Certainly a prelude can stand on its own merits. The music that is often played before a worship service hopefully helps set your heart and mind in a proper frame for worship. But it is still only what comes first. Worship isn't complete until the rest of the service runs its course.

Job saw this so very clearly, almost as if he saw a shaft of bright light beaming from heaven onto his ash heap. With his body covered with boils and sores, draped loosely with ill-fitting clothes, feeling his very skin peeling away almost as if it had been burned, Job suddenly breaks out in an exclamation of faith and praise. In the prelude he hears the beginning of the postlude at the end of the service. The tune that is played ever so cautiously in his pain and sickness lays the foundation for the full symphonic version that will follow. He is again sure of God's vindicating power. God will make this right. He will redeem. He will save. Job could clearly see God standing right in front of him. How his heart yearned to be with his Savior!

Those who are nearing the end of their earthly life sometimes have a deep spiritual sense of God standing near them. They may even see him. Many people report seeing a bright light right before death. We really don't know how God will make himself known to us during those last days or moments. But we can take a lesson from Job—a lesson of faith and confidence that we will see our Savior with our own eyes.

Job's statement of praise comes approximately halfway through the story. A little more of his earthly journey had to be completed before the eternal song could actually begin. But it finally came. For Job, the blessing came not only in receiving more gifts from God than he had in his earlier life but in dying "full of years." His life was complete. He eventually died in peace.

Death is no stranger to those who love Jesus. The trauma associated with death will certainly be our common experience. But death is contrary to God's original design, and he has engaged in a battle with Satan to finally wipe it out. This decisive battle was fought and won by Christ himself on the cross of Calvary. But the final victory day has not yet arrived. As you approach the end of your own life, that V-day is getting nearer. The final victory will be yours. As this life of preludes comes to a close, you can hopefully begin to hear the beautiful strands of the full orchestra playing the main selection of the concert. You have heard the words of the eternal song, haven't you? They go like this:

> Worthy is the Lamb, who was slain,
> to receive power and wealth and wisdom and strength

and honor and glory and praise! . . .
To him who sits on the throne and to the Lamb
be praise and honor and glory and power,
for ever and ever!

Revelation 5:12–13

PRAYER: *Dear Lord, many people hold Job up as an example of patience. I'm not so sure of that because of all the arguing he did with his friends and with you. But I am encouraged that you still put his story in the Bible because through it you give me some assurance that my lack of patience (at least sometimes) is perfectly normal. I want either to get better or to be done with all this suffering. Getting better doesn't look very realistic right now. Please, dear Father, strengthen my patience. Do it at least in part by helping me understand a little better the grand drama behind Job's story and how it relates to my story. Amen.*

Ashes to Ashes; Dust to Dust

*For he understands how weak we are; he knows we
are only dust. Our days on earth are like grass; like
wildflowers, we bloom and die. The wind blows, and we
are gone—as though we had never been here.*

Psalm 103:14–16 NLT

What happens to my body when I die? May a Christian be cremated?

or more than two decades, we both enjoyed the love of our first marriage partners. Susan's relationship with Rick was intertwined with his illness because eighteen of the twenty-four years of their marriage were spent intermittently battling a brain tumor. Char, Bob's first wife, fought cancer for four of the twenty-eight years they were married. In spite of the illnesses, we both had happy, fulfilling, and loving relationships. A healthy marriage means to us being intimate with each other emotionally, spiritually, and physically. The physical body is an integral and important part of who we are, and in union with each other two people experience each other's bodies in the most intimate of ways. Physical intimacy is so meaningful and special because it connects two people like no other relationship.

Our physical presence, however, is important in any relationship we have with others. Brothers give each other hearty hugs or wrestle on the floor. Mothers and daughters hold hands, cry on each other's shoulders, and embrace heartily after they have been apart for a period of time. Grandparents' laps are extremely important resting places for grandchildren. Friends place their hands on each other's shoulders to express support and caring.

Death takes that all away. The body—the physical presence of the other person—is gone. Even if you opt for a traditional funeral with an open casket, your corpse (doesn't that word stick in your throat!) will be lifeless. No longer can your loved one lay their head on your chest to hear your gently beating heart, feel the warmth of your exhaling breath, and caress your soft hair. What should they do with the body—this earthly house that for so many years was animated by the presence of the one they loved?

In Christian circles, at least in Europe and North America, the most traditional parting gesture has been, of course, the embalming and burial of the body. The family takes great care to clothe the body in a favorite dress or suit, comb the hair properly, and have the funeral personnel attempt to cover up the gray pallor of death with heavy makeup. Then during the visitation at the funeral home, many people feel compelled to say something like, "Oh, doesn't she look good?" or "Didn't they do a nice job?" or "His smile isn't just right." We want to replicate as closely as possible in the casket what we experienced when the person was alive.

In the United States, people are increasingly choosing cremation as a means for the disposition of their loved one's body. According to recent research, the percentage of Americans who prefer to be cremated after they die is on the rise. But for some Christians, the thought of intentionally destroying the body by fire is a challenge. Does the Bible allow cremation? Does it forbid it? Actually, does the Bible say anything about it at all?

Our passage for this meditation reminds us (as do many other passages as well) that once the soul has left the body, the body deteriorates and returns to the ground. Whether you use the familiar "dust to dust" phrase or quote this psalm about the wind blowing over the flowers of the field, the point is that once death occurs, the earthly body slowly deteriorates. The physical elements of our body return to the earth. The Bible does not stipulate a preferred way for this to happen. The Bible is clear that God will create for us an entirely new body at our resurrection. He is not going to need or use the old one as a model or mold.

What, then, are the factors that you as a Christian might keep in mind when deciding the disposition of your body? What wishes are you going to convey to your family? Consider the following list of biblical principles you might want to keep in mind. Notice that this list also still leaves open the choice of burial or cremation. The biblical principles apply to both.

First, we believe that the Bible honors the human body as an important creation of God. God was actively involved in the very creation of the human body—both for Adam from the dust and Eve from Adam's rib (Gen. 2:7, 22). The body is not just a disposable container to be easily thrown out at the end of its usefulness. God took special care in creating man and woman. He called them his image. Throughout our lives we are to take care of our bodies. We are to treasure them and be good stewards of the skills and abilities inherent in these earthly houses. When death comes, we should still see the body as something to be respected and honored.

Second, we must also recognize, however, that the purpose or usefulness of the body has come to an end with death. The body no longer serves the function for which God designed it. Therefore, what happens to it after death is really of no earthly consequence. A person who dies in a fiery plane crash or who is lost at sea does not present any bigger challenge to God than someone who dies quietly at home with the body fully intact. God will remake us regardless of the condition of our old bodies. In the resurrection we will have an entirely new body—a "spiritual body" as the apostle Paul calls it (1 Cor. 15:44).

Third, because this earthly body serves no function after death, we recognize that keeping the body is no longer necessary. Whether a person cremates the body or buries it six feet under the ground in a metal casket and cement vault, the body is gone from our daily lives. Just because someone may have an urn of cremated ashes on the mantel over the fireplace does not mean the deceased person is any closer or more present than the person buried in a local cemetery or whose ashes were scattered in a favorite location. The psalmist says that, like wildflowers, we bloom and die, "The wind blows and we are gone—as though we had never been here" (Ps. 103:16 NLT). If we are truly gone, the condition and/or the location of our physical remains are no longer important.

Fourth, the important thing to focus on is that when you die you will be with Christ. You will be totally remade with a new "spiritual" body. You will continue to be a unique, identifiable person. You have entered into the joy of your new existence (1 Cor. 15:44).

One parting gift you can give your family and friends is to make certain that whether you opt for a burial or cremation, you allow them time to say good-bye to the physical body they loved so much. Keep the casket open for a while, or delay the cremation long enough so they can touch you one more time. Let them feel your hair and give you a gentle good-bye kiss. Then you can let the body fade away, like the flowers of the field, and eventually it will be no more—not on this earth. But we will be with Christ in a new body and a new life. We will be in a place where death is no more, and the new life will begin.

PRAYER: *Creator God, the one who shaped us from the dust of the ground, how I hate to leave this earthly body! I have grown accustomed to it. But I know I will shed this earthly frame and receive the new spiritual body promised to us by Christ himself. In the meantime, grant me and my loved ones the wisdom to decide how my body can best be returned to the dust where it came from. Thank you for giving it to me for these years on earth. Help me now get ready to receive a completely new body from you after I die. Amen.*

Comfort

Praise be to the God and Father of our Lord Jesus Christ,
the Father of compassion and the God of all comfort, who
comforts us in all our troubles, so that we can comfort
those in any trouble with the comfort we ourselves have
received from God.

2 Corinthians 1:3–4

How can I use my dying to help others?

ertrude was sixty-eight years old. For the past three years she had valiantly battled cancer, but now her body was weakened to the point at which she was confined to a hospital bed set up in the dining room of their home. Her mind was still very sharp and clear, but her body was slow to respond, often racked with pain. She knew she was going to die, probably within a couple of months. She lamented that she no longer seemed to be of any use to anyone. All her life she had tried to be helpful to others. She certainly had been a good mother and more recently a grandmother. She had done her share of work at church. She also was the one who always organized the neighborhood garage sales, collected for charity, and held potlucks in her backyard. "Now," she complained, "it's over. I'm no longer of any use to anyone else."

Her sensitive pastor tried to help her see things differently, using 2 Corinthians 1 as a starting point. Maybe you can relate to this situation. You might be reading this meditation specifically because you have only a limited amount of time left on this earth. Perhaps your abilities and strength are ebbing away.

The first thing we would like you to consider is that your experiences are unique. That includes your experience of dying. Try to look at the process you are going through as something special. No one else will have exactly the same experience you are having. Your personality, your faith, and your disease all combine into a drama that will be played out as the unique final act of your life.

The second thing we would encourage you to consider is that this drama does have an impact on others. We do not live in isolation from others. We do not rejoice alone, nor do we weep alone. Changes in our personal, unique dramas affect the other players on our stage—whether those people be our children, a spouse, parents, or close friends. Read Tolstoy's classic *The Death of Ivan Ilyich*.[30] As Ivan's health deteriorates, you can see in his drama the wide variety of reactions and responses. Some people were angry because of the unexplained change in his behavior. Others were eager for his death because they were human vultures hungry for his job or holdings. Still others were fearful because they thought death might happen to them. And some were brought closer, touching a part of their heart and compassion that might not have been exercised in that way before. What happens to you affects your family and friends. The choices you make in the dying process will have wider implications for the people around you.

Third, try to remember to share your experiences with others in reference to God's activity, not in terms of other people's experiences. Because each person's experiences are unique, comparing your pain or your condition to what some aunt or uncle may have had is of little value. The point of comparison is how you understand the grace and power of Christ. When our first spouses died, both of us learned something deeper about joy in the middle of our sorrow and strength in the middle of our weakness. We couldn't have learned that by comparing our experiences to those of other people. We learned it by reflecting on God's presence and activity in our lives during those tough times.

Finally, share your experiences with others in order to better understand your own story. We are still baffled by how many people face death silently and stoically. That's not how we say our temporary good-byes at the airport or train station. We hug and kiss and even weep a little. We tell people we love them. And we wish them a safe journey. You can comfort others around you by talking about the experiences you are having. You can help them understand your fears, your anxieties, and hopefully your sense of God's presence.

Hebrews chapter 11 is often referred to as the "heroes of the faith" passage. Each story is unique. But they all had faith in God, and they all died. And then the writer adds this strange verse: "These were all commended for their faith, yet none of them received what had been promised. God had planned something better for us so that only together with us would they be made perfect" (Heb. 11:39–40). The image is that of a relay race. We are all in the race together, and the race isn't complete until the last runner crosses the finish line. Those heroes who went before us have run their leg of the race. But the race isn't over. As we approach our own death, we near the end of our personal leg of the race. The time comes to hand the baton off to someone else. And the race goes on. If we die quietly, without talking about our experiences and without testifying to God's grace and power working within us, how will the next runners of the race be prepared to run?

Gertrude's pastor said she had one more opportunity to serve her family and her friends, one more gift to give. That gift was the explanation and testimony of the comfort she was receiving as she rounded the final turn and made her way to the finish line. If she could do that, she would then take her place with the other heroes of the faith who now form that "great cloud of witnesses" (Heb. 12:1) waiting for the rest of us to run our leg of the race.

PRAYER: *Eternal God, the giver and sustainer of all life, make clear the purpose you still have for my life on this earth. I am so tempted to turn in on myself. Sometimes I'm too weak to think or too consumed by pain to talk. I appreciate others who come to comfort me. Show me how I can comfort others, especially as I prepare to hand off the baton of life to those who come behind me. Please, Lord, give me strength as I sprint the last leg of this journey. May my witness encourage others to run the race valiantly. Amen.*

Patience

I waited patiently for the LORD; he turned to me and heard my cry.

Psalm 40:1

Why is it so hard to be patient?

*D*eveloping patience is tough for many of us. Patience is a virtue—something that may not come very naturally. King David wrote Psalm 40, the text for this meditation. The opening verse is the main theme of the entire psalm. David recalls all the trouble he has had in his life. He confesses his sins against God. He actually pleads with God to "come quickly to help" him (Ps. 40:13), but deep inside his heart he confesses, "I waited patiently for the LORD; he turned to me and heard my cry." That's why the psalmist portrays patience as a virtue. He was able (unlike so many of us!) to wait patiently for the Lord.

The need for patience when you or a loved one is nearing the end of life is obvious. Whether you are the one afflicted by a terminal disease or the one caring for such a person, you tend to count the days and weeks. At some points time moves too slowly, as when you are waiting for test results or relief from pain. At other points time moves too quickly when it seems like your disease is exploding before your very eyes. You would do anything to slow it down or stop it. Yet regardless of what you do, the clock keeps ticking, the body gets weaker, and you know that time is running short.

"How long, O Lord!" is a common cry. How long will this go on? How long will the pain last? How long do we need to wait for an answer to our prayers? Don't let the first verse of Psalm 40 fool you. This psalm isn't the sweet melody of some saint who has quietly capitulated to the will of God. This is King David, likely writing some time after he realized his dreadful sin in committing adultery with Bathsheba and killing Uriah (2 Samuel 11). The first half of the psalm does praise God for giving David an escape from his predicament. But the last half of the psalm, beginning at verse 11, is still the pleading of a needy heart. "Do not withhold your mercy from me," he writes (Ps. 40:11). "Troubles without number surround me; my sins have overtaken me, and I cannot see. . . . O LORD, come quickly to help me" (Ps. 40:12–13). Those sound more like our prayers! The entire psalm ends with the plea, "O my God, do not delay" (Ps. 40:17). So how do the two themes of this psalm fit together? Is David a patient man or not?

We suspect that David is no different than the apostle Paul or than you or us. Paul lists patience as one of the fruits of the Spirit (Gal. 5:22). Patience is a result of allowing the Holy Spirit to work with us in our lives; it is not really something we can create on our own. But we rarely allow the Spirit's work to go unobstructed. Paul also knew that the good he wanted to do, he didn't do; he often did the evil he didn't want to do (Rom. 7:19). We tend to feel that conflict between what we want to do and what we really do. That takes patience with ourselves as well.

So why is patience so hard for some of us to attain? Why is it especially hard when we are not doing well physically? One of the reasons being patient is so difficult is that we get restless when we hear the clock ticking. We keep looking at our watch while seated in the waiting room. We check the calendar to count how many more days must pass before the next chemo treatment. We lie in our bed, fully conscious of our surroundings but too weak to get up or to concentrate enough to be productive, and we wait. And what is it we are waiting for? We're waiting for something to happen in a time and manner that we think are right and proper. The challenge of patience implies a challenge of control. As long as I assume that I am in control, I can get very impatient with people who don't do something my way. David made certain that God knew how he wanted things to go in his life. But patience came when he turned control over to God. "You're in charge. Do it your way. I'll wait." When we use those words, they are sometimes spoken with a little bite to them—a touch of sarcasm revealing our hesitancy or difficulty in really wanting to turn control over to someone else.

But we really don't turn control over to God. He is *already* in control. We just have to accept that fact. Nothing happens without his providential permission. That is what David is teaching us through what he learned from his own experiences. He is also teaching that the "bad stuff" is as much under God's control as the "good stuff." This doesn't mean that God creates evil—it does mean that he is all powerful so that even when bad things happen, he can turn them around for us. God can use the evil things that happen to us for the good of us and others. But it means we must trust him. Remember also the famous assurance of Paul of God's promise to us: "And we know that in all things God works for the good of those who love him, who have been called according to his purpose" (Rom. 8:28). "All things" means just that—everything, including a terminal illness or what seems to be endless caregiving.

Patience actually becomes an evidence of a deeper trust. I can be patient in waiting for a promise only to the degree to which I trust the person making the promise. God doesn't make empty promises. So we can be certain of God even though we are at times uncertain about what will happen next. In writing to the Colossians, Paul prays that they may be strengthened in the Spirit "so that you may have great endurance and patience" (Col. 1:11) in living the life of obedience.

Patience can also be difficult when we live so much in the future that we don't embrace the present moment. We may be like the grandchild who so desperately wants to get to Grandma's house that she fails to enjoy all the other sights and activities involved in getting there, or like children at the zoo who want to see the monkeys so badly that they don't take time to look at the lions and elephants on the way.

Sometimes when we put our hand in God's hand, we try to pull him in the direction and at the speed we want to go. We tug at his arm, pulling with all our might, but it seems that he doesn't move. If patience is becoming more of a challenge in your life, perhaps it is time to consider where you see God's face in the present moment. God doesn't always make himself known to us in spectacular ways. Elijah learned that lesson. He had to wait through tornado-like winds, earthquakes, and fire before he could hear the Lord speak to him in a whisper (1 Kings 17:11–13). Can you see God where you are?

Patience comes in recognizing who is really in control. The Christian knows that person is God himself. Patience also comes from recognizing his presence in places and ways we might not have seen him before. David knew in the end that God was in control. God still is. Hold on to his hand tightly—but let him lead.

PRAYER: *Hold my hand, dear Lord. Lead me even though I must go down strange and scary paths. Speak comfort to me so I can be patient as I wait to see you in your full glory. I get tired of waiting. Teach me how to wait patiently. Amen.*

My God, My God, Why Have You Forsaken Me?

About the ninth hour Jesus cried out in a loud voice,
"Eloi, Eloi, lama sabachthani?"—which means, "My God,
my God, why have you forsaken me?"

Matthew 27:46

So do not fear, for I am with you; do not be dismayed, for
I am your God. I will strengthen you and help you; I will
uphold you with my righteous right hand.

Isaiah 41:10

Will God really be there when I die?

either one of us authors knows what it is like to actually be on the brink of death. But between us we have had several experiences of being with someone we loved as they died. Both Rick and Char, our first spouses, were devoted Christians. In some ways that gave them a lot of peace as the day of death approached. But both of them were terribly weak physically as the end neared. They each slipped into unconsciousness hours before they actually died. Death then came as quietly and easily as sleep.

Weeks and months before their deaths, however, we both had several lengthy conversations with our spouses about dying and death. We are grateful that we were able to talk about death with them and that they were open and willing to share their thoughts and feelings about what was happening. Their responses to our inquiries were amazingly similar.

242

The prospect of death was not terribly frightening. Of course, dying was an unknown experience. Doing anything for the first time often raises the anxiety level several notches. You would think that would be all the more true about this final act of life! But their confessions actually paralleled the words of Isaiah 41:10. They truly believed that God would give them his strength, that he would help them, and that Christ would be waiting on the other side to greet them. As Christians they even had a certain kind of eagerness to be done with all this suffering and pain so they could enjoy this final glory.

What both of them feared more were the events that would lead up to their final death. Each, in his or her own way, feared what might be the final onslaught of pain. They were very sad at the prospect of having to say good-bye to us, to our children, and to our families. They were also worried about us. How would we do? Could we take care of ourselves? What would our lives look like? Both of them also encouraged, almost insisted, that we get married again. They knew how much we enjoyed married life with them, and they did not want their deaths to be the end of marriage for us.

We have no way of knowing what your personal situation is right now. On the one hand, you may be like Isaiah, confident of God's presence and strength as you walk the final leg of your earthly journey. Or you may be more like Christ himself on the cross, feeling totally forsaken. There is something unique, of course, about Christ's experience that makes it completely different than anything a Christian has to endure. We run headlong into a mystery too deep to explain. The Bible clearly indicates that Jesus was 100 percent divine and 100 percent human. As the divine God he could, of course, endure anything and fear nothing. As a human being, he was just like us except that he did not sin (Heb. 4:15). He likely experienced all the same emotions we do. He even endured temptations, as we have pointed out in these meditations. So the mystery deepens when we realize that Christ carried with him to that cross the burden of sin for the whole world. His was not an ordinary death. As he hung on the cross that Friday afternoon, he not only felt the physical pain of the crucifixion, he also felt the terrible anger of God the Father for the sin of the world. That was the agony that wrung from him the cry, "Why have you forsaken me?" (Matt. 27:46).

As believing Christians, we *never* have to experience that agony in our dying. Christ did it for us, once for all. That is why Paul could boldly proclaim, "There is now no condemnation for those who are in Christ Jesus" (Rom. 8:1) and that we are now "more than conquerors through him who loved us" (Rom. 8:37).

Isaiah 41:10 fits our situation much better than Jesus' cry. God may not remove the pain of dying—neither the physical pain that sometimes needs morphine to blunt its steely presence nor the deep-ripping emotional pain. We will still experience the pain of saying good-bye, that pain of separation. But once we finish looking over our shoulder at what we are leaving, we can turn our face toward the Son of Eternity and know that he is waiting for us. Not only is he waiting, but he has staked out the way. He put up the markers for us so we can follow his path. He will certainly lead us home.

PRAYER: *Lead me home, dear Jesus. I can hardly imagine what this experience will be like, but one thing I am coming to believe is that I will never experience, even in dying, the same agony you had on the cross of Calvary. Help me tolerate my physical pain and manage my emotional pain. But thank you that in my death I will never have to cry out, "Why have you forsaken me?" the way you did, because you did it for me. Help me follow the path you have laid out through this valley of death. Amen.*

Standing on the Front Porch of Heaven

After this I looked, and there before me was a door standing open in heaven. And the voice I had first heard speaking to me like a trumpet said, "Come up here, and I will show you what must take place after this."

Revelation 4:1

What does heaven look like?

In the early 1950s, Bob's neighbors across the street from his boyhood home purchased one of the first television sets on the block. It was a big square box with a very snowy picture. These neighbors were generous people. They invited Bob and his three older brothers to stand on their front porch once a week to peer through the window and watch *The Howdy Doody Show*. The children couldn't hear the sound, but seeing the marvel of a picture on a television set was magnificent enough.

The apostle John was having a similar experience, only at a far deeper and more profound spiritual level. He was invited to stand on the front porch of heaven, peer through the front door, and see what was inside. Isn't that a rather common yearning among all of us, especially as we approach our final days on earth? We want to see a little more clearly where we are going! So John gives us a report.

You really need to read all of Revelation 4 and 5 to get the entire picture. John sees amazing sights and hears amazing sounds while standing on tiptoe looking in heaven's open door. What does he see? Majesty, power, beauty, glory—all those words that have little physical reference here on earth. We have to look into heaven to understand what they really mean. John reports that he sees a huge throne encircled by a rainbow.

In front of that throne are seven golden candlesticks representing the seven spirits of God. There is also something like a sea of glass, pure as crystal. The people (if you can call them that) were all very strange. Whoever was sitting on the throne couldn't be seen very clearly, but he had the appearance of jasper and carnelian. Surrounding him were four strange-looking creatures: like a lion, an ox, a man, and an eagle. They were surrounded by an even larger ring composed of twenty-four elders, likely representing the twelve tribes of Israel from the Old Testament and the twelve apostles from the New Testament. They were all worshiping the One seated on the throne, singing, "Holy, holy, holy is the Lord God Almighty, who was, and is, and is to come" (Rev. 4:8) and

> You are worthy, our Lord and God,
>   to receive glory and honor and power,
> for you created all things,
>   and by your will they were created
>   and have their being.

> 4:11

Can you see the throne from where you are? You may not be able to even stand up physically if you are terribly ill, but spiritually you may be able to stand on tiptoe a little more, strain your neck a bit, and catch a glimpse of this glory. Many Christian believers who are aware that they are nearing the end of their lives on earth testify that they begin to sharpen their focus on this glory of God. They actually pay less attention to the routines around them. Food may lose its appeal. People might even become less important. The yearning of the soul to find its rest in the bosom of the Father takes over. The desire of the heart slowly becomes a desire to be with Christ and to leave this earthly life behind.

But just as John is swept up into this vision, something very strange happens. Beginning with chapter 5, this beautiful scene seems shattered. John looks again and sees that the one seated on the throne holds a scroll in his hand. The mighty angel is calling out, "Who is worthy to break the seals and open the scroll?" (v. 2). But no one could be found. Then the most amazing thing happens. While John is getting a glimpse of the beauty and majesty of heaven, he actually begins to weep—not for joy but out of deep disappointment. No one, he believes, is worthy to open the scroll. Just then, one of the elders sees John's sorrow. "Do not weep!" he says. "See, the Lion of the tribe of Judah, the Root of David, has triumphed. He is able to open the scroll and its seven seals" (v. 5).

You know who the Lion is—Jesus Christ. As a matter of fact, the vision now immediately shifts from the image of a Lion to a Lamb (Rev. 5:5–6). Just as John responds to the elder's invitation to see the Lion,

John turns to see the wounded, bloody Lamb. But a new song emerges from the elders:

> You are worthy to take the scroll
> and break its seals and open it.
> For you were killed, and your blood has ransomed people for God
> from every tribe and language and people and nation.
> And you have caused them to become God's Kingdom and his priests.
> And they will reign on the earth.

> 5:9–10 NLT

When you turn your eyes toward heaven, what do you see? Sometimes we imagine that we are going to see all those loved ones who have preceded us in death. "Won't it be good to see Mom and Dad again?" we ask. Our desire to get to heaven to see our loved ones can be overwhelming. We want to shed everything that holds us back so we can be in heaven with them.

But we invite you to look again. Stand next to John. Look at what he sees. He's not talking about friends or relatives. He is talking about God, a Lion, and a Lamb. You might suddenly realize that this is really what heaven is all about. Your eyes are now turned toward heaven because Christ is there. Your desire to be *with him* is now so great that you want to shed everything to be there—to join that crowd around the throne to sing his praises.

John was still standing on the porch. He wasn't in heaven himself. While the vision was magnificent, eventually he had to turn away and go back to his life here on earth. The vision lasted only a little while. As you approach the end of your life, these visions may come. They will be comforting. But we still need to get off the porch and move inside. Death is the doorway, and Christ has opened the door for us. He is waiting for all of us to come inside.

PRAYER: *Dear Lord, my days on this earth are numbered. Part of me would really like to see what John saw. I think I will actually see it as soon as I die, but thank you for giving me this eyewitness report from your disciple. Right now I am surrounded with medicines and other treatments. Someday I hope to be free of all of the trauma related to my illness and fly away to the heavenly home you have specially prepared for me. Stay close by me all the way home, dear Lord. Amen.*

In the Beginning

He died for us so that, whether we are awake or asleep, we may live together with him. Therefore encourage one another and build each other up, just as in fact you are doing.

1 Thessalonians 5:10–11

When does eternity begin?

n 1999 the countdown clock became very popular. This was the digital clock that counted backward indicating how much time was left before the new millennium began. You could watch the months, days, hours, minutes, seconds, even tenths of seconds whiz by as the turn of the century approached. In some ways, you might want a clock like that to know exactly how much time you have left before you die. On the other hand, we wonder how helpful that really would be—waking up each morning to see the countdown clock ticking away the days and hours left in your life.

Looking at time as if it were a sequence of equally divided segments of clock time is only one way to understand time. The Bible in the original Greek language uses two words for time: the first word is clock time, which refers to the ticking away of the seconds and minutes of our lives. The other word is better translated as *timing*—waiting for the precise moment when an event would best occur. Think, for example, of baking a cake. Once you put it in the oven, you can set a timer to happily tick away the minutes. When it finally dings, you check to see if the cake is really done—to see if the "timing" is right to take it out. Even if the timer has gone off, we need to see if the cake is done properly.

Paul is attempting to console some of the members of the church in Thessalonica who were concerned about how the death of their loved ones might affect their sense of eternity. His argument is very simple: Christ died for us. Therefore, death no longer makes any difference. Whether we are alive (on this earth) or have already died (and are with Christ), we still live together with him. Of course, we easily assume that those who have died and have gone to heaven are living with Christ. Many of us have pictured heaven as the place where eternity begins. But Paul is saying in this passage that eternity has also already begun for those of us on the earthly side of death because we won't ever die spiritually, although we still experience evil and brokenness in this world and eventually die a physical death.

As you or your loved one faces the end of life, this matter of time can be tricky. Many times we find that the closer we sense we are to death, the more we begin to think about life eternal. This world is controlled by the clock. Heaven is endless time or perhaps even the absence of time. What is your idea of "eternity"? Does eternity start only after you die? We suggest a different view: that once you are a Christian you have already begun your "life eternal." We no longer need a countdown clock to tick away the minutes before we get to heaven in order to begin eternity. We invite you to consider the fact that your eternal life has already begun! Once you are in Christ, there is an unbroken continuity between this life and the next. You will not die spiritually. You will change your physical form if you die before Christ returns, but as a person you will live forever. The Apostles' Creed asserts belief in "life everlasting," which is explained by one of the church's confessions in this way:

58 Q. How does the article concerning "life everlasting" comfort you?

A. Even as I already now experience in my heart the beginning of eternal joy, so after this life I will have perfect blessedness such as no eye has seen, no ear has heard, no one has ever imagined: a blessedness in which to praise God eternally.[31]

Note the phrase "even as I already now experience in my heart the beginning of eternal joy." In a very real sense, those who are Christians have already begun life eternal. Death is no longer the end. We certainly still experience it, and we may dread having to go through it. Death will cause those whom we love to grieve. But death is not the end. It is the transition. In God's timing, the time comes for us to be translated from one form of existence to another.

Another way to think about eternity in contrast to this world's sense of time is to recognize that clock time is not separate from God's timing. Clock time serves God's time, but God is not bound by clock time. He made that clear in saying that to him "a day is like a thousand years, and a thousand years are like a day" (2 Peter 3:8). To this Peter adds: "The Lord is not slow in keeping his promise, as some understand slowness. He is patient" (2 Peter 3:9).

So what do you think time will look like in heaven? Will there be clocks there? While we cannot answer that question with any certainty, remember that our definition of time as a sequence of minutes is a function of this earth. Time comes from the rotation of the earth and moon around the sun. That may or may not happen when God creates the new heaven and the new earth. We can say this much, however: This type of clock time is of secondary importance to God's sense of "timing." Time now has no end point—no matter how you define it. Because Christ has conquered death, he has also conquered the tyranny of the clock. Our life does not end at death. God's clock keeps ticking. We keep on living. And our life goes on forever—eternal life.

PRAYER: *Eternal Father, help me understand how you are eternal, how you never had a beginning and you will never have an end! Everything I know has a beginning—a baby born or an acorn growing into a mighty oak. Everything also has an end—the baby grows to adulthood and eventually dies. But now you say that although this body may return to the ground, I will live eternally—I will never cease to be the person I am because you have made my life eternal! I am humbled by such a thought. You are indeed a great and glorious God. Amen.*

Day 38

Cry No More, My Friend

He will wipe every tear from their eyes. There will be no more death or mourning or crying or pain, for the old order of things has passed away.

Revelation 21:4

What is the meaning of shalom, this heavenly peace?

Our time together in this book is almost over. Perhaps you also sense that your time on earth is nearly finished. So we turn our attention to the very last book of the Bible. Here we once again find the apostle John standing on the front porch of heaven peering through the open door to see what he can see. In Revelation 21, the second to the last chapter of the entire Bible, John now catches a glimpse of one of the most magnificent sights a person could imagine. This is the same vision, we believe, that each of us will see as we approach the heavenly gates. John saw something new put in place—a new heaven, a new earth, a new Jerusalem (v. 2). "The old order has passed away," declared a voice (v. 4).

Centuries before, God called this entire cosmos into being. By the word of his mouth, stars were flung into place. The water and land were separated. Trees and ferns burst out of the ground. Fish and snails populated the waters. Animals and butterflies galloped and darted over the ground and air. And Adam and Eve stood, naked and unashamed, in the peace of the Garden. But things went horribly wrong. Sin, death, mourning, grief, and pain entered the world.

251

Thousands of years have passed. Christ has died and risen again. Now John sees the end of the story. "The first heaven and the first earth had passed away" in his vision (v. 1). The peace and harmony of the first creation had returned with even greater intensity. This was not just a restoration of the old earth, starting over like a movie sequel entitled *Paradise II*. No, God has started all over again. Wiped the slate clean. The old has passed away. The new has come. What does this "new order" look like?

The first thing John notices is that "there was no longer any sea" (Rev. 21:1). Don't jump too quickly to any conclusions. That doesn't literally mean there will be no water (or water sports!) in heaven. Actually, to John and the people of his day, the sea represented the edge of the world and the place where evil dwelt—the underworld. The sea was a place of threat, danger, and fear. And now the sea is no more! Safety and security are guaranteed. The threat is gone.

Then John sees a city—the new Jerusalem—being lowered down from heaven onto the new earth (v. 2). A marvelous wedding is to take place, but a strange one as well. For this wedding was between God himself and all his people. All of us who have died in Christ are gathered to the place where this new city is descending. The city is not just some new development popping up in our neighborhood. This city represents a marriage—our marriage to God through Christ! John then hears a loud voice explaining what was happening. "Look, the home of God is now among his people! He will live with them, and they will be his people. God himself will be with them" (Rev. 21:3 NLT).

Can you imagine that? Here we are on this "old" earth wondering what heaven might look like. We have a myriad of questions that no one can really answer. We begin to imagine what heaven might be like, but our images are limited to angels playing harps on the clouds, or strange-looking creatures singing songs around a throne covered with smoke and mist, or streets paved with pure gold. What John was actually seeing in his vision was that on the final day (or when we die), heaven and earth will have come together! They will no longer be separate. The wall will come down. We all will have free and direct access to God himself.

As if that were not enough, the voice then announced to John the promise that we all have prayed for with every ounce of hope within us: "There will be no more death or mourning or crying or pain" (Rev. 21:4). Isn't that amazing? Of all the things the heavenly voice could have said, why did he choose those words? He could just as easily have said there will be no more war, disease, cheating, or hurt feelings. He might have said that divorce would end, or that parents and children would understand each other better. He could have said that everyone will have equal access to jobs, have a good education, and receive equal pay for equal work. But that is what politicians promise—as if they are really able to do all those things.

In the grand scheme of things, however, those issues aren't really that important anymore. Not in heaven. They belong to the "old order." We are now entering the new order. The four things we are told we will *not* take with us are the mourning, crying, pain, and death—the things that seem to be the last experiences we have on earth, the very things you and your loved ones are probably battling at this very moment.

Most of us will enter heaven with a tear-stained face. Those tears will come from the pain of the disease or accident that caused our death. Or the tears may come from the emotional pain of having to say good-bye. Even if we die "peacefully," we may come to heaven's door with tears of grief on our cheeks because we have been torn away from our loved ones. When we arrive, God will "wipe every tear" from our eyes (Rev. 21:4). How wonderful and how sensitive—the almighty God, the Creator and Redeemer of the world, touching our face with heavenly Kleenex to wipe away the tears. But isn't that the very nature of God that Jesus himself wanted us to see as he washed his disciples' feet? He will take care of our every need.

The Hebrew word for all this is *shalom*. You may want to say it slowly to yourself several times. On the surface, the word means "peace." But as you dig deeper, you find that the word represents a deep, peaceful harmony—a place where everything is in accord with everything else. This is the shalom that Isaiah prophesied in connection with the coming of Christ:

> The wolf will live with the lamb,
>> the leopard will lie down with the goat,
> the calf and the lion and the yearling together;
>> and a little child will lead them.
> The cow will feed with the bear,
>> their young will lie down together,
>> and the lion will eat straw like the ox.
> The infant will play near the hole of the cobra,
>> and the young child put his hand into the viper's nest.
> They will neither harm nor destroy
>> on all my holy mountain,
> for the earth will be full of the knowledge of the LORD
>> as the waters cover the sea.
>
> Isaiah 11:6–9

That is heaven! That is where those who have died before us in Christ are right now. That is where you may be soon. The old order is passing away; the new is coming. This is the holy city where heaven and earth are joined together; where God lives directly with his people; a place where he will wipe away your tears; a place where death and mourning are no more; a place where by faith you are going.

PRAYER: *What a vision John must have had! What a privilege as well to be allowed to look directly into your royal throne room! As I draw nearer to the time when I hope to see this with my own eyes, John's report is very encouraging. Heaven must be a magnificent place. I will hate to leave all that I love here on earth, but, dear Lord, I can't imagine a better destination than to live for all eternity in the presence of your peace. Amen.*

When We All Get to Heaven

*At the resurrection people will neither marry nor be given
in marriage; they will be like the angels in heaven.*

Matthew 22:30

*Then the angel showed me the river of the water of life, as
clear as crystal, flowing from the throne of God and of the
Lamb down the middle of the great street of the city. On
each side of the river stood the tree of life, bearing twelve
crops of fruit, yielding its fruit every month. And the leaves
of the tree are for the healing of the nations. No longer will
there be any curse. The throne of God and of the Lamb will
be in the city, and his servants will serve him. They will see
his face, and his name will be on their foreheads.*

Revelation 22:1–4

Will we see and know each other in heaven?

*S*usan's grandparents and brother are already there. So is
her first husband. Bob's older brother is there, as well as
both his parents, his grandparents, and his first wife. When
people think about heaven, they often think about the family members
and close friends who have taken up residence there. They think in terms
of the earthly relationships they had. We can understand that since we
really don't know what it is like to live in heaven. We do have a number

255

of Bible passages that give us some hint about it, but no one on earth really *knows* what it is like. So we ask all kinds of earth-oriented questions such as, "Will we be able to play tennis in heaven?" or "Will there be boats on the sea of crystal?"

Maybe those questions seem a little far-fetched. We asked them for a reason, however, because we often assume that once we get to heaven a lot of what we have experienced on earth will continue—particularly the relationships. As our life on earth comes to a close, we often want to cling to the relationships we have here. We don't want to let go. Those of us who stay behind on this earth to deal with our grief particularly want some assurance that the ones we loved so dearly here will recognize us and love us when we all get to heaven.

The problem with all this, however, is that the Bible gives no indication that the relationships we have on earth will continue in heaven. The Bible doesn't say anything about brothers and sisters, aunts and uncles, or even parents. What it does say about earthly relationships in heaven is pretty negative with respect to marriage. There won't be any! In the passage cited above, Jesus is responding to a riddle posed to him by the Sadducees. They were a Jewish sect of Jesus' time who actually came from a line of priests in Israel. But by the time of Christ, they no longer believed in a personal Messiah nor in any form of resurrection from the dead. In this passage they were goading Jesus by posing a dilemma: "Let's say," they said to Jesus, "that a man died, so his brother married his wife, and then he died. Actually seven brothers all married this woman and then died. When she finally died, whose wife would she be in heaven?" (see Matt. 22:23–28). Jesus cut to the heart of the dilemma quickly and simply: There is no marriage in heaven. Wow! Some people celebrate sixty or seventy years of marriage on this earth, and you mean to say that they won't have that same relationship in heaven?

First, remember that heaven will be a place that is far greater and more beautiful and peaceful than this earth ever could be. We can hardly imagine what it will be like. We must be careful about transferring the good things we have experienced on earth to this heavenly dwelling. Actually, this is part of the emotional pain of dying. We may be happy to leave all the tough stuff behind—the pain, the crying, the alienation, the hurt. But we also leave all the good stuff as well, including marriage and family.

However, that does not mean we will not have meaningful and fulfilling personal relationships in heaven. On earth we define relationships most often by bloodlines or through legal contract. Siblings, parents, and children come either through a natural bloodline or a legal contract of adoption. We generally don't choose those relationships; we are born into them. Marriage, of course, is a legal contract that begins another bloodline. In the new world, however, relationships are organized around a different type of bloodline; they are organized around the blood of the Lamb. John the Baptist already made this very clear before Jesus' public ministry began. The Sadducees challenged John the Baptist, claiming that they didn't need his baptism. After all, they were children of Abraham! They could trace their bloodline straight back to the father of the covenant! John's reply was: "I tell you that out of these stones God can raise up children for Abraham" (Matt. 3:9). Bloodlines are not what counts; what counts is who God calls to be his children. Not only is heaven a far more perfect place than this earth, relationships are now defined through the bloodline of Christ and not through a natural parental bloodline.

Third, the focal point of all relationships is the throne of God and the Lamb. The passage from Revelation 22 quoted above is the beginning of the final chapter of the Bible, which describes the total peace of the New Jerusalem. In heaven there are no family squabbles, divorces, stepfamilies, widows, or orphans. In heaven we are all related through God our Father and Christ his Son. We are all brothers and sisters in the Lord—and "all" means people from every tribe and tongue and nation across the face of this earth. While we have to work hard at creating and maintaining healthy relationships on earth, the depth and beauty of those relationships is guaranteed in heaven. The image of those healed relationships is the river of the water of life that flows straight from the throne. The tree of life, which Adam and Eve were banned from eating after they ate from the tree of the knowledge of good and evil, is now in full bloom. The tree has multiplied and is readily available to everyone, bearing its eternal life-giving fruit all year long!

Leaving our loved ones behind or saying good-bye to a dying family member is extremely difficult. We may well recognize each other once we all get to heaven. After all, we will be the same people in many important ways. But the way in which we relate to each other will be so much better than anything we can imagine here that we cannot describe it in words. This is one of the few times when "it sounds too good to be true" and it really is true!

The Bible ends with these verses. The apostle John, privileged to be caught up in this vision to see heaven and the end of time, leaves us with this message from Christ himself:

He who testifies to these things says, "Yes, I am coming soon." Amen. Come, Lord Jesus. The grace of the Lord Jesus Christ be with God's people. Amen.

Revelation 22:20–21

PRAYER: *For centuries Christians have prayed, "Maranatha"—come quickly, Lord. Even if you don't come soon to mark the end of this world, please come quickly for me. Quiet whatever trouble I have in my soul. Give me peace deep within my heart. Help me let go of this life and seek my final rest in you, for you alone are eternal. I believe you have prepared a place for me in your beautiful heavenly home. Take me there in your timing. Amen.*

Ministering Angels

Then the devil left him, and angels came and attended him.

Matthew 4:11

Are ministering angels near me now?

It's over. Finished. For forty days Jesus had been alone in the wilderness. Near the end of these five and a half weeks, Jesus was engaged in a direct assault by Satan himself. Already weak and tired from having no food, Jesus had to withstand a series of temptations that pushed him to the very brink of breaking. We have used these temptations as the backdrop to consider the challenges of living, of dying, and of death itself. This may not be the end of your life, although that might be coming soon. Maybe you are the loved one who is still reading this book even after your dear one has died. In either case, you may be yearning for one more word of comfort and direction.

Notice the two movements in this short concluding verse. Movement number one is that the devil left Jesus. Satan was gone. We don't know if he ran away with his tail between his legs or just shrugged his shoulders in disgust and walked quietly back home. In either case, the devil left. Then the second movement: No sooner had Satan left Jesus than ministering angels appeared. We don't know what they actually did or how they ministered to him. But we are left with the impression that as Jesus slumped into his corner of the ring exhausted from the fight, the angels took care of his every need.

Angels are interesting beings. Some religious traditions focus on them more than others. In the Reformed tradition from which we come, most people think of angels with a bit of curiosity. They are interesting little beings whose pictures adorn greeting cards or are made into little cherub statutes to put around the house. But some of us are not quite certain what they really do. All we know is that sometime before the creation of the world, God created these heavenly creatures.

Certainly one thing they do is clearly expressed in this passage. They take care of us. They ministered to Jesus, and we can have confidence that they also are God's ambassadors of mercy to care for us as well. Sometimes they may "appear" in the faces and hands of other people. We are encouraged, for example, to be hospitable to others, because in doing this we may be entertaining an angel (Heb. 13:2). In fact, Hebrews also asks this simple question of readers: "Are not all angels ministering spirits sent to serve those who will inherit salvation?" (Heb. 1:14).

If you are reading this meditation with the full awareness that your life is going to end soon, you may also be considering who will help you with that transition. Of course you will want your doctor involved, and perhaps visiting nurses or hospice workers. You will want your family and maybe some close friends. Someone may need to take care of you. Both of us were intimately involved in the physical care of our dying spouses. But we also wanted to be there to provide emotional and spiritual support. In both cases, as life began to ebb away, communication became more difficult. We wondered, *What is Rick thinking about now? Does he know what is happening? How is Char feeling? Is she scared?* The realization that God's angels minister to us gives us confidence to know that even when human communication fails, God's presence is still felt. We believe those who are making their way toward the new heaven and new earth are guided and deeply comforted by these special beings called angels.

Angels also perform another important function: They are messengers for God. The Bible is filled with examples of angels coming to earth with special words from the throne room of heaven. Think of just a few of God's saints who had direct encounters with angels: Abraham and Sarah, Moses, Gideon, David, Elisabeth and Zechariah, Peter, Paul, and of course Mary the mother of Jesus. But the angels' appearances—their shape and form—varied greatly. Angels are spirits, and it seems that they can take any shape or form they wish as they come with a message from God. You may want to see an angel dressed in silver robes with gossamer wings hovering like a hummingbird over your bed or chair. But an angel is just as likely to appear in the form of a dream. Or as a vision in your mind. You see, God sends his messengers to us in many different ways. Some people who have come very near to death and were subsequently revived reported seeing what they believed to be angels deployed to help them on their journey.

The third thing angels do is join us in our eternal worship of God in heaven. That is their home base. In his vision of heaven, John saw many angels. We read about them first of all as ones assigned to each of the seven churches singled out for special attention in the book of Revelation. Angels stand before the throne of God in Revelation 8 and appear later holding seven golden bowls (Revelation 16).

Angels assure us of God's presence on every step of our journey through life. Maybe you believe in having your own personal "guardian angel." That may be how God does it. Or you might be skeptical about all these winged spirits flying around. Don't let that block you from the real message. What happened to Christ in the wilderness is what will now happen, through Christ, to each one of us. After we have gone through our trials on this earth, the devil (and all that is evil and corrupt) will leave us, and God will send his ministering angels to show us the way home.

On the cross Jesus said, "It is finished" (John 19:30). He meant it then. He conquered Satan and evil through the terrifying event of the crucifixion and his miraculous resurrection on Easter morning. Forty days later he returned to his heavenly throne. The story has come to a conclusion. Christ reigns. His saints are being gathered around his throne. They are coming one by one, each as his or her time comes. Your time may be coming soon. You have run the race. You hopefully have found new life through Christ. His angels now surround you with God's love and compassion, and they whisper God's own words in your ear: "Well done, good and faithful servant. . . . Come and share your master's happiness" (Matt. 25:23).

PRAYER: *O Lord, send now your angel of mercy to minister to me. As this trial ends, help me see clearly your angels caring for me just as they cared for Christ after his ordeal in the wilderness. Whether I have only hours or perhaps weeks or months left on this earth, surround me with your angelic messengers to encourage, calm, and comfort me now. In Christ's name I pray. Amen. ·*

EPILOGUE

We have journeyed from the daylight through the shadows of dusk into the heart of the darkness of midnight. The journey is difficult because we all want to walk in the light, not in the darkness. But just as a new day dawns following the darkness of midnight, so Christians believe that our pilgrimage ends in the eternal light of the new heaven and the new earth ruled by Christ, the Lion of the tribe of Judah (Rev. 5:5). C. S. Lewis captures this image in his delightful children's series *The Chronicles of Narnia*, in which four young children find their way into the fantasy world of Narnia. The hero of the story is Aslan, a mighty Lion. Aslan is killed, only to reappear later in the epic. The final book of the series ends on the same theme that Scripture ends. Lewis writes:

> For us this is the end of all the stories. . . . But for them it was only the beginning of the real story. All their life in this world . . . had only been the cover and the title page: now at last they were beginning Chapter One of the Great Story, which no one on earth has read, which goes on forever and in which every chapter is better than the one before.[32]

Hear also these words of comfort from Isaiah 60:19–20 as your death is now imminent and you begin your Chapter One of the Great Story:

> The sun will no more be your light by day,
>   nor will the brightness of the moon shine on you,
> for the LORD will be your everlasting light,
>   and your God will be your glory.
> Your sun will never set again,
>   and your moon will wane no more;

> the LORD will be your everlasting light,
>   and your days of sorrow will end.

Believe this with all your heart and face your death with the confidence that God will be with you every step of the way, and Christ through his blood will usher you into your eternal home.

APPENDIX

RECOMMENDED BOOKS TO HELP CHILDREN, ADOLESCENTS, AND YOUNG ADULTS DEAL WITH DEATH AND GRIEF

For Parents:

The Dougy Center, located in Portland, Oregon, is dedicated to helping children grieve the death of loved ones. Check them out at www.dougy.org or (503) 775-5683. Some of their publications include: *Helping Children Cope with Death; What about Kids? Understanding Their Needs in Funeral Planning and Services;* and *Helping Teens Cope with Death.*

Johnson, Kay. *Keys to Helping Children Deal with Death and Grief.* Hauppauge, N.Y.: Barrows, 1999. Deals with grief, funeral arrangements, and life after death.

For Parents and Children:

Grollman, Earl. *Talking about Death: A Dialogue between Parent and Child.* Boston: Beacon Press, 1990. An updated version of the 1970 classic; contains illustrations and a comprehensive list of resources. Also includes a read-along section for parents to use with children and another section to help parents explain death to children.

Schwiebert, Pat. *Tear Soup: A Recipe for Healing after Loss.* Portland: Grief Watch, 1999. A story for children and adults in an allegory form

265

of making soup from tears. This book teaches the uniqueness of one's grief, underscoring the need for expressing feelings and encouraging children to remember the deceased.

For Preschool and Elementary Aged Children:

Brown, Laurie Krasny, and Marc Brown. *When Dinosaurs Died: Understanding Death.* New York: Little Brown, 1996. The book is written like a comic strip in the style of a Richard Scarry book. Visually stimulating, religiously and culturally sensitive.

Buscaglia, Leo. *The Fall of Freddy the Leaf.* Thorfare, N.J.: Charles B. Slack, 1982. A classic that explains death by using the analogy of the changing of seasons as well as the metaphor of a journey.

Cohn, Janice. *Molly's Rosebush.* Morton Grove, Ill.: Albert Whitman & Co., 1994. Uses many illustrations to help children understand issues of miscarriage and stillbirth.

Heegaard, Marge. *When Someone Very Special Dies: Children Can Learn to Cope with Grief.* Minneapolis: Woodland Press, 1988. For preschool and early elementary schoolchildren, this activity book invites children to draw pictures to express their thoughts and feelings. The book emphasizes that change is a part of nature.

Mills, Joyce C. *Gentle Willow: A Story for Children about Dying.* Washington, D.C.: Magination Press, 1993. The story is about a squirrel who sees a favorite tree dying. The story helps normalize death as a part of life. The book contains a helpful introduction to parents and concludes with instructions for making a "My Pain Is Getting Better" book.

Stickney, Doris. *Water Bugs and Dragonflies: Explaining Death to Young Children.* Cleveland: Pilgrim Press, 1997. Suitable for all ages although written for children. The story of the transition of a water bug into a dragonfly shows that death is a transition to another form of life with no return to the previous form possible.

Thomas, Jane Resh. *Saying Good-bye to Grandma.* New York: Clarion Books, 1988. Addresses the death of a grandmother, including all the activities following the death through the funeral, with special ways to remember a grandma.

Vigna, Judith. *Saying Good-bye to Daddy.* Morton Grove, Ill.: Albert Whitman & Co., 1991. This book deals with the reality of death and the funeral as well as the feelings associated with these events.

For Middle School Aged Children:

Greenlee, Sharon. *When Someone Dies*. Atlanta: Peachtree Publishers, 1992. Helps children express emotions and promotes the idea that healing can occur.

Paterson, Katherine. *Bridge to Terabithia*. New York: Harper Trophy, 1977. This Newberry Award winner has become a classic for early teens on the death of a friend.

For Teenagers and Young Adults:

Grollman, Earl. *Straight Talk about Death for Teenagers: How to Cope with Losing Someone You Love*. Boston: Beacon Press, 1993. This book for adolescents is honest and forthright. An easy read for teens with places for them to write about their feelings in response to what they are reading. Uses many bullets and other devices to make the format appealing to teens.

O'Toole, Donna. *Facing Change: Falling Apart and Coming Together Again in the Teen Years*. Burnsville, N.C.: Compassion Books, 1995. This book lists seventy-five brief explanations of what a teenager can do to address grief. The book acknowledges the spiritual side of life in a nonoffensive, nonsectarian way. Contains a very positive outlook with several reflective poems.

Zonnebelt-Smeenge, Susan, and Robert DeVries. *The Empty Chair: Handling Grief on Holidays and Special Occasions*. Grand Rapids: Baker Book House Company, 2001.

Notes

1. Robert M. Herhold, as quoted in Helen Nearing, *Light on Aging and Dying* (Gardiner, Maine: Tilburg House, 1995), 67.

2. Susan J. Zonnebelt-Smeenge and Robert C. DeVries, *Getting to the Other Side of Grief: Overcoming the Loss of a Spouse* (Grand Rapids: Baker, 1998). Susan J. Zonnebelt-Smeenge and Robert C. DeVries, *The Empty Chair: Handling Grief on Holidays and Special Occasions* (Grand Rapids: Baker, 2001).

3. *Webster's New World Dictionary*, 3rd College Edition (New York: Simon & Schuster, 1988).

4. John Bunyan, *The Pilgrim's Progress* (London: Folio Society, 1962).

5. Elisabeth Kubler-Ross was a significant researcher in the area of dying. Among her more influential writings are: *On Death and Dying* (New York: Macmillan, 1969), *Questions and Answers on Death and Dying* (New York: Macmillan, 1974), and *Living with Death and Dying* (New York: Macmillan, 1982).

6. For a special consideration of grief and the holidays, see Zonnebelt-Smeenge and DeVries, *The Empty Chair*.

7. For more information on the theory of multiple intelligences, see Howard Gardner, *Frames of Mind: The Theory of Multiple Intelligences* (New York: Basic Books, 1983), and Thomas Armstrong, *Multiple Intelligences in the Classroom* (Alexandria, Va.: Association for Supervision and Curriculum Development, 1994).

8. To respect gender inclusive language, some quotations from Scripture are taken from the *Holy Bible*, New Living Translation, 1996. Used by permission of Tyndale House Publishers, Inc., Wheaton, IL 60189. All rights reserved.

9. Richard J. Foster, *Freedom of Simplicity* (San Francisco: Harper & Row, 1981).

10. Charles Wilson, *Sojourners in the Land of Promise: Planning, Theology and Surprise* (Downers Grove, Ill.: Spiritual Growth Resources, 1981), 72–73.

11. C. S. Lewis, *A Grief Observed* (Greenwich, Conn.: Seabury Press, 1963).

12. "Cats in the Cradle," music by Harry Chapin, lyrics by Sandra Chapin. Originally recorded on the album *Verities & Balderdash* by Harry Chapin, 1974.

13. Doris Stickney, *Water Bugs and Dragonflies: Explaining Death to Young Children* (Cleveland: Pilgrim Press, 1997).

14. "Amazing Grace" by John Newton, 1779. This stanza written by John Rees, 1859.

15. Stuart Hample and Eric Marshall, *Children's Letters to God: The New Collection* (New York: Workman Publishing, 1991).

16. The identity of Seniab is obscure. He most likely lived around 1450–1400 B.C. in the Middle East. His saying is one of many that has been collected in various "Books of the Dead" from Tibet, Egypt, and other locations throughout the region. This saying is now considered part of the public domain.

17. Kathleen Walczak, "NFDA's 2001 General Price List Survey," *The Director*, August 2002, 36–38.

18. Ibid.

19. For a much more complete discussion of this, see our book *Getting to the Other Side of Grief*.

20. Ira Byock, *Dying Well: The Prospect of Growth at the End of Life* (New York: Putnam/ Riverhead, 1997).

21. *The Westminster Larger Catechism*, Q & A #1, as contained in Johannes G. Vos, *The Westminster Larger Catechism: A Commentary*, ed. G. I. Williamson (Phillipsburg, N.J.: Presbyterian and Reformed Publishing Company, 2002).

22. Harold S. Kushner, *When Bad Things Happen to Good People*, reissue edition (New York: Avon, 1997).

23. Edith Schaeffer, *Affliction* (Old Tappan, N.J.: Revell, 1978).

24. Winston S. Churchill, *Never Give In: The Best of Winston Churchill's Speeches* (New York: Hyperion, 2003), 307.

25. World Health Organization, "Cancer Pain Relief and Palliative Care," Technical Report Series 804 (Geneva, Switzerland, 1990).

26. You will find these facts and many others in M. J. Field and C. K. Cassel, *Approaching Death: Improving Care at the End of Life*, Report of the Institute of Medicine Task Force (Washington, D.C.: National Academy Press, 1997); J. Lynn, J. L. Schuster, and A. Kabcenell, *Improving Care for the End of Life: A Sourcebook for Health Care Managers and Clinicians* (New York: Oxford University Press, 2000); and National Hospice and Palliative Care Organization, *Hospice Fact Sheet* (Alexandria, Va., 2000).

27. Mitch Albom, *Tuesdays with Morrie* (New York: Doubleday, 1997).

28. Consider as an example the song "I Bowed My Knees and Cried Holy" on the Brooklyn Tabernacle Choir's CD *Live . . . Again*. The arrangement copyright by Dayspring Music (a division of Word, Inc.)/BMI, 1989.

29. *The Heidelberg Catechism*, Q & A #1, in *Psalter Hymnal* (Grand Rapids: CRC Publications, 1987), 861.

30. Leo Tolstoy, *The Death of Ivan Illych and Other Stories* (New York: The New American Library, 1960).

31. *The Heidelberg Catechism*, Q & A #58, in *Psalter Hymnal*, 885.

32. C. S. Lewis, *The Last Battle* (New York: Collier Books, 1970), 184.

Index

(Page references in italics are found in the sections of Christian meditations.)